Rabbits
FOR
DUMMIES®
2ND EDITION

by Connie Isbell and Audrey Pavia

Wiley Publishing, Inc.

**Rabbits For Dummies®, 2nd Edition**

Published by
**Wiley Publishing, Inc.**
111 River St.
Hoboken, NJ 07030-5774
www.wiley.com



Published by Wiley Publishing, Inc., Indianapolis, Indiana

Published simultaneously in Canada



For general information on our other products and services, please contact our Customer Care Department within the U.S. at 877-762-2974, outside the U.S. at 317-572-3993, or fax 317-572-4002.

For technical support, please visit www.wiley.com/techsupport.

Wiley also publishes its books in a variety of electronic formats. Some content that appears in print may not be available in electronic books.

Library of Congress Control Number is available from the publisher.

ISBN: 978-0-470-43064-4

Manufactured in the United States of America

10 9 8 7 6 5 4 3 2

# About the Author(s)

**Connie Isbell,** the author of *Rabbit Adoption For Dummies,* grew up in rural New York State, where she spent time with creatures of all kinds — companion, farm, and wild alike. Connie carried this interest in animals and nature into her work as an editor and writer for *Audubon* magazine. She has also edited countless pet books, on everything from adopting an ex-racing greyhound to caring for rabbits and parrots. Connie now works from her home on the coast of New Jersey, where she lives with her husband, two daughters, and an assortment of pets.

**Audrey Pavia** is a former pet magazine editor and an award-winning freelance writer specializing in animal subjects. She has written articles on various rabbit topics in *Rabbits, Critters,* and *Pet Product News* magazines. She has authored 21 other animal books besides *Rabbits For Dummies*, including the *Owners Guide to the Rabbit.*

Audrey has been involved with rabbits since the age of 10, when she first joined her local 4-H rabbit project. She currently resides in Norco, California, with her husband, two Rex rabbits, and a house full of other pets.

# Dedication

**From Connie:** To my parents, who have inspired me in so many ways.

**From Audrey:** To Doey and Rusty, who introduced me to the world of rabbits and loved me despite my inexperience.

# Acknowledgments

**From Connie:** Many thanks go out to the knowledgeable and dedicated volunteers of the House Rabbit Society, editors Kelly Ewing and Erin Calligan Mooney, technical editor Angela M. Lennox, DVM Dipl. ABVP-Avian, Stacy Kennedy, and Ingrid Pearsall; Cream Puff, Cupid, and Coconut deserve extra treats for their expert bunny antics and input.

I am grateful to my husband and daughters — Eric, Alice, and Lila Nathanson — for their endless love, patience, and encouragement throughout this and every one of my projects.

**From Audrey:** I would like to thank the following people for their assistance with writing this book: Wayne Kopit, DVM, of Brook-Ellis Animal Hospital in Fountain Valley, Calif.; attorney Roberta Kraus; my editors Tonya Maddox Cupp and Tracy Boggier; my sister Heidi Pavia-Watkins, DVM; Margo DeMello of the House Rabbit Society; Caroline Charland of the Bunny Bunch; my always supportive husband Randy Mastronicola; and my very helpful parents, Haydee and John Pavia.

## Publisher's Acknowledgments

We're proud of this book; please send us your comments through our Dummies online registration form located at `http://dummies.custhelp.com`. For other comments, please contact our Customer Care Department within the U.S. at 877-762-2974, outside the U.S. at 317-572-3993, or fax 317-572-4002.

Some of the people who helped bring this book to market include the following:

***Acquisitions, Editorial, and Media Development***

**Project Editor:** Kelly Ewing

(Previous Edition: Tonya Maddox Cupp)

**Acquisitions Editor:** Tracy Boggier

**Assistant Editor:** Erin Calligan Mooney

**Editorial Program Coordinator:** Joe Niesen

**General Reviewer:** Angela M. Lennox, DVM Dipl. ABVP-Avian

**Senior Editorial Manager:** Jennifer Ehrlich

**Editorial Supervisor and Reprint Editor:** Carmen Krikorian

**Editorial Assistant:** Jennette ElNaggar

**Cover Photos:** © Radius Images/Alamy

**Cartoons:** Rich Tennant (`www.the5thwave.com`)

***Composition Services***

**Project Coordinator:** Katherine Key

**Layout and Graphics:** Christin Swinford, Christine Williams

**Proofreaders:** Melissa Cossell, Evelyn W. Gibson

**Indexer:** Potomac Indexing, LLC

---

**Publishing and Editorial for Consumer Dummies**

**Diane Graves Steele,** Vice President and Publisher, Consumer Dummies

**Kristin Ferguson-Wagstaffe,** Product Development Director, Consumer Dummies

**Ensley Eikenburg,** Associate Publisher, Travel

**Kelly Regan,** Editorial Director, Travel

**Publishing for Technology Dummies**

**Andy Cummings,** Vice President and Publisher, Dummies Technology/General User

**Composition Services**

**Gerry Fahey,** Vice President of Production Services

**Debbie Stailey,** Director of Composition Services

# Contents at a Glance

# Table of Contents

# Introduction

Welcome to *Rabbits For Dummies,* 2nd Edition, the one and only book that you need to get started in the wonderful world of rabbit ownership. Of course, when it comes to rabbits, you can never stop discovering. Although they may seem like simple little creatures, rabbits are actually physically and emotionally complex and they never cease to amaze those who live with them.

If you're interested in rabbits, you came to the right book. Whether you're thinking about getting your first rabbit or you already have a bunny and want to find out more about how to take care of him, this book can be a great help.

How hard is owning a rabbit? *Rabbits For Dummies,* 2nd Edition, is designed to be a useful reference for those who aren't experts, as well as those who know zero about rabbits. Even people who know a thing or two about bunnies can benefit from this book because it's a reference for behavior and health.

Rabbits are nothing like cats and dogs, the two most common pets. The rabbit's digestive system is more akin to a horse than a feline or a canine. And the psychological makeup of a bunny is closer to that of a bird than that of a cat or dog.

In order to understand your rabbit and care for him properly, you have to know the details specific to rabbit ownership. By finding out about rabbit psychology, rabbit physiology, and basic rabbit care, you'll have what it takes to take care of a rabbit just right.

## About This Book

*Rabbits For Dummies,* 2nd Edition, is like a department store: You're able to enter on whatever floor you like. You don't have to walk past that smelly perfume counter to get to the housewares section on the third floor. You just walk into the housewares section. Likewise, you don't have to start reading this book at the beginning, going through each page until you reach the end. You can turn to any section of the book that interests you and begin reading at that point and not feel lost. You don't have to remember what you read yesterday, and you don't have to read chapters or sections in order. Just find something that interests you, read it, do it, and put the book back on your shelf. (No one expects you to read from cover to cover except maybe your high school English teacher, but you can ignore her this time around.)

Each part of the book is divided into chapters that address basic questions about rabbits and their care. You'll find answers to questions like

- Am I really cut out to be a bunny owner?
- How do I prepare my home for my rabbit's arrival?
- How do I communicate with my bunny?
- What's the best way to make sure that my rabbit is healthy and happy?
- What do I do in the event of a medical emergency?

# Conventions Used in This Book

*Rabbits For Dummies,* 2nd edition, makes information easy to find and use. To help you navigate through the text, we've used certain conventions:

- *Italics* are used for emphasis and to highlight new words or terms that are defined.
- **Boldfaced** text is used to bring attention to key words or highlight points in a series.
- `Monofont` is used to set apart Web sites and e-mail addresses.

In this book, we refer to rabbits with the male pronouns (he, his, him) and the female pronouns (she, her). This convention is merely for readability's sake. We don't call rabbits "it" because they're living creatures.

# What You're Not to Read

From time to time in this book, we share information that may be interesting but isn't essential to the complete understanding of the topic at hand. You can find this nonessential information in two places:

- **Sidebars:** The gray shaded text boxes contain supplementary information that you can skip or read later.
- **Technical Stuff:** Paragraphs highlighted with the Technical Stuff icon contain technical rabbit facts and tidbits that are interesting but not required reading.

# Foolish Assumptions

In writing *Rabbits For Dummies,* 2nd Edition, we made some assumptions about our readers:

- You know a rabbit when you see one.
- You're one of the many people who think about adopting a cute, fur ball of rabbitness, but you want to make sure that a rabbit is the right pet for you and your family.
- You're lucky enough to own a rabbit, but you want to be certain that you're doing all you can to properly care for him.
- You care about rabbits and want to treat them with kindness, especially when it comes to housing them in your home.
- You're allowed to keep rabbits in the area where you live.
- You know that the best way to find out about things is to read about what the experts have to say on the subject.
- You're no dummy, despite the title of this book. In fact, you're pretty smart — otherwise, you wouldn't have bought this book.

# How This Book Is Organized

This book is put together in a way that allows you to find the information you need quickly and easily. *Rabbits For Dummies,* 2nd Edition, is divided into five parts made up of several chapters relating to that specific rabbit topic.

## Part I: Bringing on the Bunny Basics

Before you even get a rabbit, you need to know what rabbits are all about. This part offers information about whether a rabbit is right for your lifestyle, how rabbits are put together, how to go about choosing a rabbit, and the best places to find one.

## Part II: Taking Care of Creature Comforts

Housing, grooming, and feeding — these three important elements for keeping a rabbit are all covered in this part of the book. You can find out why rabbits are happier and healthier as indoor pets, how to litter box train your house rabbit, why keeping your pet clean and groomed is so important, and how best to feed your bunny.

Because rabbits are prone to illness, bunny healthcare is an important matter. In this part, you can find out how to recognize common rabbit illnesses, how to prevent them, and when to go to the vet. You also get help putting together a bunny first-aid kit, and you discover how to handle rabbit emergencies. Finally, this part discusses how to say the final goodbye when that inevitable moment comes.

## Part III: Rabbit Psychology: Behavior and Training

Rabbit personality is what makes living with a bunny so much fun. Find out how to understand bunny body language. (They can't speak English.) Discover helpful tips on training, as well as how to train your pet to do a few fun tricks. This part also includes invaluable information on how to deal with common behavior problems, such as biting, chewing, and digging.

## Part IV: Enjoying Your Fun Bunny

Think rabbits don't do much except sit in a cage all day? Wrong! You can have all kinds of fun with your rabbit. Part IV discusses playing with him, getting involved in rabbit clubs and shows, and even traveling with him. This part also covers the unique sport of rabbit hopping, along with details on how to get involved with rabbit social issues.

## Part V: The Part of Tens

In the Part of Tens, we tackle three different subjects: health emergencies, useful rabbit Web sites, and ways of enhancing a pet rabbit's life. In the health chapter, you find an overview of the ten signs that require emergency action. Follow the advice, and your rabbit is likely to live a long, healthy life. Chapter 18 has the best links on the Internet for rabbit lovers. And last but not least, the final chapter offers ten ways to make your bunny's day special.

### Appendix

The Appendix in this book contains a plethora of rabbit resources, including rabbit rescue groups, purebred rabbit clubs and registries, rabbit activity groups, educational organizations, rabbit publications, and other useful resources for rabbit owners.

## Icons Used in This Book

As with all the other books in the *For Dummies* series, this book has useful little icons in the margins to call your attention to specific types of information. See the following explanations of what each of those icons means:

You see this icon throughout this book because when it comes to rabbits, you need to do plenty of remembering. We place this icon next to important information that you won't want to miss or forget.

When you see this symbol, beware! This icon highlights information about dangers that can cause your rabbit harm.

Occasionally, rabbit information gets a bit technical, hence this icon. When you see it, put the left side of your brain in high gear. But if you're short on time, know that this information is interesting but not essential.

This icon alerts you to helpful hints regarding rabbits, pertaining to their care and handling. If you read the information next to this icon, you'll have a happier, healthier rabbit.

## Where to Go from Here

Go wherever you want. You can start at Chapter 1 and read all the way through to the final appendix, or you can hop, skip, and jump around — much like a rabbit.

If you're going to do that skipping around thing, can we at least ask you for a favor? Before you start jumping from place to place, take a few moments to read through Chapter 1, which contains the most important questions you want to ask yourself before you embark on the responsibility of rabbit ownership:

- If you're considering getting a rabbit, hop over to Chapter 1.
- If you've decided that you're going to buy a rabbit, Chapters 2, 3, and 4 help you find the right one.
- If you already have a rabbit or two and want to get the latest perspective on a healthy bunny diet, see Chapter 6.
- If you want to train your rabbit, Chapter 12 can help you.
- If you want to participate in rabbit-related activities, Chapter 15 can get you started.

# Part I

# Bringing on the Bunny Basics

"Oh, it was so cute. He looked at me with those big ears, his nose twitching, and he started hopping up and down. That's when I said, 'Arthur, stop hopping up and down! We'll go pick out a rabbit this afternoon.'"

## *In this part . . .*

If you're just starting out with a rabbit, you need the basics. This part gives them to you. You find details on how to tell whether a rabbit is the right pet for you, the different breeds and types of rabbits available, the benefits of adopting a rabbit who needs a home, and how to find a healthy rabbit. You also see details about how the rabbit's body works and receive pointers on how to choose the right rabbit for you.

# Chapter 1

# Jumping into Rabbit Ownership

### In This Chapter

- Finding out about rabbits before you get one
- Discovering the realities of rabbit ownership
- Examining your rabbit readiness
- Parceling out duties to family members

The two most common pets in North America, if not the world, are cats and dogs. Rabbits, on the other hand, aren't as common (although they have enjoyed a recent rise in popularity and now rank fourth after cats, dogs, and birds). As a result, many folks don't know too much about them.

Rabbits are complicated creatures, both physically and psychologically. In addition to a uniquely designed social structure, their bodies have helped them to survive as a species for eons. As the caregiver to one of these special animals, it behooves you to understand the inner workings of the rabbit. If you do, you'll not only be able to take better care of your pet, but you'll also have a greater appreciation for this special member of the animal kingdom. (See Chapters 9 and 10 for more information about the health of your rabbit.)

Because they're so misunderstood, rabbits are the unfortunate victims of much neglect, mostly by well-intentioned folks who simply weren't properly suited or prepared for sharing their lives and homes with these fine long-eared creatures. In addition to providing a primer on the rabbit form, this chapter guides you through the process of looking at your own life and how well a rabbit might fit into it. Those who fit the rabbit profile are fortunate, indeed.

## Admiring from Afar

Rabbits are mammals, which means that they're in the same general classification as dogs, cats, horses, sheep, tigers, elephants, humans, and a lot of other animals. To be a *mammal* means that you're *warm blooded* — that is, your body regulates its own temperature (as opposed to a reptile who needs an outside heat source to maintain its body temperature). Your species also gives birth to live young and nurses them with milk produced by mammary glands (hence the name mammal).

The rabbit's body, shown in Figure 1-1, is uniquely designed in large part to escape predators. The rabbit is also put together in a way that helps him take in food, which in turn provides energy for escape and reproduction.

## Digesting this information (and that carrot)

One of the most interesting aspects of a rabbit's body is his digestive system. Unlike cats or dogs, rabbits can eat a wide variety of plant material. They can process and extract nutrients from many plants that are indigestible to less adaptable herbivores or omnivores. This flexibility helps make them highly successful in a variety of environments around the world. Understanding how your rabbit's digestive system functions is important so that you feed him in a way that's most efficient for his body. (For more on feeding your rabbit, see Chapter 6.)

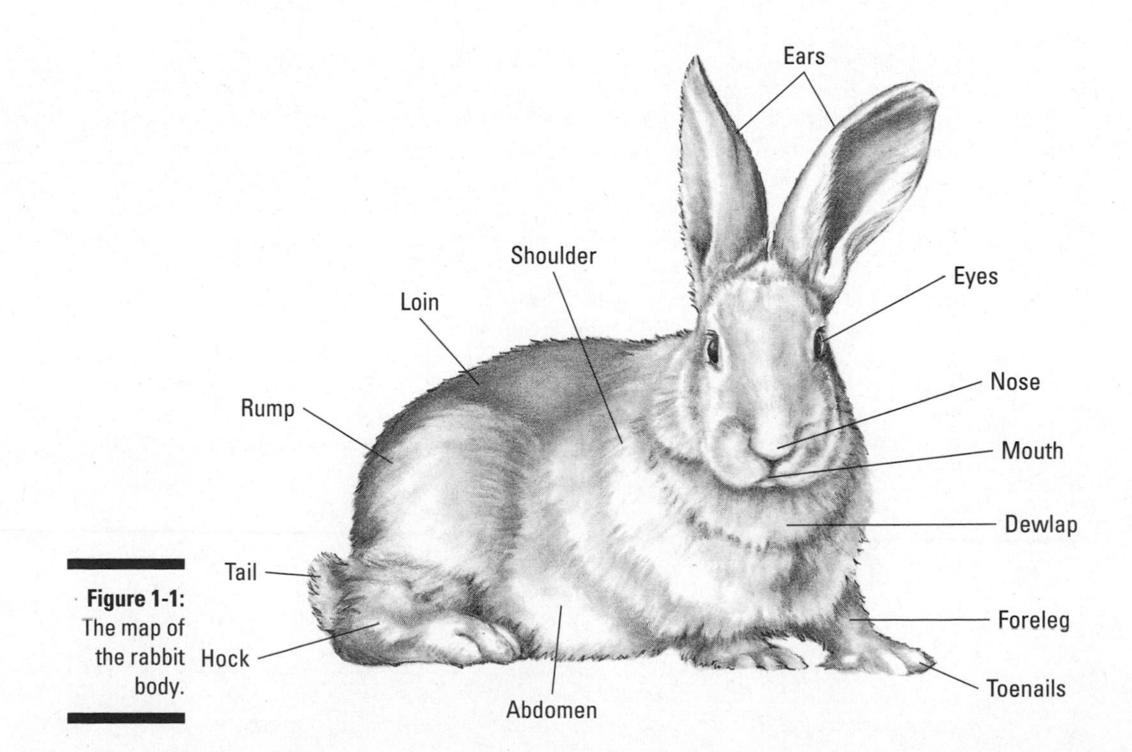


**Figure 1-1:** The map of the rabbit body.

## Munching on fiber

Rabbits are *herbivores,* meaning that they dine only on plant material. A rabbit has an esophagus, stomach, and intestinal tract like other mammals. However, because they often dine on plants that are high in fiber, rabbits have developed a strategy for dealing with the high fiber foods called *hind gut fermentation.* This area of the digestive system is where the indigestible materials are broken down into manageable chemicals. (We talk more about this interesting process in a minute.) Many other herbivore friends, including horses, guinea pigs, and chinchillas, have this specialization of the digestive system.

Rabbits have a large stomach for their body size to enable them to eat large amounts of plant material quickly. They are *crepuscular,* meaning they eat primarily at dawn and at dusk. They don't need to eat small amounts all day long. They graze primarily in the morning and evening with little food intake during the rest of the day, depending on what's available, the weather, and so on. Rabbits can do nicely eating a large meal twice a day.

The digestive process begins in the rabbit's mouth. The rabbit's *prehensile* lips grab the plant material first, and then the front teeth called *incisors* — four upper and two lower — neatly slice off pieces of plant matter. The food is then passed to the molars (the back teeth), where it's chewed into small particles and finally swallowed.

All of the rabbit's teeth grow continuously throughout its life. If he's on a good diet, like the one described in Chapter 6, and is given some additional materials to munch on throughout the day, your rabbit is less likely to pick something else to eat, such as your couch legs, your bed legs, or your legs. (Chapter 14 lists some fun toys for rabbits.)

Rabbits have a very large blind sac called a *cecum* that is located where the small intestine and the large intestine join together. The cecum contains a wonderfully diverse population of healthy bacteria, yeast, and other organisms working to help the rabbit digest his food.

When the food in the small intestine reaches the cecum and large intestine, the gastrointestinal tract knows which materials to divert into the cecum for further break down. The materials that were already digested in the small intestine and that don't need to make this little side trip to the cecum pass directly into the large intestine as waste. This waste then leaves the body as the little round droppings you see in your rabbit's litter box.

What is happening in the cecum? The microorganisms are breaking down the indigestible fiber and turning it into digestible nutrients. In order for the rabbit to use these nutrients, he must take this material and move it through the digestive tract one more time. So, at certain times of the day (which coincides with several hours after a rabbit eats a big meal), the material from the cecum is packaged up into small round moist pellets called *cecotropes.* The rabbit gets a signal in his brain about when these little delicacies are ready to be passed out of the body; he eats them the minute they emerge. Your rabbit will often look like he is grooming his hind end, but actually he is taking in these nutrient-rich cecotropes.

The various types of fiber in a rabbit's diet is not only there to be used for nutrition, but they're vital to keeping the rabbit's gastrointestinal tract in excellent working order. The indigestible fiber is particularly important in making the intestines move along smoothly. You can think of the fiber as a tool to sort of "tickle" the lining and keep things moving smoothly. A diet that is low in appropriate types of fiber and too high in rich carbohydrates can lead to a sluggish intestine and cecum and subsequent serious disease (see Chapter 9).

Normally you will not see any cecotropes in your rabbit's cage or at the most a rare one here or there. They're soft, green to brown, mucous coated, and have a stronger smell. If you see a number of them in your rabbit's cage, it may indicate a diet too rich in protein or another more serious condition. Please consult your vet.

## Taking advantage of skin and bones

Watch rabbits run and leap in play, and you get a sense of the complexity and flexibility of their skeletons and muscles. Nature equipped rabbits with this kind of flexibility to allow them to make lifesaving maneuvers when being chased down by predators. Basically, the rabbit's bones and muscles are what keep it ahead of the game.

Unfortunately, poor diet, inadequate housing, lack of exercise, and improper handling can be a deadly combination for rabbits. Accidental injuries to the spine can occur in any rabbit, but are extremely rare in rabbits on proper diets who get plenty of exercise to strengthen bones and supporting muscles.

For this reason, it's important that

- Rabbits who are outdoors for a period of exercise must be well protected from predators. (See Chapter 8 for more information about outdoor safety.)
- You handle your rabbit properly (see Chapter 7). Incorrect handling or lifting can result in serious, if not fatal, injury.

Rabbits are excellent swimmers, but taking them for a dip in the pool with you isn't a good idea. Although the rabbit's skeleton and muscles allow it to swim effectively, swimming is reserved for life-and-death escapes. Needless to say, your bunny won't enjoy any excursions in the pool.

## Taking a whiff

Rabbit noses are always on the go. They wiggle almost incessantly. Although much of this wiggling is a result of the rabbit's rapid breathing, it also helps facilitate taking in certain odors when the rabbit needs to do so. Rabbits can tell much about a situation just by taking a good whiff.

Rabbits are like cats and dogs in that their olfactory sense gives them access to an entire unique world that humans aren't privy to. Rabbits can smell even the faintest odor and use their noses to do the following:

- Distinguish one rabbit from another or one sex from another.
- In the case of males, find out whether a female rabbit is ready to breed.
- In the case of a mother rabbit, identify her own babies.
- Determine whether they want to eat a particular food.
- Detect danger from predators and from weather conditions.

Also, given your rabbit's sensitivity in the olfactory department, refrain from using harsh chemicals, perfume, or anything particularly strong smelling in his presence or around his cage. His nose will thank you for it.

## Putting those ears to good use

Rabbits haven't survived for eons just on their good looks. Their profound sense of hearing has served them well over time. (For a prey animal like the rabbit, being able to hear predators approaching and detect the warning thumps of other rabbits is crucial to the *colony,* a group of rabbits living together in a *warren,* a series of dens and tunnels.)

The shape of a rabbit's ears allows them to pick up barely detectable sounds in its environment, sort of like radar dishes. The large exteriors intercept sounds and funnel them into the ear canal where the ear drum is located. Rabbit ears are also flexible. They can pivot around at the base to help detect the exact location where a sound is coming from.

What does all this great hearing mean to you, the rabbit owner? Be aware of the sensitivity of your rabbit's ears and treat him accordingly. Spare him loud music, screaming children, barking dogs, and any other nerve-frazzling racket. Your rabbit is less stressed if his environment is free of harsh, jarring noises.

Rabbits also use their ears to release excess body heat. Applying cool wet cloths to his ears (if he hasn't gone into shock already) can help cool down an overheated rabbit. Thus, cool blood circulates through his body and lowers his body temperature. (For more on heatstroke, see Chapter 9.)

# Figuring Out Whether a Rabbit is Right for You

Rabbits are cute and fuzzy and make great pets, but these truths alone aren't good enough reasons to own one. If rabbits are so wonderful, why not have one? The answer is simple: Though rabbits are terrific companions for many reasons, they also demand plenty of work and a serious commitment.

For example, Sarah works eight hours a day at an office job and spends another hour a day commuting back and forth to work. She's gone from her home a good nine hours a day, and that's on the days when she comes right home from work. Often, Sarah, who is single, meets her girlfriends after work or heads off to the gym to exercise. On those nights, she doesn't get home until 9 or 10 p.m. Because Sarah's schedule doesn't give her enough time to spend with a dog, she opted for a rabbit. A rabbit, however, is a very social animal and will be just as unhappy as a dog in this situation.

## Asking yourself whether you're rabbit-ready

Fantasizing about owning a rabbit is quite different from actually being ready to take one on. Think hard about your lifestyle and whether it's the right time to be adding such an animal to your household. Ask yourself these questions:

- **Do I have at least three hours of free time a day?** Your rabbit needs at least two hours of exercise, which we describe in Chapters 15 and 17.

That leaves another hour to clean his hutch and to groom, feed, and water him. Are you embroiled in something right now that's taking up much of your time or energy, like the holiday season, a move, or a personal transition, such as a baby, a new marriage, or a divorce? Are you putting in long hours at work on a special project? Do you travel often for work?

Adding a new pet to the household during an already stressful time can be disastrous for all involved. Wait until things settle down and are back to normal. That's the time to bring a new rabbit into the home.

- **Do I have the space to house a rabbit?** Can I put him in my yard or in my house? Does my apartment complex allow pets? Rabbits require adequate cage space (see Chapter 5 for more information), and you must have the room to accommodate this need. You must also do some investigating to find out whether you're zoned for rabbit ownership. Rabbits aren't allowed in some residential areas. Check with your local zoning board.
- **Does anyone in my household have allergies?** Those who have allergies know how miserable and even debilitating they can be. Chapter 5 offers some tactics to minimize the evil effects of bunny-related allergens (rabbit fur, rabbit saliva, rabbit hay, and so on), but people who have serious allergies may want to spend some time with rabbits before making the decision to adopt.
- **Can my kids handle the responsibility?** Kids and rabbits can make fine companions, providing the children are old enough to respect the rabbit and are properly supervised; the general consensus is 7 years of age, but all children should be considered individually. Mishandling can result in serious injury or even death of the rabbit. Likewise, rabbits who kick — or even bite — when held improperly can hurt children. See Chapter 7 for a more detailed discussion of how to properly handle a rabbit.

Give serious thought to whether your children are old enough to behave responsibly around a rabbit and whether you have the time to properly supervise their interaction time with the new pet. Children can't be expected to be in sole charge of the rabbit. In fact, an adult must oversee the rabbit-caring tasks that children are given for the sake of the rabbit.

- **How will my other pets get along with a rabbit?** Rabbits can get along with other pets, depending on the type of pet they're being asked to live with. Introducing your pet rabbit to another strange rabbit may jeopardize one or both pets, putting them in serious danger. (Chapters 2 and 11 offer tips for how rabbits can coexist with other pets peacefully.)
- **Am I willing to alter my lifestyle?** Rabbits are notorious diggers and chewers and can make short work of your backyard or your wooden furniture legs if you don't make certain changes to your home environment. You have to thoroughly rabbit-proof your home and/or backyard if you bring a rabbit into your life. And in many cases, the results of your rabbit-proofing won't exactly be an asset to your home decor. (Chapter 5 can help you figure out how to rabbit-proof your home.)

- **Do I have enough money to set up and sustain my rabbit?** You need cold, hard cash (or a warm credit card) to purchase any rabbit, plus the cage and supplies that your rabbit must have to be comfortable. You should also have money on hand to pay veterinary bills for the annual preventative physical exam, in the event of an illness, and the health difficulties that becomes more likely as the pet ages. (See Chapters 9 and 10 for details on rabbit health.)
- **Am I ready for the emotional commitment?** Rabbits are friendly, sociable creatures who need plenty of attention to thrive in a domestic environment. Think about whether you can make the emotional commitment to a rabbit.

What happens if you don't ask yourself these questions and just go out and get a rabbit because you *think* you want one? If it turns out that rabbit ownership isn't really right for you, then the rabbit will ultimately suffer. Typically, when people don't want their rabbits, they end up taking them to an animal shelter or turning them loose in the woods in the hopes that the rabbit can get by on its own. Sadly, rabbits are put to death in animal shelters, just like their canine and feline counterparts, and domesticated rabbits that are set free to fend for themselves are rarely capable of doing so. Finding another home for him is an option but not an easy one. Prospective rabbit owners don't grow on trees, as you'll quickly find out when you start trying to find another home for your rabbit. So spare yourself and the rabbit all the heartache and probe deep into your psyche before taking the plunge.

## Considering the right reasons to own a rabbit

People are drawn to rabbits for different reasons. Most of them think rabbits are cute (and they're right). Others want to breed and show them for enjoyment and prestige. Some are looking for a pet that's less work than a dog yet different from a cat. The fact that rabbits are cute and fuzzy may motivate you to explore the possibility of rabbit ownership. But before you acquire a rabbit, you need to find out as much as you can about rabbits and what's involved. Only then can you have a thorough understanding of rabbit ownership really means. This book can help you do that.

The only truly legitimate reasons to get a rabbit are for companionship and/or to get seriously involved in the purebred rabbit community. Any other reason bodes trouble — for the rabbit.

## The downside of the Easter Bunny

Easter is a time of joy for children everywhere, but for those running rabbit rescue groups and shelters, Easter is nothing to celebrate. In their holiday excitement, many people impulsively buy a cute pet bunny for their children. Sadly, a family's enthusiasm quickly wanes after these little bunnies turn into teenage rabbits, when a variety of troublesome but natural behaviors emerge (see Chapter 2). It's not long until children lose interest and parents tire of the chores. Enter those rescue groups and shelters. This annual deluge of unwanted rabbits is an event that organizers and volunteers dread. Faced with an overwhelming number of rabbits, many groups are forced to euthanize — certainly not what the Easter Bunny had in mind.

Check out the following few reasons *not* to own a rabbit:

- It's Easter time, and you think getting a rabbit would be a fun way to celebrate the holiday.
- You think a rabbit would look good sitting in a hutch outside in your backyard. A bunny in the yard may lend a rural feeling to your garden decor.
- You want to breed rabbits, so you can make a pile of money.
- Your child wants one, and you plan to teach him responsibility by making him care for the rabbit.
- Your dog needs a companion, but you don't want to get another dog.

If these reasons don't apply to you, then you may be one of the fortunate folks who are suited for a life with rabbits. Of course, before you go out and get that rabbit, make sure that you did your homework and know *exactly* how to take care of this delightful creature. (See Part II in this book for more on housing, nutrition, and healthcare.) Find out about rabbit breeds to make sure that you know what kind of rabbit you want. Study up on rabbit behavior so that you can understand your pet right from the get-go and be sure to make that all-important decision about whether your rabbit will live indoors or outdoors before you bring your pet home. (They should live indoors.) Find a veterinarian experienced in the treatment of rabbits before you make your purchase rather than *after* an emergency arises.

# Knowing What You Want in a Furry Friend

Like many other animal companions, rabbits come in all shapes, sizes, and colors — not to mention breeds, ages, and gender. Some people are happy with whatever rabbit needs a home, which is great for rabbits at shelters who need adopting. Other people may have a particular rabbit in mind. It's good to remember, however, that when it comes to living with a rabbit, what matters most is personality — and that has little or nothing to do with breed or color.

That being said, you have to consider a variety of options when it comes to choosing a rabbit:

- **Mixed breed or purebred:** If you're not interested in breeding or showing, a mixed breed bunny is likely to do the trick. Chapters 2 and 3 provide loads of information about the differences between bunny mixed and the many recognized breeds of purebred rabbits available.
- **Age:** Although rabbits of all ages can be wonderful companions, it's a good idea to understand a bit about the challenges that typically come with babies, teenagers, and even older rabbits. Chapter 2 has the details.
- **Gender:** Ask rabbit people whether they prefer male or female rabbits, and you'll hear great arguments for both. See Chapter 2 for some of the conventional wisdom about differences in gender.
- **Coat type:** With rabbits, coat type comes down to this question: Longhair or shorthair? Your answer should be based on how much time you have for grooming. Read more about the coat types in Chapter 2 and the grooming involved in Chapter 7.
- **Size:** The question of size can matter for those who have children or who have physical limitations when it comes to lifting. (Rabbits don't care much for being carried, but it will have to be done.) Although you may think a smaller rabbit would be best for a child, the opposite is in fact true: Small rabbits are too fragile, really, for most children; a larger, sturdier rabbit is a better bet for most families with kids. Chapter 2 has more on size considerations.

# Providing Shelter

Not just any home will do for a rabbit. All rabbits deserve safe, comfortable, and inviting accommodations. Responsible rabbit caretakers will

- **Set up house indoors:** Rabbits are increasingly being brought in from lonely outdoor hutches so that they can live indoors with their human companions. Indoor living is a brilliant idea for many reasons: better health, a longer life, protection from predators, and more fun for all. Read Chapter 5 for more on this happy trend for bunnies and their humans.
- **Get equipped ahead of time:** Rabbits require some basic equipment, including a cage, nest box, litter box, as well as food and water vessels. Chapter 5 outlines a basic shopping list to guide you in your interior design efforts.

- **Take care of rabbit-proofing:** To create a successful indoor living situation, you must first take precautions to protect your home from your rabbit and your rabbit from your home. Chapter 5 details those measures, which involve electrical cords, furniture, and carpeting.

# Feeding Your Rabbit

This chapter's earlier "Admiring From Afar" section delves into the fascinating world of the rabbit gastrointestinal system. Rabbit nutrition is the subject of much discussion and debate, leaving many new owners to puzzle over pellets and parsley. Practically speaking, your rabbit's nutrition is a critical part of caring for your rabbit. Chapter 6 covers this topic in detail, but here's a glimpse at what's in store for you and your bunny kitchen:

- **Making hay:** Fiber is critically important to a rabbit, and hay is the ultimate in rabbit fiber. The average rabbit should be given an unlimited supply of grass hay (such as timothy). Keep it fresh and keep it coming!
- **Keeping it fresh:** Leafy greens and some vegetables are another vital part of your rabbit's diet and should be fed daily. Chapter 6 discusses those veggies considered to be good for bunnies, as well as recommended quantities; fruits, which are high in sugar, should be fed sparingly.
- **Considering pellets:** Much of the discussion about rabbit nutrition is centered on the subject of pellets. It now appears that alfalfa-based pellets, which are convenient and have been used by those breeding rabbits, are probably not the best choice for companion rabbits. See Chapter 6 for more on this debate, as well as for guidelines for using pellets that are timothy-based as one part of a rabbit's diet.

- **Tempting with treats:** Commercially prepared rabbit treats are the rabbit equivalent of junk food, and so are best avoided. Instead, when feeling the need to treat your bunny (maybe once a day or during training), opt for a bit of fresh fruit. Suggested treats are listed in Chapter 6.

# Grooming Your Rabbit

Rabbits are pretty good about taking care of their own grooming and personal hygiene (that's what all that licking and preening is about). Most human companions need to lend an occasional hand, however, when it comes to coat, nail, and ear care. Chapter 7 includes a list of grooming tools you should have on hand, as well as guidelines for

- **Brushing:** The amount and frequency of brushing you need to do will depend on your rabbit's coat. Longhaired rabbits, such as angoras, often require daily brush sessions; short coats, like rexes, may need brushing only once or twice a week.
- **Clipping nails:** This grooming chore is probably the most intimidating, but with a bit of guidance (from a vet) and practice, most owners do fine when it comes time to tame unruly rabbit nails. Chapter 7 outlines the steps to a successful clip session.
- **Cleaning ears:** Making the ears a regular part of the grooming process can help detect problems such as ear mites or infection. These are no regular ears, however, so treat them with care, as discussed in Chapter 7.
- **Bathing:** Rabbits rarely need bathing, which is a good thing because rabbits aren't fond of being bathed, and bathing causes them undo stress. Typically, you can handle the need for a bath with a spot treatment to clean the offending area (usually the hind end). Keep in mind that rabbits are susceptible to cold when they're wet; Chapter 7 describes bathing precautions to prevent your bunny from catching a chill.

Many rabbits don't like being handled, but grooming will become easier as you build a trusting relationship with your rabbit. Chapter 7 also offers tips for proper handling and bonding.

# Keeping Up with Chores

Having any pet is going to add a certain amount of work to your to-do list around the house. Staying on top of chores, such as food prep, cleaning, and litter box maintenance, is a critical part of keeping both your home and your rabbit healthy and happy.

All rabbit owners must do a number of tasks that take time, but you must also determine who can perform them. If you live alone, you'll obviously perform them. (No rabbit likes to clean his own litter box.) If you have a family and the rabbit will belong to everyone, then tasks must be delegated. Before your rabbit comes to live with you, sit down with your family and have a meeting. Discuss the tasks described in this chapter, as well as who will perform them, and when. A written schedule can do wonders to encourage slackers to keep up their end of the bargain. This meeting is a great way to find out whether your family is committed to owning a rabbit. If they're not, then you can put off any plans for a new pet rabbit and thus spare your family and the rabbit from going through the hassle.

However, for the family that's willing to undertake a few extra chores for the sake of a furry new pet, taking care of a rabbit isn't too hard, especially if everyone in the family agrees to pitch in. Table 1-1 has tips on who may best be able to perform the various tasks required of rabbit owners. (All these tasks are described in detail in Part II.)

**Table 1-1 Divvying Up the Tasks**

| *Task* | *How Often* | *Who* |
|---|---|---|
| Feeding the rabbit | Daily | Kids of all ages can easily perform this task as long as an adult monitors them and makes certain that the child is performing this important job. An adult should wash and cut up fresh foods for the child's safety and measure out pelleted feed. |
| Changing the water | Daily | Older children can make sure that the rabbit has fresh water daily; adult supervision ensures the job gets done. |
| Exercising | Daily | A child of any age can help a rabbit exercise by playing with the bunny or simply watching to see that the rabbit doesn't get into anything he isn't supposed to as the rabbit runs around on his own. It's important that adults be the one to lift and carry the rabbit if the children are young. Children should be monitored when they're playing with the rabbit to ensure that they don't chase or accidentally hurt the bunny in any way. |
| Cage cleaning | Weekly | Depending on the type of cage, an adult or an older child should do this job. |
| Grooming | Varies | Adults or older children can tackle this job, which entails brushing (daily for longhaired rabbits and weekly for others), nail clipping, and ear cleaning. |

# Monitoring Your Rabbit's Health

Like any other animal companion, rabbits can become injured, contract diseases, or get infections. Of course, your rabbit is going to be less likely to become ill or injured if you follow the advice in this book and provide her with a proper diet, a clean home, and plenty of exercise. But even the best cared for rabbits can become sick, and your best defense is to be prepared for whatever comes your way. You should

- **Find a vet.** Don't delay. Chapter 9 discusses how to find a vet who can care for rabbits. If your rabbit is intact, make spaying/neutering a primary topic of conversation.
- **Keep up with annual checkups.** Even though rabbits don't require annual vaccinations, an annual checkup is a critical part of your rabbit's healthcare regiment.
- **Put together a first-aid kit.** Having basic medical supplies on hand may mean the difference between a minor health situation and a medical emergency. Consult Chapter 9 for how to put together a first-rate first-aid kit.
- **Be on the lookout for symptoms of illness.** The better you know your rabbit, the better you're able to spot unusual behaviors or symptoms associated with bunny illnesses. By conducting regular home checkups, as described in Chapter 9, you're more likely to detect problems early on.
- **Respond to issue of aging.** Thanks to better care and living conditions, house rabbits can live 10 years or longer. Unfortunately, geriatric bunnies have their own health problems. Arthritis, kidney disease, cancer, and blindness are among the ailments you should look for as your bunny ages.

# Training Your Rabbit

Whether it's to use a litter box, come when called, or stop chewing the carpet, training is a rewarding part of living with a house rabbit. Chapter 12 covers some basic ideas of training, with stops for training rabbits to do "tricks" like sit, jump, and come. Chapter 13 goes a bit deeper into training to cover troublesome behaviors such as kicking and biting. Consider the following:

- Many "problem behaviors" are simply the result of your bunny acting on natural urges — digging, chewing, urinating, for example.
- Take time to bond with your bunny by "listening" to your rabbit's body language and sounds, which are described in Chapter 11.
- The success of your training efforts will depend a great deal on how good of a trainer you are. Are you consistent? Patient? Firm but kind?

Though people are surprised to hear it, rabbits are quite capable of being litter box trained, which is a goal for many rabbit owners. Most rabbits take to litter boxes quite readily, but Chapter 5 outlines the steps to success, with advice for those who come across stray pellets in the parlor.

# Thinking Like a Bunny

You may love your rabbit, and your rabbit may love you, but underneath your bunny's overt affections, a worried creature still exists. Think about it: For thousands of years, humans have hunted rabbits for food and fur. In fact, they still do!

The genetic makeup of the wild rabbit enables him to recognize human beings as predators. Try walking up to a wild bunny and see what happens. Although your pet rabbit is tame and comes from a long line of domesticated rabbits, that innate fear of humans still prevails. You can win your bunny over to the point where he's incredibly comfortable with you, but be aware that he's still easily frightened by quick movements, loud noises, and rough handling. In fact, some rabbit experts believe that even lifting a rabbit off the ground can be terrifying to the animal because this sensation normally comes with being carried off by a predator.

For this reason, treat your rabbit gently at all times. You can get more details about how to ease your rabbit's fears and build a trusting relationship by reading Chapter 11.

A large part of building that trust will come from reading your bunny's body language and sounds. Whether he has an urgent message or is just being social creature that he is, your rabbit has a lot to say! Chapter 11 describes the sounds and movements you'll come to recognize and understand.

# Having a Good Time with Your Pet

Living with a rabbit is so much more than chores, rabbit-proofing, and training — be sure to make time for some fun! Rabbits and their people love to have a good time, and they've come up with some fairly ingenious ways of doing so.

- **Playing games and tossing toys:** It's natural for rabbits to play, but many rabbits, especially those confined to a cage for long periods of time, may need some encouragement. Toys and games are the perfect way to keep bunnies healthy, active, and energized. Get involved in a game of tag or take a seat and enjoy the jumps, dashes, and leaps that follow a session with a new toy. Chapter 14 is loaded with ideas for games, as well as for toys, both homemade and store bought.

- **Making friends with other rabbit owners:** Like their rabbit companions, many rabbit people crave social activity. Some people love their rabbits so much that they want to share them with others, and rabbit clubs and shows are the perfect outlet. Others go a more philanthropic route and volunteer their time with a rescue organization, whether by fostering bunnies waiting to be adopting or interviewing prospective adoptees. Still others find happiness in rabbit hopping, a sport managed by the Rabbit Hopping Association of America. Chapter 15 offers details on all of these activities.
- **Traveling when you have a rabbit:** For most rabbits, travel is not high on their list of fun things to do, but you can make unavoidable trips more pleasant for your bunny companion. Safety is first, of course, and Chapter 16 offers guidelines for auto and air travel, with tips for finding hotels that accept long-eared guests. The chapter also includes helpful advice for finding someone who can care for your rabbit at home while you're away.

# Chapter 2

# Choosing the "Right" Rabbit

### *In This Chapter*

- Discovering the differences in age and sex
- Bringing home more than one rabbit
- Getting a grip on variations in coat type, size, and head shape
- Choosing between a purebred or mixed-breed rabbit

So you're certain you want a rabbit for a pet, and you're ready to go out and get your bunny. Finding and choosing the rabbit who can ultimately be your companion may be one of the most exciting aspects of entering into rabbit ownership.

To be honest, this process can also be one of the most daunting parts of getting a rabbit. Is it possible that just one bunny is the perfect match for you? Probably not. Even people who've had and lost "the best rabbit in the world" usually end up with another equally amazing rabbit sooner or later.

A large part of the selection process is deciding whether you want a purebred rabbit or a mixed breed. You have good reasons for choosing each. If you're starting out with only one bunny at first, then you have to make a choice.

In choosing your pet, you also have to make decisions about her age, sex, and size. Whether you have a particular rabbit in mind or you're still weighing your options, you can discover a lot about the different types of rabbits, which can help you through what may be a confusing, even emotional, process.

So, with all the rabbits out there, how do you know which one to get? In this chapter, you find out everything you need to know to select the rabbit that's best for you.

# Pinpointing the Right Age

Regardless of whether you plan to get a purebred or mixed-breed rabbit, you need to think about the age of the rabbit you want. Many rabbits live ten years or longer, so you should factor that into your decision-making process. Rabbits of all ages can be terrific pets, but it's helpful to know ahead of time about some of the challenges that come with each age.

- **Baby bunnies (younger than three months):** Baby bunnies are cute, and saying no when you see one is difficult. However, baby bunnies should also come with a warning label: Not as easy as they look. Though they're notorious for destructive chewing, the most serious problem associated with baby bunnies has to do with their health; combining the stress of moving to a new home to the stress of being weaned can result in illness and even death. Plus, baby bunnies are, well, babies, and prone to litter box accidents. Finally, you can't be sure what kind of personality your baby will have when she grows up. If you've considered all these factors and still want a young rabbit, look for one — preferably from a shelter or rescue group — around 12 weeks old who should be better able to adjust to change.
- **Adolescent rabbits (typically 5 to 12 months):** Before a baby rabbit can become an adult, he must go through the dreaded adolescent stage — the rabbit equivalent to being a teenager. Many people prefer to skip this rather bratty period in rabbit development by adopting an adult rabbit. Keep in mind that these hormonally charged behaviors — chewing, digging, spraying (see Chapter 13), aggressiveness, and territoriality — are part of a phase that should pass or at least diminish. Though not an instant fix, spaying or neutering your pet, which we cover in Chapter 9, can also help.
- **Adult rabbits (1 year and older):** At this point in a rabbit's life, he has probably emerged from adolescence and has mellowed a bit. Without all the hormonal surges, you'll be able to get a good sense of his personality and temperament. As far as litter box training goes, an adult rabbit is not too old to learn new tricks, and many can adapt to indoor life with litter boxes.
- **Senior rabbits (generally 4 years and older):** Like other senior animals, older rabbits may be slowing down, but they're still a wonderful choice for a companion, delighting owners with their curiosity, cuddles, and leaps. And take heart, because your older rabbit can still make good use of a litter box. Depending on the breed, the average lifespan of a companion rabbit is generally between 7 and 12 years.

## Is it a boy or girl?

Though you're most likely going to have a vet determine your bunny's sex, knowing how to do it yourself can't hurt. It's a good idea to be sure of your rabbit's sex because males should be kept apart from females, even when they're babies. Rabbits as young as 4 months old are capable of reproducing.

To determine your rabbit's sex

1. **Gently place the rabbit on his back in your lap.**

   If the rabbit panics, let him rest a minute and then try it again. If he continues to resist, leave this exam up to your vet.

2. **Using your thumb and forefinger, spread apart the hair on the area just beneath your rabbit's tail.**

3. **Push down gently in this area, and the vulva of a female or the penis of a male becomes visible.**

   You can see the difference in the accompanying figure. The male is on the left; the female is on the right.

Mature males (over 6 months) have scrotal sacs with testicles under the tail. They can pull the testicles up into the body at times, but you can still see the wrinkled area of the sacs.

You can perform this procedure on rabbits as young as a few weeks. The older the rabbit, however, the easier it is to tell whether you're looking at male or female reproductive organs.

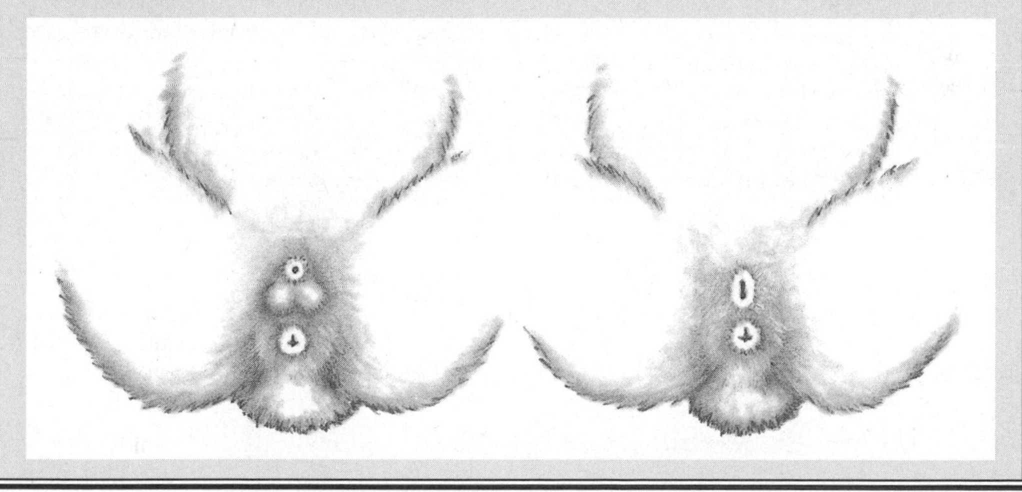

# Deciding Between a Boy or Girl

Another decision is whether to get a male or female rabbit. Depending on whom you talk to, both genders have their benefits, and the final decision is usually a matter of personal choice. Each sex generally has the following characteristics:

- **Bucks (males):** Having a reputation for being aggressive with people and other rabbits, males also tend to be distracted by their constant impulses to breed. This generalization isn't true of every buck, of course, but enough male rabbits act that way to make it a valid one. Bucks also have the unpleasant habit of marking their territory, spraying urine around the house on vertical surfaces.
- **Does (females):** Often said to be territorial and aloof, females care about reproducing to the point that they even conjure up false pregnancies if they aren't bred. Much like the buck, some female rabbits spray urine to mark their area.

Face it — neither one of these options sounds particularly appealing. In fact, if you read them again, you may start to wonder why anyone would ever want to keep *either* gender for a pet. It seems that raging hormones are the problem for both genders and are a large part of the reason that rabbits are so well known for reproductive tendencies. Luckily for those who love to share their lives with rabbits, a solution exists. Simply have your buck neutered or your doe spayed (see Chapter 9), and you're relieved of many of these behavioral problems. In fact, the sooner you spay or neuter your rabbit, the more likely your pet will never develop any of the unpleasant behaviors discussed here and in Chapter 13.

# Opting for an Only Rabbit or a Bunny with a Built-in Companion

More than one bunny means all the more fun, right? Sure it does, but it also means more work and a bit of planning and thought, too, for several reasons:

- **Most rabbits love other rabbits.** Rabbits are social creatures and love the companionship of their own species. If the time that you have to spend with your rabbit is limited, providing a home to at least two bunnies can ward off loneliness for both pets.
- **Some rabbits don't like other rabbits.** Although rabbits are social creatures and enjoy the company of other rabbits, like people, each has its own personality as well as likes and dislikes. In other words, not all

rabbits get along well together. Putting strange rabbits together, whether intact or not, is serious business and should be done with great care. Some rabbits *never* get along.

Unless two rabbits grow up together, they're likely to fight or at least be disagreeable toward each other in the beginning. Introductions need to be made slowly and carefully to ensure that the rabbits don't get into a literal bunny free-for-all. Putting several rabbits together requires a large space. See Chapters 5 and 6 for more details on housing your rabbits.

In fact, rabbit fights can be downright dangerous, and rabbits have been known to seriously injure and sometimes kill each other. Keeping siblings together is the best bet for rabbit harmony, as long as both pets are spayed or neutered.

- **Two rabbits mean double work.** When it comes time to clean up after your rabbits, two rabbits are twice as much work as one. You have much more to do when you have two rabbits sharing a hutch or two rabbits in their own cages. Also, you need to feed two rabbits, provide water to two rabbits, and give exercise and vet care to two rabbits. All these extra chores are more time-consuming and costly.
- **If you want a rabbit for a companion, stick with only one rabbit.** Rabbits who spend more time with other rabbits than humans tend to have a stronger bond with members of their own species rather than their human caretakers. If you want your rabbit to be more focused on you rather than a rabbit companion, have only one rabbit and spend a considerable amount of time with your pet.
- **Littermates do well together.** However, if they're male and female, as soon as they're of age (4 months), littermates do what rabbits do — incestuous or not.

If you plan to have more than one rabbit, introducing the bunnies carefully to avoid a fight is important. Rabbits are territorial, and it may take some convincing to get your resident bunny to accept a newcomer. Also, because rabbits have strong hierarchies in their social groups, your rabbits will probably scramble to see who is going to be the boss (see Chapter 11).

The first step toward a successful friendship between rabbits is spaying and neutering. Raging hormones can cause rabbits to fight when they might otherwise get along. Altering your rabbits means getting rid of those pesky hormones, resulting in a calmer and more docile bunny.

When deciding whether two rabbits can become friends, keep in mind that sex can be an important factor, too. Spayed females tend to get along best with neutered males. If you end up with two of the same sex, some rabbit folk report that two females are a better match than two males, who can be more territorial. Of course, like anything with rabbits, much of this dynamic has to do with individual personalities.

When making the initial rabbit-to-rabbit introduction, follow these guidelines:

1. **Make the introduction on neutral territory.**

   Pick a spot where neither rabbit has had a chance to stake a claim, such as a room in the house where neither has ever been. Placing the rabbits on unclaimed turf will temper their instinctive urge to defend territory.

2. **Keep the rabbits in individual cages at first and put the cages next to each other so that they can see one another**.

   Leave them together in this arrangement as often as possible.

3. **After the rabbits seem comfortable with each other through their cages, place them together in the neutral territory while they're wearing leashes and harnesses.**

   Make sure your rabbits have plenty of hiding places to allow escape should it be necessary. Let them spend time together (as much as you can) but don't allow them to get too close to each other.

4. **Look for signs of trouble.**

   Be aware of the signs that a rabbit is ready to attack: Ears will be bent back at a 45 degree angle, and the rabbit's tail will be raised. Rabbits that are biting or screaming during a scuffle should be separately immediately.

5. **When the rabbits seem comfortable together and you don't detect any aggression, allow them to get a little closer while still on their leashes.**

   If they do start to fight, you can separate them more easily because they're leashed.

6. **If you don't see any signs of hostility, you can let the rabbits loose together in the neutral space.**

   If they do squabble, break it up by squirting a water gun or spray bottle at them. Provided that you're dealing with neutered rabbits, the two can eventually work things out between them. If they do fight in the beginning, their personalities may be such that they never become best friends, but they at least need to tolerate each other.

After considering these factors, you may opt to just keep one rabbit for now. You can always add another bunny to your household later on. Or you may find that one rabbit is just right for your family and your situation. Again, if you're sure that you want to add more than one rabbit to your household, study up on the best way to make the transition for successful results. For more on how on how rabbits relate to each other and to help your bunny get along with your other pets, see Chapter 11.

# Mixing it Up: Bunny Mutts

A mixed breed is just that — a mix of different breeds that results in a unique, maybe surprising, kind of rabbit. If you're simply looking for a companion rabbit and have no notions of breeding or showing (see Chapters 10 and 15, respectively, for more on these topics), a mixed-breed rabbit is a wonderful choice. In fact, you're more likely to find a mixed breed in need of a home at animal shelters or rabbit rescue groups than a purebred.

Here are some good reasons to bring home a mixed-breed rabbit:

- If you go to a shelter or rescue group to adopt a rabbit, you'll be providing a home to a bunny who desperately needs one. This feeling is great!
- Rabbits within a breed tend to all look alike to the untrained eye, but mixed-breed rabbits are truly unique. No two are exactly alike.

If you choose to adopt a rabbit from a rescue group or animal shelter (a terrific idea that's covered in Chapter 4), you're likely to end up with a rabbit of unknown parentage. However, if you study photographs and descriptions of each rabbit breed in Chapter 3, you can use your detective skills and probably see purebred elements in your mixed-breed rabbit. Known in the rabbit world as *scrubs,* rabbits who are obviously not purebreds to a trained eye are assumed to be a mixture of breeds.

Of course, you don't need to know your mixed breed's ancestry to love her, but it may come in handy when dealing with issues such as coat care, ear care, and size. Mixed-breed rabbits come in a variety of shapes and sizes as a result of their varied bloodlines. If you want to adopt a mixed-breed bunny, you should think about its coat type, ear type, head shape, and its size.

## Rabbit coat types

Generally speaking, rabbits come in two different coat types: longhair and shorthair, both of which are shown in Figure 2-1.

Longhair rabbits need frequent grooming. If your rabbit seems to have fur that looks similar to an Angora's coat (see Chapter 3 for more information on what that looks like), your bunny probably has some Angora breeding and should be treated like an Angora when it comes to grooming. Brush a longhair rabbit to keep the hair from matting, which can lead to skin disease. In the case of matting around the anal area, brush out the hair to avoid the accumulation of stool and urine that can burn the skin.

Shorthair rabbits, on the other hand, do need grooming but not as often as a longhair rabbit.

**Figure 2-1:** Longhairs to the left, please. Shorthair? To the right.

## Head shape

The breeds that have shortened faces or small heads have a higher incidence of dental disease caused by *malocclusion* (the upper and lower teeth aren't properly aligned). Rabbit teeth grow throughout their lifetime, and they must wear properly on each other in order to stay in alignment. Therefore, in rabbit breeds such as the lop-eared, which has a flatter face, and the dwarf, which has a smaller head, pay particular attention to the appearance of the teeth when looking for a pet.

Some dental disease won't show up until the rabbit is 4 months old. It's therefore important to have your rabbit checked by an experienced veterinarian within its first year of life.

### Myth of the hairballs

Contrary to popular myth, hair is normally in a rabbit's stomach because rabbits are constantly grooming themselves. In a normal rabbit, this hair leaves the stomach and moves on through, ending up in the litter box. The malady traditionally called *hairballs* is really a dehydrated mass of hair and food that doesn't want to move. This condition can be caused by any illness that results in dehydration, but is more common in rabbits eating a diet that is low in certain types of fiber. The hair in itself is not the problem, but the diet is, and the situation demands immediate attention. For more on rabbit diet, see Chapter 7; Chapter 9 discusses gastrointestinal issues in detail.

## Size

Just like with purebred bunnies, you're likely to see a wide range of sizes in mixed-breed rabbits. Mixed breeds can range from 4 to 12 pounds. Most mixed-breed bunnies fall somewhere in between:

- **Small** is 2–6 pounds.
- **Medium** is 6–9 pounds.
- **Large** is 9–11 pounds.
- **Giants** are over 11 pounds.

Size is an important consideration because the larger the rabbit, the more space the pet needs. On the other hand, the smaller the rabbit, the harder the rabbit is to handle because small rabbits tend to be flighty and nervous. Although the 2-pound Dwarfs (see Figure 2-2) are a problem to handle, rabbits that are 4 to 5 pounds are a better choice for children.

Young children shouldn't be permitted to lift and carry any rabbit because of possible injury to the bunny. (See Chapter 8 for more on lifting and carrying rabbits.) A smaller rabbit is particularly vulnerable — not necessarily just due to its size but because of its temperament. Conversely, older children who are gentle, responsible, and carefully monitored should be able to lift and carry both medium-size and smaller bunnies without a problem.

**Figure 2-2:** A dwarf is a dwarf, of course, of course. . . . A giant breed is to the left, a dwarf breed to the right, as compared to an apple.

# Living the High Life: Bunny Bluebloods

In the last hundred years or so, rabbit fanciers around the world have worked hard to create the various breeds of rabbits that exist today. But not all breeds are easily available in North America and in many other parts of the world.

If you lean toward a purebred, you have many rabbits to select from. The American Rabbit Breeders Association, Inc. (ARBA) recognizes 47 rabbit breeds (purebred rabbits other than the 47 ARBA breeds are out there, too), and if you want a purebred rabbit, you'll most likely be choosing from one of these fascinating types. However, you'll be happy to know that even though so many rabbit breeds exist, each one is distinctive enough in appearance to make your decision easier. (The breed descriptions are outlined in Chapter 3.) Size, coat type, and color — even personality — can differ significantly between rabbit breeds.

Don't forget that you have all the various mixed-breed rabbits to pick from as well, with characteristics of the breeds, but each different from the other.

## Purebred reasoning

Before you decide on a mixed-breed or purebred rabbit, give the following issues some consideration:

- **Appearance:** If you prefer a rabbit with a particular type of fur or general appearance, you can get exactly what you want if you go for a purebred. Also, keep the coat type in mind. Different rabbit breeds have different coat types. English Angoras and Jersey Woolies, for example, are known for their profuse coats. These coats are beautiful to look at but require considerable time and care to keep groomed. Shorthair breeds, such as the Rex and Dutch, on the other hand, need little grooming. Think long and hard about whether you have enough time and interest for a longhair rabbit.
- **Breeding:** If you've done your research and are certain you want to get involved with rabbit breeding, you should get a purebred. Please keep in mind that the world has many bunnies out there in need of homes, so breeding rabbits for a hobby without the purpose of improving the breed is irresponsible. Responsible rabbit breeders are involved in the business of purebred rabbits, understand the ins and outs of rabbit husbandry, and have good homes lined up for the rabbits before they breed.
- **Disposition:** Many breeds of rabbits have distinct dispositions that are unique to them. If you want a quieter rabbit, opt for one of the larger breeds, which are known for their more gentle temperament (see Table 2-1). If you prefer a challenge, go for a smaller, feistier breed. (Of course, all rabbits are individuals, and temperament can vary even within a particular breed.)

- **Showing:** If you plan to show your rabbit in the American ARBA shows, you must have a purebred. (For more on the ARBA, check out the resources in the Appendix.) If your child wants to show rabbits in 4-H, a purebred offers more opportunities for showing than a mixed breed. See Chapter 15 for more showing details.
- **Size:** With a purebred rabbit, you know exactly what size the bunny will be when he's grown; Table 2-1 has the breakdown. For example, if you buy a young purebred New Zealand rabbit, you know that it will grow up to weigh about 10 pounds, max, because that's typical of the New Zealand breed. Purebred rabbits come in an assortment of sizes, from the tiny 2-pound Netherland Dwarf to the huge 14-pound Flemish Giant and a number of sizes in between. The smaller breeds are easier to house than the larger breeds. The large breeds require bigger cages and bigger biceps to lift. The majority of breed sizes is in between, which is the typical size that most people think of when they imagine a pet rabbit.

**Table 2-1 Rabbit Breeds According to Size**

| *Small (2–6 lbs.)* | *Medium (6–9 lbs.)* | *Large (9–11 lbs.)* | *Giant (11 lbs. and Over)* |
|---|---|---|---|
| American Fuzzy Lop | American Sable | American | Checkered Giant |
| Britannia Petite | Belgian Hare | American Chinchilla | Flemish Giant |
| Dutch | English Angora | Beveren | French Lop |
| Dwarf Hotot | English Spot | Californian | Giant Chinchilla |
| Florida White | French Angora | Champagne d'Argent | |
| Havana | Harlequin | Cinnamon | |
| Himilayan | Lilac | Creme d'Argent | |
| Holland Lop | Rex | English Lop | |
| Jersey Wooly | Rhinelander | Giant Angora | |
| Mini Lop | Satin Angora | Hotot | |
| Mini Rex | Silver Marten | New Zealand | |
| Mini Satin | Standard Chinchilla | Palomino | |
| Netherland Dwarf | | Satin | |
| Polish | | Silver Fox | |
| Silver | | | |
| Tan | | | |
| Thrianta | | | |

## You pure about that?

You may be wondering what exactly makes a rabbit purebred. A *purebred* rabbit or animal of any kind is a member of *breed* — a group of individuals within a domesticated species that has common ancestors and characteristics that are different from other groups of individuals within the same species. Rabbit breeds are similar to dog breeds, such as Cocker Spaniel and Collie, in that respect. Both dog breeds and rabbits breeds have distinct body types, head shapes, colorations, and other traits that when combined result in a unique kind of dog or rabbit.

## Different breeds, different looks

Rabbits come in a vast array of colors and patterns according to ARBA. The group declares that a few coat variations exist within the breeds, too. "What's the difference?" you ask. Well, I'll tell you:

- **Coat:** The kind of fur a rabbit has. Rabbits come in one of four different kinds of fur, the first three of which are considered shorthair:
  - **Normal** rabbit fur is the kind of coat that you see on most rabbits. It comes in two layers: an overcoat and undercoat. Both layers are about an inch in length. The undercoat is soft and serves as insulation to keep the rabbit warm.
  - **Rex** fur is found only on Rex rabbits and breeds with Rex lineage. This fur looks and feels like velvet and is shorter than normal fur. Cottony and airy to the touch, Rex fur stands upright instead of laying flat against the rabbit's body.
  - **Satin** fur has a silky, shiny appearance, the result of its fine, somewhat translucent hair shafts. Satin coats are about the same length as normal fur coats but can be distinguished by their distinctive luster.
  - **Angora** coat is long (2 to 3 inches in length) and fluffy and is often used for spinning because of its warmth. Because it's used to make clothing, the Angora coat is often referred to as *wool.* The fur stands away from the rabbit's body, giving it a fuzzy, puffy appearance.
- **Color:** Rabbit colors are arranged in pattern groups. Individual colors exist within each pattern group. (Some have the same name as the pattern group, but are considered distinct colorations and not just pattern

groups.) Each breed has its own breed standard and allowed color varieties, but a host of common colors can be found in many different breeds.

- Patterns are made of the following:
  - **Agouti:** Agouti-colored rabbits have three or more bands of color on each guard hair shaft, usually with a dark gray base. (*Guard hair* is the coarse, outer hair on most mammals.) Two or more alternating light or dark rings are also present. The head, feet, and ears of a rabbit of this color are usually *ticked* (darker), while the circles around the eyes, the fur on the belly, and the fur under the jaws tend to be lighter. Agouti-colored rabbits come in chestnut, chocolate, sable, lilac, and smoke pearl.
  - **Brindle:** Brindle, a color also seen commonly in certain dog breeds, such as the Greyhound and American Pit Bull Terrier, is an intermingling of two solid guard hair colors, a dark and a light. Black and orange as well as black and white are the prevalent color combinations. The brindle pattern appears consistently throughout the body.
  - **Broken:** Two different subdivisions can be found within the broken pattern: bicolor and tricolor. A bicolored broken pattern consists of any normal rabbit color appearing with white. For example, a bicolored rabbit may be white with black spots. A tricolored rabbit, on the other hand, has white along with two other colors.
  - **Marked:** Rabbits of marked patterns are usually white with patterns consisting of another color throughout their bodies.
  - **Pointed white:** Much like a Siamese cat, this type of rabbit is all white with a darker color on its nose, ears, feet, and tail.
  - **Self:** Used to describe solid-color rabbits, this term applies to those bunnies who have a uniform color throughout their entire body.
  - **Shaded:** Shaded rabbits show a gradual shift in color, beginning with a darker color on their backs, heads, necks, ears, legs, and tails. This color eventually turns into a lighter version of the same color when it reaches the rabbit's sides.
  - **Solid:** Similar to the self-pattern, described earlier in this list, this pattern may also include agouti and other mixed-color fur, as long as colors don't create a pattern or marking.
  - **Ticked:** Contrasting the rabbit's main color, solid or tipped guard hairs throughout the coat distinguish this pattern.
  - **Wide band:** Rabbits of this coloration have the same color on their bodies, heads, ears, tails, and feet. Their eye circles, underside of tail, jaws, and belly have a lighter coloration.

- **Common colors:** In addition to black and white, the colors in the following list are those you'll see most often:
  - **Beige:** Rabbits of this color have a beige pigment throughout their bodies except for the napes of their necks, which is lighter. They have a bluish-white color on their bellies, along with *eye circles* (coloration around the outside of the eye) of the same color. Their eyes are brown with a ruby glow.
  - **Blue:** The blue coloration in rabbits is best described as a medium shade of gray with a blue or lavender cast. The eyes of a blue-colored rabbit are blue-gray.
  - **Castor:** A rich dark chestnut color, castor has also been described as mahogany brown. Castor fur is lightly tipped with black evenly distributed over the body, head, and legs. The belly of a castor rabbit is white or tan, and the eyes are brown.
  - **Chinchilla:** Chinchilla-colored rabbits possess a blend of black and pearl hairs with a dark gray base. Named after the coloring seen on actual chinchillas, a rodent known for its lush fur, chinchilla rabbits also come in a chocolate version.
  - **Chocolate:** A deep dark brown, the chocolate coloration features a light gray undercoat. The eyes are brown with a red cast in subdued light.
  - **Fawn:** Fawn-colored rabbits are a deep golden color over their backs onto their flanks and chests. Their eye circles, insides of ears, under jaws, tails, and bellies are white. Fawn-colored rabbits have gray or brown eyes.
  - **Lilac:** This coloration features a medium-gray hue with a pinkish tint over the rabbit's entire body. The eyes are the same color as the fur and have a ruby glow in subdued light.
  - **Lynx:** The body and the top of the lynx-colored rabbit's tail are tinged with lilac and light orange with a sharper orange color showing through. Areas underneath the tail, belly, and jaw are white. The eye circles and insides of the ears are also white. The eyes of a lynx-colored rabbit are blue-gray.
  - **Opal:** Opal-colored rabbits feature a pale bluish color on the top of the hair shaft with a fawn band below it and a dark gray undercoat. The ears of the opal are laced with blue. The eye circles and underside of the rabbit are white with a dark gray undercoat. The eyes are gray.
  - **Siamese:** Not surprisingly, Siamese-colored rabbits look much like seal-point Siamese cats. They have dark brown color on their ears, head, feet, belly, and tail with a lighter body color so that the dark points can be seen. The eyes are brown.

- **Squirrel:** Although it's a strange color name for a rabbit, squirrel is often used nonetheless. The hair shaft of rabbits with the squirrel coloration consists of a blend of gray and white bands. This color extends from the rabbit's back down to its sides, where it's met by white on the belly and top of the hind feet. The nape of the neck, chest, and eye circles are a lighter version of the original color. The upper part of the ears has a dark blue edge. The eyes are gray.
- **Steel:** This interesting color pattern comes in black, blue, chocolate, lilac, sable, and smoke pearl. The entire body of the rabbit features one of these colors, the hairs of which are diffused with a small amount of gold or silver tipping, depending on whether the rabbit is a gold steel or a silver steel. The eyes are brown or gray.
- **Tan Pattern:** Different from beige, the tan coloration features a solid color on the head, back, sides, outside of ears, back legs, front of forelegs, and top of the tail. A lighter color appears on the eye circles, nostrils, jaw, chest, and underside of the rabbit's body.
- **Tortoiseshell:** Rabbits with this coloration don't have a shell that they can duck into, but they sport a lively orange on their bodies, which mingles into a grayish-blue shadowing over the rump and haunches. The top of the tail matches the orange color, but underneath is the color of the shadowing. Tortoiseshell-colored rabbits have brown eyes.

Even though it may seem hard to visualize the patterns and colors listed in descriptions of these breeds, they can be broken down into more simple terms. Start with the various types of coats that rabbits have and then move on to the different colorations and patterns.

# Chapter 3

# So Many Breeds, So Little Time

### *In This Chapter*

- Listing the rabbit breeds
- Discovering the differences between the breeds

If you're thinking that a purebred rabbit may be the right choice for you, you've taken your first step toward finding your pet. Your next step is to consider the nearly 50 breeds recognized by the American Rabbit Breeders Association, Inc. (ARBA), which governs the business of purebred rabbits in the United States. (See Chapter 15 for more ARBA information.)

Each breed has a unique appearance, with differences in size, coat type, and color. Even a rabbit's personality can vary according to breed. So, you ask, how are you ever going to sort through it all? Well, go to the experts. All the ARBA rabbit breeds have a unique history and a set of fans who believe their breed of rabbit is the absolute best. You'll find many of these experts in *breed clubs,* groups of people who specialize in each of the ARBA breeds.

Take a look at these breeds and judge for yourself. Then see the Appendix of this book for ARBA contact information and the recognized breed clubs.

## American

Compact in appearance, the American is a medium-size rabbit, weighing around 10 pounds. Its mandolin-shaped body provides a slight arch over the loins and hindquarters and a taper from the hindquarters to the shoulders. In existence nearly 100 years, the American breed comes in two color varieties: blue or white. The blue variety has blue-gray eyes, and the white version has pink eyes.

# American Fuzzy Lop

The Fuzzy Lop, which is related to the Holland Lop and the Angora, is available in many colors. This color choice, along with its furry coat and long, floppy ears, make it a popular breed with rabbit lovers. The American Fuzzy Lop is shown in six different groups based on its color pattern: broken, pointed white, wide band, agouti, shaded, and self. Within those groups are the agouti colors of chestnut, chinchilla, opal, and lynx. The broken colors of any recognized rabbit breed are allowed, as are the solid colors of black, white, lilac, blue, and chocolate. A number of other color patterns are also available in this small rabbit, whose body is short and stocky. This cobby (stocky) little rabbit's coat is long and woolly, requiring frequent grooming.

# American Sable

The ears, face, legs, and tail of the American Sable are darker than the main part of its body. This rabbit is well named because its coat is a beautiful dark brown — the result of crosses with the Chinchilla. A medium-size rabbit sporting a slightly arched back, the American Sable is an attractive pet, weighing around 9 pounds.

# Angora

Angora rabbits come in one of four types:

- **English Angora:** Originating in Turkey, the English Angora breed is at least 200 years old, if not older. This rabbit comes in six color groups: the pointed white, self, agouti, shaded, wide band, and ticked. Within these groups, the colors available are white with black; blue lilac or chocolate points; solid blue, black, chestnut, agouti, chinchilla, chocolate agouti, chocolate chinchilla, copper, lilac, lilac chinchilla, lynx, squirrel, opal and wild gray; shaded blue cream, chocolate tortoiseshell, dark sable, frosted pearl, lilac cream, smoke pearl, sable and tortoiseshell; solid cream, red and fawn; and ticked chocolate steel, lilac steel, steel and blue steel. Compact in size and stature, the English Angora weighs in at around 6 pounds.
- **French Angora:** The French Angora was developed before the English Angora, specifically for its wool. The French people used to hand pluck its wool and spin it for clothing. This breed comes in the same four-color varieties as the English Angora and in the identical colors. While the

two breeds are similar, the French Angora is somewhat bigger than the English, weighing in at around 9 pounds. The French Angora also has less hair on its head, ears, and legs.

- **Giant Angora:** Bathed in fur, the Giant Angora, with its dramatic appearance, tends to stand out among the rest of the Angora breeds. Unlike the other Angoras, the Giant is available only in white, with blue eyes or ruby eyes. It's larger than the English or the Satin, weighing in at around 9 pounds. Its coat is similar to the English Angora in that it has longer *furnishings* (hair on its ears, face, and legs).
- **Satin Angora:** Slightly smaller than the English Angora, Satin Angoras usually weigh around 7 pounds. The Satin Angora comes in the same color varieties as the English and French Angoras. The main difference between the Satin and the other Angoras is its coat. The Satin, as its name would imply, has shinier, silkier hair than its counterparts.

Each one of these Angoras is a separate breed and has the characteristic long, woolly hair typical of this rabbit family. Angoras come in a vast array of beautiful colors and come in two color classifications: white and colored.

Because of the Angora's dense coat, which measures about 3 inches in length, this breed needs plenty of grooming. You should only consider owning an Angora if you have the time and patience to spend brushing its luxurious coat. Chapter 8 offers grooming information.

# Belgian Hare

Europeans developed the Belgian Hare in the late 1800s specifically for the lean, racehorselike appearance. Despite its name, the Belgian Hare isn't really a hare but is actually a domestic rabbit. However, its long legs and ears give it the appearance of a hare, hence its name. Only available in red chestnut, the Belgian Hare is a large-size rabbit of about 9 pounds.

# Beveren

A large rabbit of about 10 pounds, the Beveren has a thick, silky coat. It's of medium length and has a slightly arched back. Not as frequently seen in the United States as some other breeds, the Beveren was developed in Europe and comes in the color varieties of white, blue, and black.

## Britannia Petite

Known for being curious and alert, the tiny, fine-boned Britannia Petite can make a good pet for older children who can treat this light-stature breed gently. This rabbit is all white or black otter-colored and weighs only about 2 pounds.

## Californian

Originally bred in the Golden State in the 1920s, the Californian is related to the Himalayan, which is similar in appearance. This popular rabbit looks much like a Siamese cat, with its white coat and black-tipped ears, nose, feet, and tail. Somewhat large in size, the typical Californian weighs about 9 pounds. Its body is plump and firm to the touch.

## Champagne d' Argent

The Argent, an old breed, was originally bred in the Champagne province of France for its fur and meat. Weighing about 10 pounds, the medium-size Argent is a popular pet in the United States. The Argent coat contains a marvelous mix of colored hairs that has a silvery effect.

## Checkered Giant

The Checkered Giant was first brought to America from Europe in 1910 and sports a long, well-arched body. This popular breed comes in black and blue color varieties. The breed is typically white with dark markings, including a "butterfly" on the nose, dark ears, dark circles around the eyes, spots on the cheeks, and various other dark patches on the body. Weighing a solid 11 pounds or more, the Checkered Giant is related to the Flemish Giant.

## Chinchilla

The Chinchilla comes in three breeds: the Standard, the American, and the Giant. All three types have the coloring of an actual chinchilla and are popular pets because of their attractive coats.

- **Standard Chinchilla** is the foundation of the Chinchilla breed, weighing around 6 pounds. Reportedly developed in France by crossing a wild gray rabbit with some domestic strains, the breed was first shown in 1913. It has a medium body with a slight arch to the back.
- **American Chinchilla** is the middleweight of the three Chinchilla breeds, coming in at around 10 pounds. It was bred down from the Standard variety for its size.
- **Giant Chinchilla** is the largest in this family and the result of a cross between the Flemish Giant and a smaller Chinchilla by an American breeder sometime after World War I. It was developed as a meat rabbit, but makes a nice, albeit large, pet at about 14 pounds.

# Cinnamon

This breed comes only in a reddish color synonymous with its name. The ears, face, and feet bear a darker shade of this same color. Occasional shades of gray on various parts of its body contribute to this breed's unusual appearance. Cinnamons, which are related to the New Zealand White, the Checkered Giant, the Californian, and the Chinchilla, weigh approximately 10 pounds.

# Crème d' Argent

The Crème d'Argent, which originated in France, is a handsome rabbit with an exquisitely colored coat of pale orange. Lighter guard hairs give this rabbit a smooth and silky appearance. Typically, the Crème d'Argent weighs about 9 pounds.

# Dutch

Originally from Holland, the Dutch is one of the oldest established rabbit breeds. Small and compact, these rabbits weigh around 4 pounds. The Dutch is an extremely popular rabbit and easily recognizable because of its markings; they have a band of white around the chest. Available in six color varieties, the Dutch has a dark head with a white nose, a white *blaze* (a white stripe starting at the nose and going upward toward the face), and dark *britches* (the back half of the rabbit). Its dark eyes blend into the color on its face, which can be black, blue, chocolate, tortoiseshell, steel, or gray.

## Dwarf Hotot

Only seen in white with dark eyes, the Dwarf Hotot weighs about 3 pounds and was bred down from the Hotot in the 1970s. At first sight, the tiny Dwarf Hotot appears to be wearing eyeliner. The breed's characteristic black eye bands give it this look.

## English Spot

An old breed whose popularity began in England in the late 1800s, the English Spot is still a favorite breed and makes a good pet. The English, for short, is reminiscent of a Dalmatian with its white coat and dark spots. The breed comes in seven different color varieties of which the breed's markings are made: black, blue, chocolate, gold, gray, lilac, and tortoiseshell. A capped nose, dark ears, eye rings, and a stripe along the back are all characteristic of this breed, which weighs about 8 pounds.

## Flemish Giant

Seen quite often at rabbit shows, the Flemish Giant originated in Belgium as its name suggests. Massive in size, the Flemish Giant is the largest breed of rabbit and weighs over 14 pounds. Available in steel gray, light gray, black, blue, white, sandy, and fawn, this breed is popular as a pet because of its large size.

In general, the larger the rabbit, the greater the tendency to be more laid-back and relaxed than the dwarf breeds.

## Florida White

This breed — a cross between the Dutch, Polish, and New Zealand White — is relatively new; the American Rabbit Breeders Association accepted this breed in the early 1960s. Sadly, the Florida White is one of the breeds commonly used for laboratory research. This breed comes in white only, as its name implies, with pink eyes. It weighs about 5 pounds.

# Harlequin

The Harlequin, developed in France in the 1800s, is an interesting, medium-size rabbit of about 8 pounds with unusual markings. Available in two color groups and four actual colors, the Harlequin is best described as having an "ice-cream sundae" look to its coat. Different colors swirl and blend in unique configurations. The heads of Harlequin rabbits are split in half by color, making them look like a different rabbit from one side to the next! Harlequin base colors are black, blue, lilac, and chocolate and come in two types:

- **Japanese Harlequin** sports a coat that has a base coloring that interchanges with strips of orange or a lighter version of the base color.
- **Magpie Harlequin** base coloring alternates with strips of white.

# Havana

The small, shiny Havana was created from a single rabbit born to an unpedigreed doe in Holland in 1898. First appearing in chocolate, the Havana is now available in blue and black varieties as well. Prized for its coat, the Havana is short and stocky *(close coupled)*. Its weight of 6 pounds and its compact build can make it a nice pet for an older child.

# Himalayan

More widely distributed around the world than any other breed of rabbit, the Himalayan is popular in China and Russia, as well as in the United States. The breed has been around for many years, reportedly originating near the Himalayan Mountains. Distinctive because of its white coat and blue or black markings, this small-size rabbit weighs only about 4 pounds.

# Hotot

The breed was first imported into the United States in the late 1970s. In France, this breed is known as the Blanc de Hotot, which means *the white of Hotot.* Hotot is the area where the breed was developed. Available only in a frosty white color with thin black eye circles, the medium-size Hotot weighs around 9 pounds.

# Jersey Wooly

A recently developed breed of rabbit created in the 1970s through crossbreeding, the Jersey Wooly was created specifically for its luxurious coat. The fur of the Jersey Wooly is available in agouti (chestnut, chinchilla, opal, and squirrel), pointed white (black or blue markings), self (black, blue, chocolate, lilac, blue-eyed white, and ruby-eyed white), shaded (sable point, seal, Siamese sable, smoke pearl, tortoiseshell, and blue tortoiseshell), and tan pattern (black otter, blue otter, silver marten, sable marten, and smoke pearl marten) color groups. A small rabbit, the Jersey Wooly weighs about 3 pounds.

This breed is known for its gentle temperament and for being an exceptional pet. However, because of its long coat, the Jersey Wooly does require regular grooming.

# Lilac

The Lilac comes in one color: a light pinkish gray. Originally considered a deviation from the norm, the Lilac began as a result of an unusual coloration within the Havana breed. Weighing about 7 pounds, the body of the Lilac is substantial and compact. This breed makes a good and attractive companion rabbit.

# Lop

The Lop rabbits are probably the most distinctive and easily recognizable of all the breeds. The Lop has huge ears that flop down beside its head like a hound dog's ears, giving it a special look unique to the breed. Along with those big ears comes a wonderful personality. Because Lops are bred specifically for show and pet purposes, they tend to be people oriented. Owners of Lops report that they're amusing rabbits to live with and can also grow to be affectionate and sensitive to their owners' feelings.

Lops come in four different breeds, each unique in both its appearance and history:

- **English Lop:** Developed at least as early as the 1800s, the English Lop is one of the oldest breeds of domestic rabbit still in existence and the first of the lop-eared breeds. The ears of an adult English Lop measure 25 inches or more in length. Weighing approximately 10 pounds, the English Lop comes in broken and solid color patterns. Within those patterns, many of the typical rabbit colors are found. When being judged at rabbit shows, the ears are the most important aspect of this well-balanced breed.

- **French Lop:** Developed in France in the 1800s from the English Lop and the Flemish Giant, the French Lop differs from the English in that it sports a heavier stature and shorter ears. The French Lop weighs in at around 10 pounds and comes in two color varieties: solid and broken. This breed comes in many different rabbit colors. The French Lop is a close relative of the English Lop, which was used in its creation.
- **Holland Lop:** Also known as the Netherland Dwarf Lop, the tiny, compact Holland Lop weighs only about 4 pounds. The Holland Lop is a dwarf breed of Lop, created in Holland in the 1960s. It falls into the same color varieties as the French and English: agouti, broken, pointed white, self, solid, shaded, and ticked. Holland Lops are available in any recognized rabbit color.
- **Mini Lop:** Developed in the 1970s in Germany, the Mini Lop was originally called the Klein Widder until its named was changed in the 1980s, when the American Rabbit Breeders Association recognized it.

The Mini Lop, shown in Figure 3-1, is similar to the French Lop, although it's much smaller at around 5 pounds. The breed comes in the usual Lop color varieties of agouti, broken, pointed white, shelf, shaded, solid, and ticked. All recognized rabbit colors are seen in the Mini Lop.

**Figure 3-1:** The Mini Lop, a relatively new breed of Lop recognized by the ARBA in the 1980s.

*Faith Uridel Photography*

# Mini Rex

The Mini Rex breed, shown in Figure 3-2, is growing in popularity as a pet and show rabbit because of its luxurious fur, which is short yet plush, and its small size. Cottony and airy to the touch, Rex fur looks and feels like velvet and is shorter than normal fur. Their guard hairs are erect and short and the undercoat is erect, which gives it that cut fur look. (*Guard hair* is the coarse, outer hair on most mammals.)

This breed was developed using the standard-size Rex. Weighing about 4 pounds, the Mini Rex is available in the same color varieties and colors as its larger cousin, the Rex.

Rabbits with Rex fur lack the heavy protective fur on the foot pad. Rex rabbit owners need to take care to keep their pets from becoming overweight and house the pets on a surface that provides some softness.

**Figure 3-2:** With its short, plush fur, the Mini Rex is growing in popularity.

Faith Uridel Photography

# Mini Satin

Weighing in at about 4 pounds, the Mini Satin is a more petite version of the American Satin. An American creation going back to the 1970s, the Mini Satin was recognized as a breed in the ARBA standard only in February 2006, making it the 47th ARBA breed. Although color varieties can include red, broken, and white, only the white variety can compete for Best Mini Satin. Like its larger counterpart, Mini Satins are known for their brilliant color, due to a recessive trait that results in a more transparent covering of the hair shaft.

# Netherland Dwarf

Part of the Netherland Dwarf's appeal is no doubt the result of its babylike features; fully grown adult Netherland Dwarfs still resemble what's commonly known as *kits* (baby rabbits) among rabbit lovers. This popular breed is the smallest of domestic rabbits, not weighing more than 2 pounds. Its tiny stature, wide availability of colors, small ears, and large eyes make it a popular pet. The Netherland Dwarf comes in the following color varieties and colors: self (white with ruby eyes, white with blue eyes, black, blue, chocolate, and lilac); shaded (Siamese sable, Siamese smoke pearl, and sable point); agouti (chinchilla, lynx, opal, squirrel, and chestnut); tan pattern (sable marten, silver marten, smoke pearl marten, otter, and tan); and any other variety (fawn, Himalayan, orange, steel, and tortoiseshell).

This breed is definitely more prone to dental disease due to the small size of their heads and shortened jaws.

# New Zealand

Despite its name, the New Zealand was developed in the United States, where it was created for meat, fur, and research purposes. In spite of its original function, however, the New Zealand has become a popular pet and show rabbit. This breed comes in three distinct color varieties: white, black, and red. The red was the first color to appear after what experts believe was a cross between a Belgium Hare and a white rabbit. Typical New Zealands weigh about 10 pounds.

## Palomino

The Palomino's golden color is similar to the coat colors seen in the Palomino horse. (Surprise!) A newer breed, the Palomino was developed in the United States and comes in two color varieties: golden and lynx. Weighing about 9 pounds, the Palomino has a slightly arched back and makes a good pet because of its easygoing personality.

## Polish

Some experts believe that the name of this breed doesn't refer to the country of Poland but rather to this rabbit's shiny coat. A tiny bunny weighing only about 3 pounds, the Polish is believed to have developed in England in the 1800s. Commonly seen at rabbit shows, this breed comes in five color varieties: blue, black, chocolate, blue-eyed white, and ruby-eyed white.

## Rex

The Rex, which comes in a wide variety of colors, is popular as a pet and show rabbit. Rex rabbit fur looks and feels like plush velvet, as shown in Figure 3-3. Created in 1919 from a mutation, the Rex's unusual coat can be attributed to erect, short guard hairs and erect, short undercoat. Weighing approximately 9 pounds, the Rex comes in black, black otter, blue, Californian, castor, chinchilla, chocolate, lilac, lynx, opal, red, sable, seal, white, and broken group varieties. All known rabbit colors are seen in the Rex.

## Rhinelander

Developed in Europe, the Rhinelander is a medium- to large-size rabbit weighing anywhere from 7 to 10 pounds. The Rhinelander has an unusual coloration that can best be described as patches of calico, much like the coloring on the calico cat. The breed's base color is white, with markings of black and orange on its nose, ears, cheeks, eyes, back, and sides.

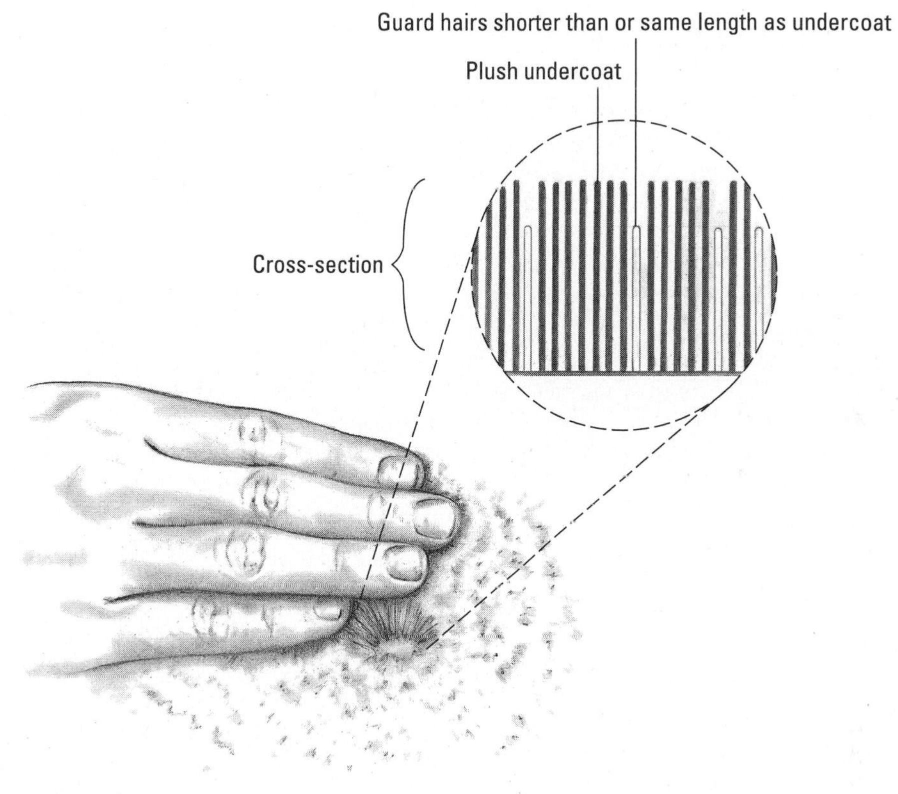


**Figure 3-3:** A Rex's hair is short but plush.

# Satin

Created in the United States from a mutation within the Havana breed, the Satin comes in ten different color groups: black, blue, Californian, chinchilla, chocolate, copper, red, Siamese, white, and broken. The Satin is so named because of its soft, shiny coat. This is a medium-size rabbit with a weight of about 9 pounds.

# Silver

Believed to have originated in India centuries ago, the Silver breed was refined in England during the height of rabbit show popularity. The Silver got its name from the silvery sheen on its coat, created by a mixture of white hairs against a dark background. Available in black, brown, and fawn, Silvers weigh anywhere from 4 to 7 pounds.

## Silver Fox

Formerly called the American Heavyweight Silver, the Silver Fox is large, weighing about 10 pounds. Originally bred in Europe for its fur, the Silver Fox has an unusual coat. Measuring an inch or more in length with a thick undercoat, the fur of the Silver Fox comes in black or blue varieties.

## Silver Marten

Created using the Chinchilla rabbit, the Silver Marten has guard hairs that are gray-tipped on a dark background of black, blue, chocolate, or sable. The area around the eye and nose are also gray. Silver Martens typically weigh about 8 pounds.

## Tan

Supposedly the result of an accidental mating between a wild buck and a Dutch doe in England during the 1800s, the Tan has been popular for decades. The color and markings of this breed are reminiscent of a Doberman Pincher, particularly the black and chocolate varieties. The top part of the body is dark, but the underside is tan. The tan coloring also appears around the eyes and nose, under the neck, and inside the brims of the ears. The Tan is a small- to medium-size rabbit, weighing approximately 5 pounds.

## Thrianta

Known to its fans as the "Fire of the Fancy," the Thrianta is a breed known for its unusual orange-red coat. The Thrianta was the 46th breed to be recognized by the ARBA and was approved in February 2006, along with the Mini Satin. Thriantas are medium-size rabbits weighing from 4 to 6 pounds, with an ideal weight of less than 5 pounds. Although the breed is relatively new to the ARBA, its origins go back to the 1930s in Europe. Because all of the breed's original stock in the United States was imported, this newer breed may be less widely available than others.

# Chapter 4

# Hiding in Shelters, Holes, and Shops

### In This Chapter

- Adopting a rabbit in need
- Knowing what to do with a stray
- Considering bunnies from breeders
- Selecting a healthy rabbit

Okay, so you can't wait to get a rabbit. You can't wait to make that furry face and long set of ears a part of your family. But because rabbits don't grow under rocks, you need to go out and find a good source for your new companion.

As a potential rabbit owner, you have several options when it comes to finding the bunny you've decided upon (see Chapter 2). The source you ultimately choose depends on exactly what you're looking for. Before you go, think about what you want to do with your rabbit — keep him as a pet or show him — and put that scenario together with the information in this chapter.

## Donning Your Cape: Rescuing a Rabbit

The true guardian angels of the rabbit world are those who take care of unwanted rabbits and struggle to find them good homes. These people are found working in animal shelters and within private rabbit rescue groups.

*Shelters* are the very same that take in unwanted dogs and cats and from where most municipal animal control agencies work. *Rescue groups* are private, nonprofit organizations mostly run by volunteers. You can look for a rescue group in your area in the Appendix, by contacting the House Rabbit Society, or by looking on the Internet for a group in your area.

By adopting a rabbit from a shelter or other organization, you're not only getting a pet, you're saving a rabbit from a gloomy, uncertain fate. Rabbit rescues and shelters are overwhelmed with unwanted bunnies, and, sadly, tens of thousands are euthanized each year. In addition, by taking one rabbit home, you're making room for another at a shelter. You're also spreading the good word about the many merits of rabbit adoption.

## Presenting the problem

You may be wondering why rabbits would need rescuing. Do that many unwanted rabbits exist? If you're familiar with the pet overpopulation that plagues cats and dogs, then you'll easily understand the situation with rabbits. It's virtually the same dilemma. A lot of domesticated rabbits are alive in this country, and not enough of them have homes.

Most of the rabbits that are homeless are in this situation through no fault of their own. Common reasons given for abandoning rabbits to shelters and rescue groups include

- The kids (or sadly, the adults) got tired of taking care of the rabbit.
- I didn't know that rabbits like to chew on everything (see Chapter 13 for training help).
- We got a baby rabbit for Easter and then it grew up (see Chapter 1).
- The adolescent rabbit's behavior is difficult to handle. I don't want to deal with it.
- My rabbit is urinating or defecating outside his litter box. (Again, see Chapter 5 for training help.)
- My rabbit has chronic health problems, and I no longer have the money or time handle them.

## Seeking the solution

When unwanted rabbits come to animal shelters or rescue groups, they're put up for adoption.

In order to ensure that you'll provide a good, permanent home for the rabbit you're adopting, be prepared to answer some questions. Each group works a bit differently, but some shelters and nearly all rescue groups

- **Screen to make sure that you have the facilities and willingness to provide a lasting home for a rabbit.** Don't be offended by their questions. Remember that these people have the best interests of the rabbit in mind. The last thing anyone wants is for a rabbit to be adopted, only to be returned when problems arise.

- **Require that you pay an adoption fee.** This is to help offset the cost of caring for the rabbit you have adopted. These fees help the groups continue to operate so they can provide help to rabbits in need.
- **Have only a few rabbits available at any given time in your area.** You'll probably be able to choose from only a handful of bunnies, but have an open mind and give all the bunnies a chance! It's worth noting that some mixed breeds are hard to place with owners simply because of their looks, such as the all-white rabbits with red eyes. (Some people think these New Zealand rabbits look "scary"; in fact, they're known to be wonderful companions.)

### Shelters

Shelters — whether run by private groups or local governments — do an admirable job of finding homes for neglected or abandoned cats, dogs, rabbits, and other pets. Not all shelters are created equal, however, and some don't even accept rabbits.

- At shelters where unadopted pets are euthanized, rabbits are destroyed if they're not adopted within a specified period of time. *No-kill shelters* keep rabbits until they're adopted (unless, in some cases, there are serious concerns about health or aggression).
- In an effort to ensure successful adoptions, some shelters screen potential adopters. They also factor into adoption fees the cost of spaying and neutering, a step that goes a long way toward preventing future unwanted litters.
- Some shelters do not screen adopters or spay or neuter rabbits. Although such shelters may charge a nominal fee as low as $1, you'll have to pay to spay or neuter your bunny, which can cost from $75 to $350. Other shelters may give you a coupon for a discounted spay or neuter.

If you make the admirable choice to go to an animal shelter to rescue a bunny, follow these steps:

1. **Call to make sure your local shelter has rabbits on the day you decide to go.**
2. **Provide the shelter with honest answers to any questions they ask about your family, other pets, schedule, and so on.**
3. **Peruse the rabbits, deciding which one most catches your interest.**
4. **Ask the staff for some information about the rabbit's personality and how the rabbit ended up at the shelter.**

   You'll probably get a good sense of who the rabbit is from talking to the people who have been caring for the bunny for a period of time.

## An oldie but a goodie

Baby bunnies are unbearably adorable, there's no doubt about that. But as cute as they are, these youngsters come with issues that older rabbits just don't have. Baby bunnies

- Need to be trained. They have to be shown how to go in a litter box (a must if you're one of those caring souls who plans to have your rabbit hop around the house).
- Will — sooner than later — become "teen-ager" bunnies. That means they go through a general phase of hormonally driven unpleasant behaviors (biting, aggression, and territoriality among them).

Another great thing about adult rabbits is that they know who they are — and that means you know exactly what you're getting. Adult rabbits have already reached their full size, so you won't get any surprises in that department. They have also developed their personalities.

Keep in mind, however, that the behavior of the adult rabbit you're considering adopting may not change dramatically, particularly if you don't have the time or experience for training. Younger rabbits may be more able to train and socialize.

5. **Interact with the bunny yourself.**

   Keep in mind that an animal shelter full of barking dogs and strange smells can be overwhelming to a rabbit, so your interactions with the bunny might be rather one-sided.

   If possible, ask the staff whether you can take the rabbit to a quiet area away from other animals. Sit on the floor and watch his behavior. Unless the rabbit is obviously aggressive or is completely terrified, even in a quiet environment the bunny will probably make a good pet. (Chapter 11 tells you more about how to read a rabbit's body language.)

6. **Check the rabbit over for signs of ill health to make sure that the bunny is in good shape.**

   For more on what to look for, see the section "Selecting the Rabbit," later in this chapter.

   If the rabbit seems sick and you're interested in adopting him anyway, talk to the staff about having the shelter veterinarian treat the rabbit at a reduced cost or for no fee if you adopt the animal.

### Rescue groups

These private nonprofit organizations usually consist of a network of foster homes that provide refuge to unwanted rabbits (many who are about to be destroyed by overcrowded and overwhelmed shelters) until permanent homes can be found. Individuals within these groups are almost always volunteers who provide this service because they love rabbits and want to help them.

The House Rabbit Society, a nonprofit organization with a network of chapters around the country and the world, leads the way in rabbit advocacy (see the sidebar "A Voice for Rabbits"), but other rescue groups out there as well. Each group may have its own variations, but a typical adoption from a rescue group would go as follows:

1. **Contact a rescue group.**

   You can find rescue groups in this book's Appendix, online, and through the House Rabbit Society and local veterinarians. You're likely going to be screened over the phone (to make certain you can provide a good — often indoor — home) before you're invited to see the rabbits. Some groups require a home visit.

   Once the group decides you're qualified to adopt a bunny, you're directed to rabbits in the area in need of homes. More than likely, the bunnies needing adoption stay in local foster homes.

2. **If you pass this initial prequalification, schedule an appointment to meet rabbits.**

   The rescue coordinator sets up one or more appointments for you to meet rabbits. In many cases, the whole family is required to attend, which is a good way for rescue volunteers to observe everyone and talk about caring for the rabbit.

3. **When meeting the foster parents, ask about the rabbit's personality.**

   The foster parent can give you his impressions of whether you (and your family) are a good match with this particular rabbit.

4. **Watch the rabbit in his element: running around the house, hanging out in his hutch, and so on.**

   Watching the rabbit provides a great way to see the animal's personality. By visiting a rabbit in a foster home, where she's comfortable, you get a good sense of who the rabbit really is. Ultimately the decision is yours, but the advice of someone who is knowledgeable about rabbits and knows an individual rabbit can be invaluable.

5. **Look the rabbit over for signs of good health.**

   For more on what to look for, see the upcoming section "Selecting the Rabbit."

   Reputable rescue groups place only healthy rabbits for adoption, so illness should not be a problem. Still, it doesn't hurt to be on the safe side.

6. **Once you've found a good match and been approved for adoption, pay the adoption fee and sign an adoption agreement.**

   The adoption fee generally runs about $65, and many rescue groups require you to sign an adoption agreement. Many times, a volunteer or the foster parents will follow up to see how things are going at home.

## A voice for rabbits

The House Rabbit Society, founded in 1988 by a group of seven rabbit lovers, serves as a true advocate for the companion rabbits of the world. The nonprofit group, which is bolstered by countless dedicated volunteers, is committed to rescuing abandoned rabbits and educating the public about rabbit care. Before HRS, many rabbits lived out their lives in outdoor hutches, isolated from human companionship and prone to illness and injury. Today, thanks to the organization's efforts to educate the public about the joys of sharing one's home with a rabbit, owners are better able to live with and care for their house rabbits.

In addition to improving bunnies' lives, the group works to reduce the number of unwanted rabbits and has rescued and found homes for 20,000 rabbits. Based in Richmond, California, the House Rabbit Society has chapters across the United States and the world. The organization's Web site offers information on adopting a rabbit as well as excellent educational materials on behavior and health problems. For more information on the HRS or to find a chapter in your area, contact the House Rabbit Society at 148 Broadway, Richmond, California 94804 or go to its Web site at `www.rabbit.org`.

## Saving a stray

It may sound strange, but stray domestic rabbits are turning up more often in urban areas. These rabbits are usually family pets that have been dumped by uncaring owners who foolishly believe that a domesticated rabbit will be able to fend for herself in the wild. Sadly, such rabbits are unlikely to survive. If you happen across a stray rabbit in your yard or neighborhood, start by determining whether she is indeed a domestic rabbit. (Tell-tale signs include lop ears or a spotted, all-white, or angora coat. And unlike a domestic rabbit, a wild cottontail is unlikely to approach you or your home.)

It's doubtful that you'll be able to safely catch the rabbit, so you'll need to call the local Humane Society to capture him or take matters into your own hands by following these steps:

1. **Buy or borrow a humane trap.**

   Typically, folks have to use a humane trap to catch a stray. The rabbit probably won't let you approach him. *Humane traps,* which bait the rabbit and hold him until you're ready to retrieve it, are available from

   • Mail-order catalogs

   • Humane societies

   • Animal control agencies

   • Fish and wildlife agencies

- Wildlife rehabilitation centers
- Local pet-supply stores (to order)

Buy a trap made of a lightweight material or that allows the tension to be set lightly on the trap door. A door that slams down hard on a rabbit's back can permanently injure the animal's spine.

2. **Take the trap to where you've seen the rabbit, set it, and use pieces of carrot, strawberry, peach, or banana as bait.**

   Try to set the trap early in the morning or evening, which is the time most rabbits feed. Avoid setting the trap at night when you won't be able to monitor it. If the rabbit is trapped and a predator approaches it in the dark of night, the rabbit may literally be frightened to death.

3. **Cover the trap with a dark towel or blanket, leaving the open door accessible.**

   The darkness gives the rabbit a sense of security once it's caught inside.

4. **Check the trap every few hours to see whether the rabbit has entered it.**
5. **Take the bunny right away to a veterinarian experienced in rabbits.**

   Ask the vet to examine the rabbit for any health problems and parasites. If the rabbit is in good health, you can take it home and provide it a good environment and diet. If the rabbit is suffering from a health problem, the vet can advise you on what is needed for treatment. (Parasites like fleas and ticks are almost certain to be present on the rabbit, especially in the spring, summer, and fall months.)

If you prefer not to capture the stray yourself, call your local Humane Society and ask it to pick up the rabbit. Keep in mind, though, that animal control may not have the manpower to trap the stray rabbit right away. Once the Humane Society retrieves the rabbit, you can begin adoption procedures. Most shelters hold new animals for a few days to see whether the pet was lost and will be claimed. Monitor the rabbit's status on a daily basis so that you know exactly when the rabbit is available for adoption. Rabbits are wonderful escape artists (they can dig their way out of just about any yard if left unsupervised), and the stray rabbit you found might actually be someone's lost pet. Once you capture the rabbit and bring it home, try

- Posting signs in the neighborhood where you found it.
- Noting your find in your local newspaper's lost and found section (which are usually free).
- Contacting local veterinary clinics that deal with rabbits, animal shelters, and animal control agencies where a person may have reported a lost animal.

If no one claims the rabbit after a month, you can feel pretty confident that you've rescued an abandoned pet.

## Run free, wee bunny!

Audrey will never forget the time that she rescued a wild baby bunny from the jaws of a barn cat at the stable where she rode. The bunny was tiny — maybe 6 inches long — and seemed incredibly helpless. His ear was sliced, and he was bleeding, so she took the baby to a local vet who specialized in wildlife care. After gluing the baby's ear back together, the vet gave the baby back to Audrey. "What do I do with him?" she asked, expecting to be told to bottle feed him and take care of him until he was fully grown.

"Just turn him loose near where you found him," the vet said. "He's old enough to take care of himself." This experience taught Audrey that although wild baby bunnies may appear tiny and helpless, unless they're newborn, they're typically able to fend for themselves in the wild.

If you come across a baby bunny whose eyes are open, has fur on his body, and is hopping around on his own, he's probably fine and better if left alone. Wild cottontails are weaned at 3 weeks of age and can fend for themselves early on.

If you find a nest of newborn baby bunnies, leave it alone. The mother is probably somewhere nearby. (Rabbit mothers have very rich milk and need to nurse their babies for only about 5 minutes a day). If you aren't sure, you can check on the newborns for the next couple of days, being careful not to disturb them or loiter around enough that you scare away the mother. If the babies are crying constantly or are developing sunken-in stomachs, they're probably orphaned. If you're sure the babies are orphaned, the best approach is to find a qualified wildlife rehabilitator in your area and turn the bunnies over to the rehabilitator. (Call your vet or local animal shelter for a referral.) *Hand-raising* (nursing a baby animal with a bottle) wild rabbits is difficult, and an experienced rehabilitator is the only person for the job.

# Considering Breeders

If you're considering going to a breeder to find your rabbit, make sure that you check out Chapters 2 and 3 and are familiar with the various types of rabbits out there.

Unless you're set on showing, consider getting a purebred or mixed breed from a shelter; more than a fair share of purebreds make their way to shelters. If you're looking for a purebred for breeding, however, please see Chapter 10, which covers some misconceptions and ethical issues related to hobbyist breeding.

If you're still interested in a purebred rabbit, probably the best place to get one is a reputable rabbit *fancier,* a person of experience and knowledge who breeds to the point of excellence. Here are some good reasons to go in this direction:

- Responsible rabbit breeders take good care of their animals and can be an excellent source for a rabbit if you're looking for a healthy, well-socialized, purebred bunny.
- Breeders usually have baby bunnies available. However, a responsible breeder will not sell babies until they're old enough to handle the stress of weaning and relocation. Typically, many of these breeders will not sell a baby until she is 12 weeks old.
- Your rabbit's breeder will be a contact for life and can help you with bunny-related questions and problems that may come up. He may even be willing to help you get started in showing and breeding rabbits, if this is your ultimate goal. A responsible breeder will also take the rabbit back if you can't keep it for any reason during the animal's life.
- You may be able to meet your future rabbit's *sire* and *dam* (father and mother) at the breeder's rabbitry (the place where the rabbits are kept), which will give you a good idea of what your rabbit's personality will be like.
- A good breeder will help you make smart decisions about whether you're ready to take on a rabbit right now.

Here are some downsides:

- Lots of shelter rabbits out there need good homes.
- Buying from a breeder can be expensive (prices range from less than $25 to more than $150).
- Breeders typically can't offer insight into the challenges associated with house rabbits.

## Getting a connection

You have these sources for finding rabbit breeders in your area:

- **American Rabbit Breeders Association (ARBA).** ARBA is a national organization, but works with national clubs for each of the breeds it recognizes. These breed clubs keep records of all the breeders in the United States, and you can contact them for the names and numbers of breeders in your area. For a list of national rabbit breed clubs, see the Appendix. Keep in mind that just because a breeder is linked to the ARBA site doesn't guarantee quality and responsibility; your own research is key.
- **Local 4-H club.** Most 4-H clubs have rabbit projects, usually run by breeders who volunteer in their spare time. You can find out who the

rabbit contact is in your local 4-H club by contacting your County Extension office. You can find your County Extension office by calling directory assistance within your area code.

- **Rabbit shows.** ARBA shows are the best events to attend because you can find breeders of nearly every type of rabbit at these shows. Spend some time at the show and make conversation with breeders to see whether they have rabbits available for sale. Be sure to wait until *after* the breeder has finished showing in his class, however, because breeders are usually busy readying rabbits just before they take the rabbit to the show ring. You can read more about shows in Chapter 15.
- **Veterinarian with rabbit experience.** These people know the responsible breeders in the area; they see these animals in their practice after they're sold as pets. Vets also receive personal recommendations of breeders from clients.

## Checking out a breeder

Once you have come up with the name of a breeder or two, your next step is to scope out his or her rabbitry and find out if this is really the person from whom you wish to buy your rabbit.

Take the following steps to help make this decision:

- Call the breeder and ask her about the breeding operation. Your job is to get a sense of who the breeder is. Find out
  - How many rabbit breeds this person is involved with. (Many breeders dabble in more than one breed and therefore may not be experts in any one breed.)
  - How many rabbits this person currently keeps. If the breeder has more than a dozen or so rabbits, ask whether the breeder has help. It's a lot of work to properly care for a large group of rabbits!
- While you're on the phone with the breeder, find out whether she shows rabbits. This question is important for two reasons:
  - A breeder involved with showing is an expert on the breed (or breeds) in her rabbitry.
  - You can't expect to buy a show-quality rabbit from a breeder who doesn't show. If you're looking to buy a rabbit you can show, the answer to this question is doubly important.

On the topic of buying a show rabbit, make sure that you tell the breeder up front that you want a rabbit you can show. Expect to pay a higher price for a show-quality rabbit, especially if you're shopping at a national rabbit show.

- Visit the breeder's facilities. Ask him whether you can come and check out the rabbitry. If the breeder says no, even with an appointment, look for your rabbit elsewhere. A breeder who won't allow buyers to see the general environment where his rabbits are kept is most likely hiding something. (However, some areas of the rabbitry may be off limits to visitors to protect from transmission of disease.)

  When you do visit the rabbitry, look for healthy rabbits in a clean environment. That means the cages should be clean, and the smell shouldn't be overwhelming. The rabbits themselves should be bright eyed, have well-groomed coats and be free of diarrhea or any respiratory ailments. (This chapter's "Selecting the Rabbit" has more on what to look for.)

If you're looking for a show prospect:

- Study the standard for your breed before you purchase the rabbit.
- Ask the breeder to select the best show animal available in the breed you're seeking. The breeder should show you the rabbit's coat and *conformation* (the way he's put together), explaining how the rabbit holds up to the breed's standard. The *breed standard* is the blueprint of the ideal rabbit.
- Ask the breeder to point out the rabbit's good points and faults before you purchase.
- Try to get the best rabbit you can afford: the one with the least amount of faults.

Be aware that if you're purchasing a very young rabbit, both you and the breeder won't know for sure whether your rabbit will grow up to be a winner in the show ring. Only time will tell. (See Chapter 15 for more information about the show ring.)

## Calling the classifieds

You may see ads for baby rabbits for sale, both purebred and mixed. You can certainly find a rabbit through the classified ads of a newspaper, but use caution with this approach for several reasons:

- Responsible breeders tend to use other methods to advertise their rabbits for sale (most often word of mouth).
- The classifieds aren't a popular place to advertise rabbits, so you won't have many ads to choose from.
- People who sell rabbits through classified ads are often not very knowledgeable about rabbits and their care, and you may not find a healthy rabbit when you arrive at the seller's home.

When pursuing these kinds of ads, be on the lookout for rabbits that may not be well cared for. Unlike rabbits placed up for adoption through reliable rescue groups, rabbits put up for adoption by individuals using classified ads have not been screened for good health. To get a sense of the rabbit's general health, ask to see where the rabbit is currently living and make sure that those quarters are clean. For more detailed health signs, see this chapter's "Selecting the Rabbit."

If the rabbit seems healthy, ask the owner whether you can take the bunny for a trial period. If the owner agrees, immediately take him to a veterinarian for a full examination. If the rabbit is suffering from a health problem, the veterinarian will let you know what treatment is needed. You then have to decide whether you want to assume responsibility for a sick rabbit or whether you want to return the rabbit to its original owner.

# Taking Precautions at Pet Shops

If you have a pet shop in your area that sells animals, an adorable baby bunny has probably lured you to a cage window. Although you can find rabbits for sale in many pet shops, especially around Easter (see Chapter 1), anyone considering a pet shop as a place to purchase a rabbit should think about the following points:

- **A lot of unwanted rabbits who currently reside in shelters need homes.** The people who run shelters and rescue groups believe that with so many mixed breed rabbits available for adoption, rabbit lovers have a moral obligation to avoid purchasing rabbits from pet shops.
- **Rabbits sold in pet shops aren't always purebred.** Many are mixed breeds of unknown ancestry (not a bad thing unless you have your heart set on showing your rabbit). The few purebreds that you do find in pet shops are almost always "pet quality," which means you can't successfully exhibit them in ARBA rabbit shows.
- **The breeding, socialization, and early health care are unknown.** You won't be able to examine the rabbitry where the bunny was born or meet its parents, so you won't know much about the rabbit you're buying or its background.
- **The rabbit care information you receive from pet shop employees may be unreliable.** Expertise on rabbits varies from pet store to pet store, and you have no way of knowing whether you're getting the right answers to your questions.
- **The fate of unsold rabbits is unclear.** However, horror stories exist in which these rabbits are sold as snake food or returned to breeders where they're euthanized. Purchasing a rabbit from a pet store may in fact perpetuate such practices.

TIP

## Pet shop adoptions: Good news?

Advocates of rabbit adoption may have reason for hope when it comes to pet shops. In recent years, Petco has made the decision to stop selling very young rabbits, and whenever possible is teaming up with rescue groups who set up in-store adoption programs for rescued rabbits. The arrangement benefits all parties: The rescue groups have a new venue for housing the rabbits and educating the public about responsible rabbit care, the rabbits have a great chance of being placed with screened families, the families get a warm, fuzzy friend and a feeling about doing something good, and the store gets a stream of new bunny owners who need to stock up on supplies. Petco is working to find local rescue groups that are able or willing to work with them. In cases where there is no local rescue, Petco will now sell only neutered or spayed rabbits.

If you'd like to buy a rabbit from a pet shop in spite of these realities, make sure that you follow these guidelines:

- **Take a close look at the conditions.** The cage should be clean and have fresh water and hay available. Groups of rabbits should not be crowded into small cages; overcrowding causes stress and increases the likelihood of disease.
- **Examine the rabbit for good health.** Follow the guidelines listed in the section "Selecting the Rabbit," later in this chapter.
- **Make certain the pet store provides a health guarantee for the rabbit.** If the rabbit becomes ill shortly after purchase (usually within 48 hours), the store should be willing to pay your vet bills. If the rabbit dies not long after you buy it, find out why it died. If the cause was related to the way the rabbit was cared for before you purchased it, you should be entitled to a refund. (A replacement rabbit is not an acceptable substitute for a refund because a dead rabbit indicates a serious illness among the bunnies available at the store.)

# Selecting the Rabbit

Whether your search has led you to a shelter, a rescue organization, or a breeder, it's time to pick your rabbit. Though there's a chance you'll find someone ready to help you with the selection, your best bet is to be educated and prepared when you arrive.

## Watching for signs of an ill rabbit

Make sure the rabbit you take home appears healthy. Unless you're prepared for the extra money, work, and heartache involved in caring for a sick or special needs bunny, disregard any tugging heartstrings and keep the following in mind:

- Consider the general condition of the body. Be wary of a rabbit who feels too fat or too thin.
- Eyes should be clear and bright, with no signs of discharge.
- Ears should be pink and free of crust or discharge; a brownish, waxy residue inside an ear can be a sign of ear mites.
- A rabbit's nose should not have any discharge; check the rabbit's breathing for signs of respiratory difficulty.
- Take a peek at the teeth. If a rabbit's lower teeth appear to extend in front of the upper teeth, or the incisors appear to be growing straight forward, sideways, or in other crazy directions, it's a sign of malocclusion, a problematic defect that affects a rabbits ability to chew properly. (Proper veterinary care can help control malocclusion.)

  In a normal rabbit, the upper incisors rest in front of the lower incisors, much like yours do when your mouth is completely closed.
- A rabbit's coat should be soft, clean, and shiny, with no bare patches. Matting, soiling, or staining around the hindquarters may indicate diarrhea or some other problem.
- Check the feet to be certain they're without sores.
- Watch the rabbit as it moves around; look for signs of lameness. A rabbit who is listless is probably not feeling well.

## Keeping character in mind

Look for a personable rabbit. Even if you plan to show your rabbit, you'll likely also want to enjoy your bunny as a pet. If possible, observe the rabbit in its home environment for clues about her personality. And although certain breeds are noted for particular personality traits, all rabbits are individuals and will behave as such. Use your detective skills to determine the following:

- How does the rabbit interact with other rabbits? Is he playful? Aggressive? Timid?
- How does the rabbit react to people? Look for a rabbit who is somewhat calm when approached and petted. Rabbits who kick repeatedly and bite when handled probably aren't well socialized and may not make good pets, especially for those with children.

# Part II

# Taking Care of Creature Comforts

"There's just something about bringing the rabbit here that makes me uncomfortable."

## In this part . . .

Properly caring for your rabbit is crucial and has many aspects. This part shows how to house your rabbit in your home and helps you navigate through the process of rabbit-proofing your house to protect both your bunny and your possessions from harm. You find out about cages and alternative accommodations for a rabbit, how to groom your pet, ways of providing enough exercise for your rabbit, and how to properly feed your bunny for optimum health. Speaking of optimum health, this part also outlines how to keep your rabbit healthy, from how to find a qualified vet to caring for special needs or geriatric bunnies. And finally, the toughest issue of all: losing your pet. This part tells you how to handle it.

## Chapter 5

# Shacking Up with an Indoor Rabbit

### *In This Chapter*

- Discovering the pluses of living with a house rabbit
- Providing the right environment
- Setting up for safety and success
- Training your bunny to use a litter box
- Maintaining a tidy house

In the old days, rabbits were considered strictly outdoor animals. Even rabbits kept as pets were relegated to hutches out in the backyard — never to put their fuzzy little bunny paws inside a human dwelling. But luckily for both rabbits and pet owners, attitudes have changed on this topic.

These days, rabbits are allowed to live indoors — in close quarters with their human companions. In fact, not only are they allowed, but they're also welcome! Many rabbit fans and advocates, not to mention veterinarians, recommend that companion rabbits be housed indoors, and this chapter outlines many of the reasons for doing so. You must be wondering how in the world this works. Rabbits inside the house? Isn't that the same as having a sheep or goat hanging around the living room? Well, not quite. This chapter explores the benefits of living with a house rabbit.

## Getting Serious about Safety

When Nature was doling out the cards to determine who would be prey and who would be predator, the rabbit got the ace of spades. Just about every predator on the planet regards rabbits as fair game.

Rabbits that live outdoors — whether in the wild or in the confines of a backyard — are constantly at risk for becoming dinner. Even in suburban areas, nocturnal predators lurk, yearning for rabbit stew.

Even if your bunny is tucked away in a hutch, he isn't completely safe. Critters, such as raccoons, are notorious for reaching their long arms between the wires of a rabbit hutch and grabbing for the terrified bunny. Other creatures — dogs, coyotes, snakes, and even cats — are attracted to a caged rabbit. Although most of these predators may not be able to gain access to the inside of the hutch, their mere presence can be enough to terrify your rabbit to death. (In the case of rabbits, "scared to death" is not an expression; rabbits can and do die of fright.)

Rabbits kept indoors are completely safe from predators that lurk in the night (provided your other pets are rabbit friendly; see Chapter 1). For that reason and others, the average lifespan of the indoor rabbit (7 to 12 years) is significantly higher (almost double) than his outdoor counterpart.

## Taking Health Concerns to Heart

Pet rabbits that live outdoors in your yard are more susceptible to illness but not for the reasons that you may think. It's not because thousands of airborne rabbit-nabbing germs are floating around your yard or because wild rabbits may drop by and spread illness. (Although in some areas, wild rabbits actually do spread illness to pet rabbits.)

The main reason that the outdoor life for a pet rabbit means a greater possibility of illness is because outdoor bunnies spend less time with their owners. For a rabbit, less time with your owner means less likelihood of someone noticing that you're sick.

### The House Rabbit Society

In 1988, a group of seven rabbit lovers got together to form an organization designed to help rabbits: the House Rabbit Society. They firmly believed, among other things, that rabbits should live indoors with their human companions.

Before the House Rabbit Society was organized, some people kept rabbits inside, but they kept quiet about it. Rabbits were traditionally considered livestock and were supposed to live outside — or so most people thought. Today, with the help of the House Rabbit Society, which promotes keeping rabbits indoors, bunny lovers around the world are finding out firsthand that rabbits make great indoor pets. The organization provides information to rabbit owners on how to best care for and live with their house rabbits. (See the Appendix for contact information; Chapter 4 also talks more about the group.)

When rabbits don't feel well, they let us know in a variety of subtle ways, such as a change in appetite or acting depressed and lethargic. Others sneeze, scratch, limp, and have changes in their stool or urine output. (See Chapter 9 for more information on rabbit health issues.) Rabbits are prey animals, and they naturally hide signs of disease, so they won't become a snack for a predator the minute they're feeling a bit under the weather. If you don't spend much time with your rabbit, you're less likely to actually see your pet limping, sneezing, or being lethargic. You're also less likely to recognize any subtle yet important difference in your pet's behavior.

Another problem for outdoor rabbits is weather. Although rabbits tolerate the cold weather, heat is a killer for bunnies. A particularly hot day can spell doom for an outdoor rabbit, and controlling the temperature in an outdoor rabbit hutch is difficult, if not impossible.

# Bonding with Bunny

For people who live with house rabbits, one of the most important reasons to keep a bunny inside is for the incredible bonding experience it offers. Sure, you can still bond with your rabbit if he lives outside in a hutch, but spending more time with your pet can be achieved only if your pet lives under the same roof and within the same walls as you.

If you live with an indoor rabbit, you and your bunny can share the following activities:

- **Watching TV:** What could be more relaxing than to come home at night and cuddle up on the couch with your favorite plant-eating mammal?
- **Reading:** Your rabbit will love it if you sit in your most comfortable chair to supervise his playtime as he romps around the room while you read a book.
- **Eating meals:** If you're a healthy eater who enjoys plenty of fresh fruits and vegetables, you can share your food with your rabbit.
- **Playing together:** You can play indoor games with your rabbit or simply sit by and watch him play on his own with his toys.
- **Cleaning house:** Watch your rabbit help you as you straighten up around the house. If he's a real people-rabbit, he'll follow you around and do his best to assist.

# Having Fun with Your Bun

Having any kind of rabbit is a hoot, but having an indoor rabbit is twice the fun. People who live with house rabbits can talk for hours about all the funny and adorable rabbit antics, such as how they hop into your lap while you're napping, stare up at you from the ground while you're making dinner, or curl up under the covers with you when you're home sick from work.

Rabbits can be really hilarious to watch, too, as evidenced in Chapters 14 and 15. Playing with their toys, chasing each other (if you have more than one), or kicking up their heels in sheer joy — indoor rabbits enjoy all these antics, and indoor rabbit owners can easily view them.

One of the many reasons for keeping your rabbit indoors is all the neat stuff that you'll witness. (Chapter 11 gives details about reading your rabbit's body language.) For example:

- **Sounds:** You get to hear all the sounds that rabbits make. They make a honking noise when they want attention from you or are begging for something to eat. A kind of purring sound resonates from a rabbit who is happily being scratched behind the ear while you're watching TV, and they "cluck" when you give them a snack that they really enjoy.
- **Body language:** A relaxed house rabbit expresses himself physically as well as vocally. A completely stretched out rabbit is happy, secure, and content. A rabbit who has flopped over on his side or back is in a deep sleep and probably dreaming. A shuddering bunny has just smelled something that he doesn't like.
- **Many moods:** Just like people, rabbits have shifting moods. Your pet may feel playful on any given day but act relaxed and sleepy the next day. One evening, he may beg for affection, but tomorrow, he's content to just huddle on a cushion nearby.

# Making Sure That Everyone's Comfy: Rabbit Essentials

To keep your rabbit indoors, you need to know how to provide the right environment. Having an indoor rabbit doesn't mean that you let your little hopper have the run of the place. Far from it. You need to provide a well thought out and careful environment for your rabbit, for both his sake and yours. That journey begins with the appropriate rabbit supplies.

You can easily find items for your rabbit if you know where to look. Pet store chains and independent pet stores are good sources, as are mail-order catalogs for pet products. A number of general online pet-supply resources carry rabbit products, and some Web sites carry goodies exclusively for rabbits. (See the Appendix for contact information on a number of these sources.)

Your indoor rabbit's cage is just one of several items that you need to pick up and accessorize at a pet-supply store before you bring your bunny home. Scope out the following house rabbit necessities:

- **Litter box:** All good house rabbits know how to use a litter box, and yours should be no exception. Get a box that's small enough to fit into your rabbit's cage yet large enough for your bunny to sit in comfortably. A small cat litter box will do, or you can find a rabbit-size box in a bunny catalog or on an Internet shopping site; a small plastic shoebox may even do the trick. Figure 5-1 is an example of a box that fits into the cage's corner. (See this chapter's "When Littering is Good: The Litter Box" for advice on litter box training your rabbit.)

  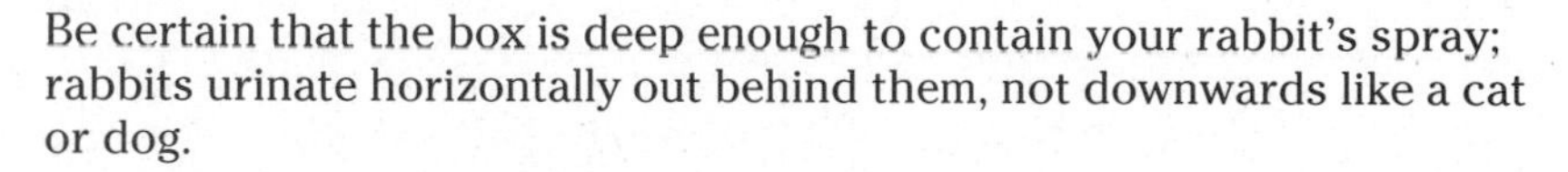

  Be certain that the box is deep enough to contain your rabbit's spray; rabbits urinate horizontally out behind them, not downwards like a cat or dog.

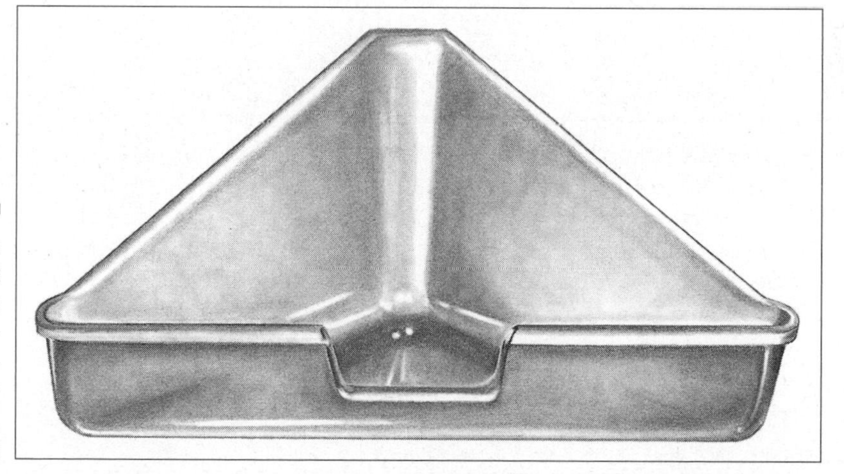

**Figure 5-1:** Please don't litter! Try a corner-hugging litter box for your bunny.

- **Litter:** You need to put something inside that litter box besides your rabbit. Your choice of litter material is important because of the amount of time your rabbit will spend in her litter box and because most rabbits tend to eat some litter along the way. Check out what rabbit folks are saying about the different litters:
  - Do not use your cat's clay-based litter. The dust irritates the rabbit's respiratory tract; some rabbits have eaten the clay litter, resulting in a fatal intestinal impaction.
  - Avoid cedar and pine beddings. Although they smell nice to the human nose, these products may cause liver damage in rabbits.
  - Pelleted bedding is more absorbent than clay and, if eaten, not harmful to the rabbit. In addition, pelleted bedding tends to draw moisture away from the surface so that it remains drier where the rabbit is sitting. Suitable bedding material includes those made of aspen, paper, cellulose, and compressed sawdust.
  - Corn cob bedding isn't very absorbent and can also cause intestinal blockages.
  - Although newspapers are absorbent, they don't control odor (and bunny urine is potent!). Some owners go with the old stand-by of lining the box with paper and then adding a layer of hay, changing both the paper and hay daily).
- **Food bowl or feeder:** You see all kinds of food bowls in the store, but the crock-style bowls are the best kind (see Figure 5-2). These ceramic containers work great because they're hard to tip over, and rabbits are notorious tippers. Make sure that the bowl you buy isn't too deep for your rabbit to reach into. Too much depth is primarily a concern with baby bunnies and small dwarf breeds. Keep in mind that bowls are easy to clean: Just throw them in the dishwasher.

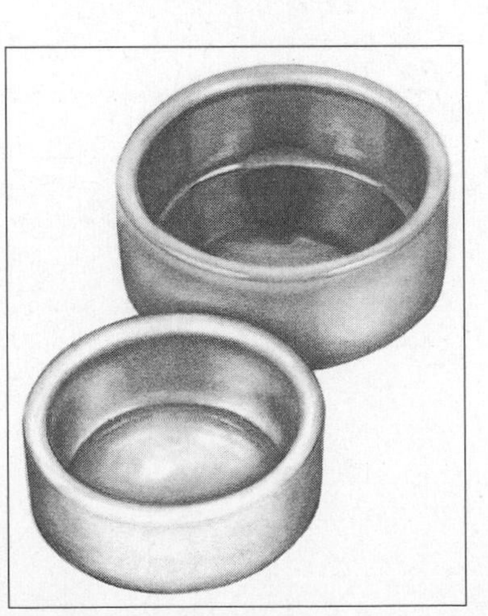

**Figure 5-2:** Subvert the notorious tendency for rabbits to tip with these ceramic food bowls.

- **Water bottle:** Instead of providing a bowl of water like you would for a cat or dog, give your rabbit a gravity water bottle, like the kind used for guinea pigs and hamsters. This bottle, shown in Figure 5-3, has a metal tube at the end with a metal ball in the tip. These bottles keep the water accessible without letting it drip. When your rabbit is thirsty, he can sip from the metal tip of the water bottle. Some rabbits prefer water bowls, but that can lead to lots of mess when the bowl gets tipped over (and over and over . . .).

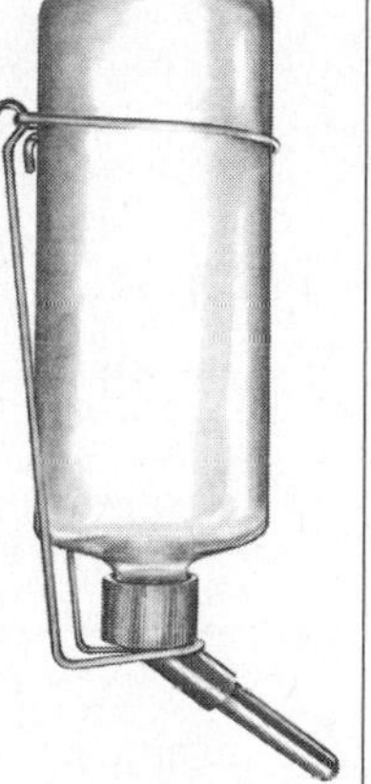

**Figure 5-3:** Honey may be the nectar of the gods, but water is pretty darn important to rabbits.

- **Nest box:** Rabbits take great comfort in having a small, dark space where they can huddle when they need time to themselves. Check out the huddling rabbit in Figure 5-4. A nest box, tucked into a corner of your rabbit's cage, can provide that comfort. You can purchase a nest box from a rabbit-supply catalog or Internet site. Get one that's made of metal with a wood floor or wood covered with metal mesh.

If you opt for a wood-only box, your rabbit will soon gnaw the box to pieces.

- **Bedding:** Put something in your rabbit's nest box to make it cozy for sleeping. You can use the same rabbit-friendly material, pelleted or otherwise, that you put in the litter box, adding a layer of hay on top to make it more nest-like. Avoid cedar or pine bedding because of the health risks. (See this chapter's section on safe litter choices.) A soft towel or T-shirt will be appreciated by bunnies who like a little extra something to nest in.

**Figure 5-4:** Who doesn't like to hang out in a small nesting box?

- **Hayrack:** Roughage is important in a rabbit's diet (see Chapter 7), and your bunny should always have a supply of fresh grass hay available for noshing. To keep the hay from being strewn all over your rabbit's house — and yours — you need a hayrack that hangs from the side of the cage. The rack, shown in Figure 5-5, keeps the hay in place as your rabbit munches on it throughout the day. Metal hayracks are available from rabbit-supply retailers.

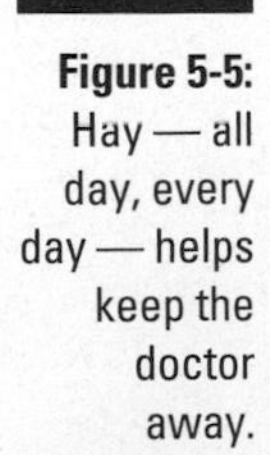

**Figure 5-5:** Hay — all day, every day — helps keep the doctor away.

- **Chew blocks:** Rabbit teeth are continually growing, and rabbits have a strong urge to gnaw as a result. Buy your bunny some chew blocks made for small animals so that he can work those teeth on the blocks (rather than your furniture); some rabbit caretakers have had success fastening a piece of unfinished wood trim to the cage. Chapter 14 has information on how to deal with rabbits who chew on your prized antique chaise lounge legs. The "Chewing," section, later in this chapter, offers tips on preventing unwanted chewing.
- **Toys:** Rabbits love to play. Pick up a few toys for your pet while you're out shopping for supplies. Rabbits enjoy most cat toys, especially balls with bells in them. You can also give your pet homemade toys, such as empty toilet paper rolls, wooden blocks, and cardboard boxes. Use toys that are safe for your pet to chew, because he most likely will! Chapter 14 talks about toys in depth.
- **First-aid kit:** A first-aid kit doesn't have much to do with a rabbit's cage, but it's still a very, very good idea. See Chapter 9 for details on what kinds of goodies you'll need in a first-rate first-aid kit.

# Craving His Cage

Yes, even though your rabbit is living inside the house, he still needs a cage. Rather than thinking of it as a jail of sorts, think of your rabbit's enclosure as a den — that is, a place that he can call his own.

A rabbit's cage is *not* where your companion will get the exercise he needs to stay healthy (at least two hours a day). Exercise, both of the indoor and outdoor varieties, is covered in Chapter 8.

The purpose of your indoor rabbit's cage is to provide a confined spot for your rabbit when you can't supervise him. Because pet rabbits have a strong desire to hide in enclosed spaces left over from their wild ancestry, your rabbit can appreciate having such a place where he can go to rest and escape from the world. You can appreciate having a private place for him to go because your rabbit shouldn't be out and about in your house unless you can keep a close eye on him. You can also use pens to achieve a sense of security (his) and peace of mind (yours). (See the section "Putting a Pen to Good Use," later in this chapter, for more on that topic.) (You also need to purchase and outfit a smaller travel carrier for trips to the veterinarian or elsewhere. (Chapter 16 covers traveling with your pet in detail.)

You can buy an indoor rabbit cage at a pet-supply store, through a catalog, or over the Internet. Shop carefully for a setup that suits your needs; look for a cage on a stand for someone with a bad back, for example, or something with drawers below for those without much space for bunny gear. (See the Appendix for shopping sites and catalogs.) Figure 5-6 shows a good example of a basic indoor cage.

Your rabbit's indoor cage should:

- **Be large enough for the rabbit to turn around comfortably and stand up on his hind legs without his ears touching the top.** If your rabbit is a baby, be sure to buy a cage that can fit him when he's grown. The House Rabbit Society recommends that a cage be at least four times the size of your rabbit, and more if he'll be in there a lot. Of course, this size is the absolute minimum. Your rabbit is much happier with even more space to call his own, and here's why:
  - Rabbits without enough space to move around often become bored.
  - Small spaces are quickly fouled with urine and feces, which creates an unhealthy environment for the rabbit.
  - Rabbits without enough room to exercise have a greater chance of becoming obese.
- **Have enough room to accommodate a small litter box, a nesting box (big enough for the rabbit to fit into), a food bowl, a water bottle, and a hayrack.** Openings should be no larger than 1 by 2 inches. Anything bigger, and the rabbit may catch his leg or head in it.

  WARNING! Aquariums or cages with solid walls don't provide adequate ventilation and are very dangerous.
- **Have a floor made of plastic slats or have a solid floor, particularly if you're planning to litter box train your rabbit.** Another option is a bottom made of wire, with square openings of about ½ inch; a slide-out tray below the wire catches waste material. Line the tray with newspaper or pelleted beddings. However, a wire bottom can be tough on a bunny's feet, so be sure to provide a resting board or a piece of washable carpet to give her tootsies a break.

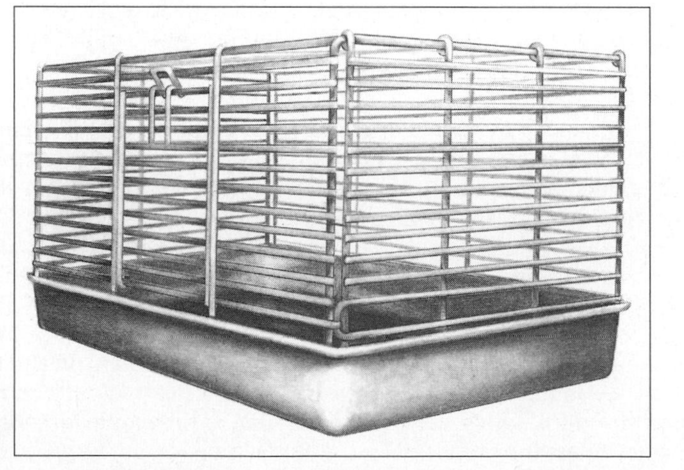

**Figure 5-6:** Not exactly a suite at the Hilton, but it's the beginnings of a bunny's favorite digs.

## Home sweet home

Even though house rabbits typically spend a good portion of the day free in your home, yours will appreciate having a place to retreat to for times of rest and relaxation. You can do several things to make your rabbit feel like her cage is a place of refuge:

- Don't use her cage as punishment.
- Make her feel safe at "home" by not doing things to her in her cage that she doesn't like.
- Keep it clean, but don't clean the cage with your bun in it.
- Don't force your bunny out of her nest box or cage against her will.
- Keep it cozy, with toys, a soft blanket or towel, and an occasional treat.

- **Include a side door for your rabbit to enter through the cage.** (How else will he hop in when it's time to take care of his bathroom business?) When the door is open, you can cover the mesh with a towel to make a more comfortable entrance/exit ramp. For your convenience, try to get a cage that also opens from the top. Being able to open the cage roof and reach inside makes feeding your pet or taking your rabbit out (if you need to) much easier.

- **Be designed for a rabbit's physique.** You may see some pretty fancy, multi-level cages on the market designed for rabbits, but buyer beware. If the ramps are too steep, injuries may result. Rabbits are land animals and don't feel safe when high above the ground. In addition, the vertical nature of the cage gives the false impression that the rabbit has enough space, when, in fact, it's the horizontal space that's important for exercise and movement. For these reasons, we caution against many-tiered cages (four-plus tiers) for rabbits, ferrets, or guinea pigs. They simply don't fit with the animals' natural physiology and psyche.

Where you put your rabbit's cage is even more important than what it looks like. Rabbits are sensitive to climate and air quality and can quickly become ill if they're exposed to the wrong things. Keep the following in mind when you think about where you place your indoor rabbit's cage:

- **Avoid placing the cage in an area of your house where dramatic and extreme temperature fluctuations take place frequently.** High heat and humidity are particularly dangerous. Rabbits, other pets, or humans, for that matter, do *not* need a constant temperature range all the time. Some fluctuation is healthy; just try to avoid the extremes (such as near heating or air-conditioning vents, which can also blow out dust that irritates your pet's respiratory tract).

- **Never expose the cage to direct sunlight.** The sun's rays when magnified through glass can become hot and can cause heat stroke in a rabbit. Even direct sunlight through a window screen can be dangerous for a rabbit.
- **An attic or basement is no place for a rabbit cage.** The dampness and lack of ventilation in these areas can prove hazardous to your pet's health.
- **The cage should be in a well-lit area where people come and go.** However, don't place it in a spot where your rabbit never has any peace and quiet.
- **Place the cage where the bunny can experience at least eight hours of darkness.** Constant bright lighting with no relief or inconsistent lighting (one night up late, next night not) can wreak havoc on a rabbit's endocrine system, which has some dependency on photoperiods for its function. At the least, cover the cage with a heavy cloth or towel that blocks light for at least eight hours out of each 24-hour period.
- **Don't put the cage near stereo speakers or a TV.** The noise may put undo stress on your rabbit's sensitive nerves.

# Putting a Pen to Good Use

Some people, especially those with multiple bunnies, opt for a different housing arrangement, such as a puppy or exercise pen. Such pens, found in pet stores or dog-supply catalogs, are comprised of 3 to 4-foot high by 2 to 4-foot long metal wire panels that quickly hook together with a long pin to make an enclosure (see Figure 5-7). You can easily step over the fencing to gain entrance, or you can remove one pin and open the fencing. You can move the panels into a variety of shapes and use them indoors or out. This option is an easy and economical way to confine your rabbit to an area of the home or outdoors, yet it's also moveable. And when the panels aren't in use, you can fold the entire apparatus completely flat and store it against a wall or in a closet in a matter of minutes. The size that you get depends on the rabbits, but, of course, the larger, the better. For large breed rabbits, we recommend the 4-foot fencing; other breeds do fine with 3-foot fencing.

In addition, if you have carpeting or want to protect a floor, you can buy a hard-plastic chair mat, carpet protector, or a sheet of no-wax flooring and place it under the fenced-in area; it doesn't have to be really high quality. The flooring can easily be rolled up and moved should you need to do so. Voilà! You have no problems with soiled carpet or digging into carpet. The rabbit can have the run of the pen and still be in the room with you without danger of getting into mischief. The mats are invaluable, and some local House Rabbit Society chapters use them in foster homes.

Another option is to leave the fencing up all the time around a cage as a permanent exercise area. This approach works great outside (better and safer with a top enclosure) as well, and you can also move it around the yard. (See Chapter 8 for more on the important benefits of fitness and fresh air.) Of course, don't leave your rabbit in his pen outside without careful supervision.

# Rabbit-Proofing Your House

A big reason for keeping your rabbit inside instead of out is so that you can share house time with your pet. But before you let your rabbit go running through the halls, you need to take some precautions. These measures aren't only for the safety of your rabbit — who can get into more trouble than you can possibly imagine — but also for the well-being of your home.

In order to adequately protect your house and your rabbit, get an idea of exactly what kinds of problems rabbits can get into when left to their own devices inside your home. Take a look at Figure 5-8 to see what areas you need to address before bringing a bunny into your home. Fortunately, you can take advantage of the clever rabbit-proofing ideas of others to make your job simpler.

**Figure 5-7:** You can use a puppy or exercise pen to house a bunny, as long as it's 3 or 4 feet tall, depending upon your rabbit's size.

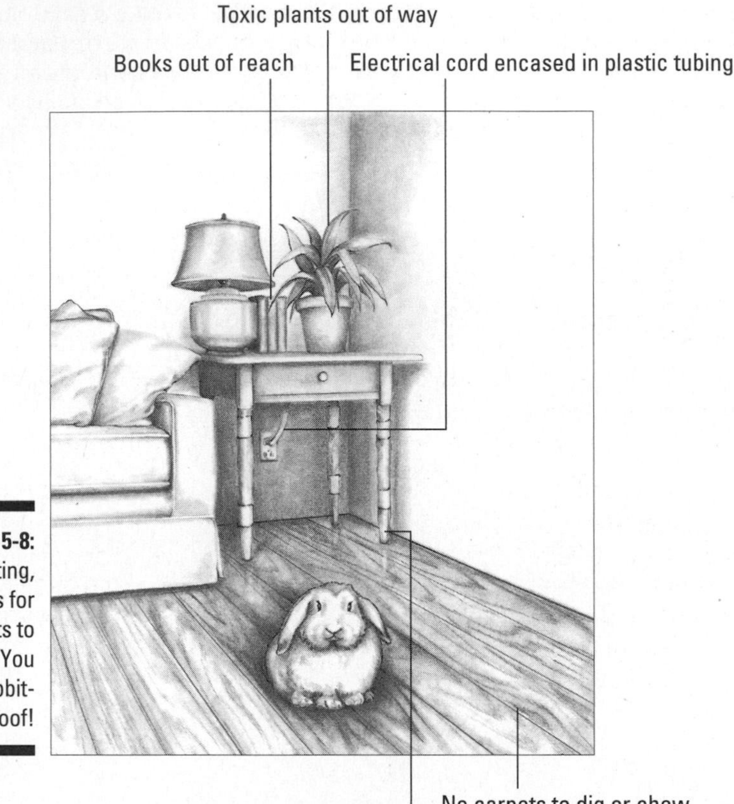


**Figure 5-8:** Tempting, tasty bits for rabbits to inspect: You must rabbit-proof!

## Identifying trouble spots

Rabbits love to tuck themselves away into little corners. They're also curious and love to investigate new places. Put this combination together, and you have potential for trouble in the house.

Before you give your bunny access to a room:

- **Get down on all fours and look around carefully.** Much like the parent of an inquisitive toddler, you should take a look at your home from your rabbit's perspective. Your rabbit won't know the difference between an interesting new snack and something dangerous, such as medicine, the contents of an ashtray, and other small not-to-be-digested objects. Better safe than sorry!

- **Find any small spaces that your rabbit may be able to get into.** Look closely — even in your kitchen and bathroom cabinets, and under and behind appliances — for gaps or holes that may look inviting to a rabbit. Your bunny is apt to crawl into one of these spots and possibly get trapped; open railings can be dangerous as well.
- **Locate all exposed electrical wires and telephone and computer cords.** It's a simple but deadly fact: rabbits are fond of chewing on wires. The next section on chewing outlines ways of preventing tragedy in this area.
- **Block nooks and crannies in furniture with heavy objects so that your rabbit won't be able to get inside and get stuck.** Rabbits have been known to burrow inside recliners and sofa beds with disastrous results; taking the proper precautions can help prevent this problem.
- **Put away and lock up toxic chemicals.** Make sure that no toxic chemicals — pesticides, cleaning supplies, antifreeze, fertilizers, and so on — are placed within reach of your rabbit.
- **Give away or relocate any plants that can make your rabbit sick — or worse.** See Chapter 8 for more information on toxic plants.
- **Be certain that trash bags and buckets are well out of bunny's reach.** Bunnies are curious and will be happy to explore the contents of your trash. Enough said.

## Chewing

Rabbits have a tremendous urge to gnaw. Although it is perfectly natural — and even necessary for healthy teeth — and loads of fun for a rabbit, chewing can result in plenty of grief for both rabbits and their owners if they chew on the wrong things.

When inside a home, rabbits tend to make a beeline for the following objects, with teeth bared:

- Carpet edges
- Electrical cords
- Telephone cords
- Wooden furniture legs

As you can well imagine, rabbit teeth can do plenty of damage to these items and more (for example, books and shoes). In a short time, wooden furniture legs can be permanently disfigured, telephone cords can be rendered useless, and carpet edges can be chomped and swallowed (a serious health risk). Electrical cords that have been chewed through can be fatal for a rabbit and may even start a fire in your home.

However, you can enjoy your indoor rabbit without having to worry about those destructive teeth:

- **Limit your rabbit's activities to one or two rooms of the house.**
- **Don't let your rabbit run loose in the house without your constant supervision.**
- **Cover wooden furniture legs in accessible rooms with bubble wrap or thick plastic (see Figure 5-9).**

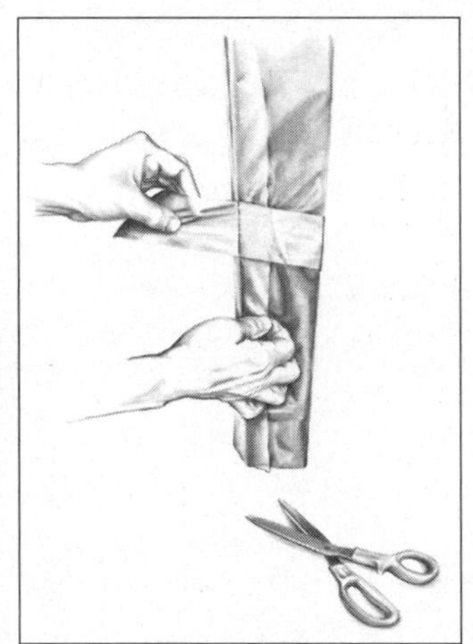

**Figure 5-9:** Plastic is pretty . . . pretty rabbit safe, that is.

- **Put telephone cords well out of reach — beyond the grasp of rabbits who like to hop up onto chairs.**
- **Cover electrical cords with plastic aquarium tubing by cutting the tube lengthwise and slipping it over the cord (see Figure 5-10).**
- **Leave chew toys around the room so that your rabbit can chew on them instead of something he shouldn't.**

## Putting off the perfume

I don't recommend spraying perfume on furniture legs to put off your chewy pet. Certain animals have been known to develop respiratory disease from perfumes, and in the case of birds, some fatalities have occurred. Highly aromatic perfumes and perfumes that contain plenty of alcohol, which helps the scent spread, have been implicated most often. Don't use these products. It has also been my experience that most products that are designed to keep dogs and cats off of furniture do *not* work on rabbits.

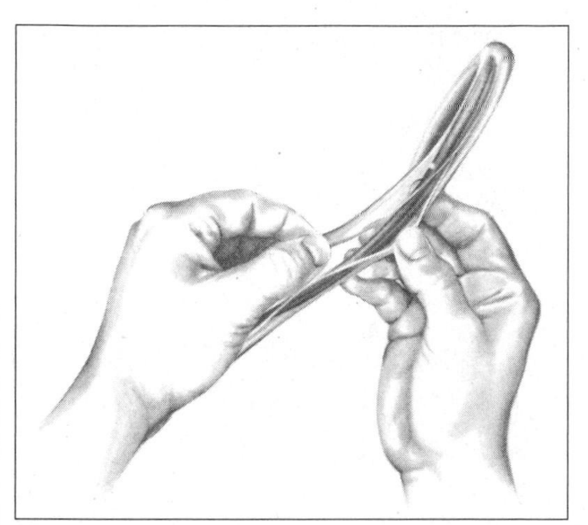

**Figure 5-10:** Wrap up that electrical wiring.

## Digging

Another bad bunny habit is digging. Rabbits love to dig. In the wild, they create their dens by excavating. A problem arises, however, when rabbits running loose in the house decide that they want to dig a tunnel through your carpeting. They usually choose a loose corner of the carpet to start their excavation. They also choose doorways if the door is closed, so you often need to protect the lower part of the door with Plexiglas or the like to keep them from damaging the wood. If this digging goes unnoticed, they can quickly tear up a good portion of the rug. In addition, if they eat the carpet, the fibers are indigestible, and the ingestion of enough of them can lead to an intestinal impaction.

To keep your four-legged shovel from messing up your carpeting:

1. **Check all the corners of the room where your rabbit will be roaming.**
2. **Place heavy objects in the corners so that your rabbit can't get a toe-hold on a loose area of the rug.**
3. **Make sure that carpet edges are securely tacked down.**

   You can cover them with a heavy plastic rug protector, such as the ones sold to protect rugs under office furniture. These rug protectors are often found in office-supply stores and are made of clear heavy plastic with spikes on the back to hold them in place on the carpet. They can be cut to different sizes and help protect carpet corners from your rabbit's digging and soiling. You can also use a clear plastic carpet runner protector found in many hardware or carpeting stores. They're all smooth enough that when the rabbit digs at them, they get nowhere.

Alternatively, you can use sheets of Plexiglas in the digging areas, but they're harder to secure.

4. **Encourage your rabbit to dig somewhere else.**

   Provide him with a box full of sand, soil, shredded paper, or old towels that he can rummage through. Make sure that the box is deep enough to keep the material inside when your rabbit starts to excavate but not so deep that your rabbit can't jump in or out.

Rabbits also like to dig at furniture. Your favorite couch, chair, or bed may be shredded. Protect these areas with a heavy cloth covering or prevent the rabbit from having access to them.

# When Littering Is Good: The Litter Box

One of the reasons that rabbits make such good indoor companions is that you can train them to use a litter box. Their denning instinct, inherited from their wild ancestors, is the reason behind this behavior. Rabbits prefer not to go to the bathroom where they eat and sleep and venture out of their dens to relieve themselves. Not unlike toddlers who are going through toilet training, some bunnies are easier to train than others when it comes to using the litter box. With these holdouts, you need to expend more time and patience.

Keep in mind that successful litter box training may be hampered by an intact rabbit's hormonally inspired territorial spraying — yet another reason to spay or neuter your rabbit as soon as possible.

When training a rabbit to use the litter box, being consistent and praising your rabbit is important. Never scold your rabbit for not using the litter box because it only frightens and confuses her.

To begin preparing for your bunny's litter box training, first purchase an appropriate box and litter. You can read more about litter boxes — what they look like, what to put in them, and how to clean them in the section "Making Sure That Everyone's Comfy: Rabbit Essentials," earlier in this chapter.

When your rabbit is first discovering how to use the litter box, don't clean up after her too often. If her box is too clean, she may forget why it's there. Clean it a couple of times a week, and that's it.

## Encouraging your bunny to go in her cage

You can start your bunny's training within a small area. Starting litter training in your rabbit's cage is best because it provides your bunny with plenty of opportunities to use the box. Gradually work your way up to larger spaces until he's using the box even when he has the run of the place.

1. **If your rabbit already has a corner of the cage where she likes to go to the bathroom, place the box in this area.**

   Putting some of her fecal pellets and urine-soaked paper in the box can help her get the idea.

2. **Attach the box to the side with a clip or twistable wire for removal when cleaning.**

3. **If she doesn't start using the box right away, put a nice bunch of grass hay in it to attract her attention.**

4. **If you see her go to the bathroom in the litter box, give her a treat and some gentle verbal praise.**

   With consistent reward, your bunny should get the idea in no time.

If your rabbit takes to sitting in the box and just hanging out there or chewing on the hay that you put there, don't be concerned. Rabbits often eat and go to the bathroom at the same time. Rabbits won't eat soiled hay, so don't worry about that. But munching on the clean hay stimulates your rabbit's digestive system and causes her to use the box in the way that you intended.

If you find that your rabbit is sleeping in her litter box instead of using it as a toilet, you should provide her with a more attractive bed than the one that she has. Try using a different bedding material or giving her a more private nest box.

## Providing 1.5 bathrooms

When you see your rabbit regularly using her litter box (which can take anywhere from a week to a month or more), you can give her more room to roam without worrying too much about her going potty outside the box. Now you're ready to train her to use a litter box in other areas of the house.

1. **Set up a special room for your bunny.**

   A kitchen, bathroom, or hallway are acceptable places. Make sure that they're small, low-traffic areas.

2. **Use a baby gate to section off the area.**

   You can also use a pen to set up an area for training. The section "Putting a Pen to Good Use," earlier in this chapter, has more information.

3. **Put the litter box in the corner of the special area.**

   Rabbits often like to pick their own areas, so your best bet may be moving the box once the rabbit has selected her favorite spot.

4. **Place your rabbit's food, water, and bedding in another part of the room.**
5. **Keep an eye on your rabbit to make sure that she uses the litter box on a regular basis.**

   Be patient! The more consistent attention you give to this process, the better.
6. **If you see her go to the bathroom in the litter box, give her a treat and gentle verbal praise.**

If your rabbit starts making mistakes at any point in this process, it may be a simple, temporary mishap. It may also have something to do with your rabbit's natural urges to mark territory as her own or the following issues:

- **You may have placed her in a bigger space too soon.** In this situation, the best approach is to take a small step back. Put the box back in your bunny's cage and reaccustom her to using the box in her cage.
- **You may have not given her enough (or the "right") litter boxes.** Buy a few more litter boxes and place them strategically around the house; try a different type of box, if necessary. You can put more than one in a room or put a box in each room that your rabbit frequents. With so many litter box options to choose from, chances are that your rabbit will get it right.

  If you don't want to keep that many boxes around the house permanently, you can try removing them one by one. See whether your rabbit seeks out the closest box, even if it's in the next room. If so, you've probably successfully trained your rabbit to use the litter box.

  If you have more than one rabbit in your household, make sure that you provide at least one more litter box than the number of rabbits in the room. Some rabbits won't use a litter box if it's been used by a more dominant rabbit.
- **A rabbit with a health problem.** A bunny who seems to be dribbling urine may have a bladder problem or an infection of the urinary tract. Consult your vet.

Once your rabbit does her business in the box on a regular basis, you can give her more room. Move the entire operation to a bigger space, such as the living room or a bedroom. Eventually, you should be able to let your rabbit have access to all the rabbit-proofed rooms in your house and count on her to use the litter box every time.

## Cleaning up

During the litter box training process, accidents are inevitable. Cleanup is easier if you protect the area under and around the litter box with newspaper or a heavy plastic carpet protector pad. If you find that your bunny's spray is missing the litter box, check that the box is deep enough for him. (Rabbits urinate horizontally out behind them.)

Clean up after your pet; pick up fecal pellets with a tissue, and wash urine marks on carpeting with a mixture of vinegar and water. You can use one of the enzyme pet accident cleaners on the market. If your bunny urinates on wood flooring, use gentle dish soap and water or cleansers made for hardwood floors.

Rabbit droppings make a great addition to your compost pile. Simply drop the goods on your heap, mix, and let it cook. For more on composting, an online search can lead you to more than you'd ever want to know about the wonders of bunny poop. (Check out the House Rabbit Network's articles at `www.rabbitnetwork.org/articles/compost.shtml`.) You can find tons of good books about composting as well.

# Keeping a Squeaky Clean Home

One of the most important factors to a rabbit's good health is cleanliness. A clean environment means a healthy rabbit. A dirty environment means the potential for a rabbit with chronic health problems.

Of course, that's not the only reason to keep a rabbit's area sanitary. In the case of the indoor rabbit, your house suffers if you don't keep up after your rabbit's hygiene.

If you perform the following duties with the frequency specified, you shouldn't have a problem with your rabbit or your house:

## Litter box cleaning

Clean the litter box every three days. If your rabbit is litter box trained, your cage-cleaning duties are much easier:

1. **If you're using appropriate pelleted bedding with one litter box per rabbit, change the litter completely.**
2. **Look for other areas in the cage where your rabbit may have gone to the bathroom (including the nest box) and clean those up, too.**
3. **Check the stools and urine daily to see whether any abnormalities are present.**

   If a rabbit is ill, use a small amount of litter and change it daily to observe any abnormalities. Changing the litter daily can be expensive. If you want to routinely change litter daily, use much smaller amounts in the box, such as 1 inch.

## Daily cage duty

You'll want to perform cage duty daily. If you're feeding your rabbit a proper diet, you no doubt have some food to clean up inside your rabbit's cage. Here's what you need to do on a daily basis:

1. **Remove any fresh fruit and vegetables that your rabbit has left behind.**

   See Chapter 7 for more on feeding.

2. **Wash out your rabbit's food bowl and water bottle.**
3. **Remove any stray pieces of hay that have fallen from the hayrack.**

## Weekly cage cleaning

In addition to your daily check of the cage, you'll want to give your rabbit's cage a good, thorough cleaning with mild disinfectant once a week. A solution of one part bleach to ten parts of water is effective against a wide range of germs. Here's what you need to do on a weekly basis:

1. **Clean surfaces of debris.**
2. **Keep the solution in contact with the surface for 30 minutes.**
3. **Rinse off the bleach solution and let the cage thoroughly dry before you place the rabbit back into it.**
4. **Soak food and water bowls/bottles in this bleach solution weekly for 30 minutes and then rinse in a good disinfectant or put through a dishwasher.**

Never clean any animal-related items, particularly those containing fecal material or urine, in the kitchen sink where food is prepared for human consumption. Use the bathtub or the bathroom sink and rinse well afterwards.

# Chapter 6

# Stocking Up on Carrots

### In This Chapter

- Understanding rabbit nutrition
- Feeding your bunny the right food
- Avoiding overweight rabbits
- Growing a garden just for Peter Rabbit

That old adage, "You are what you eat," doesn't just apply to humans. This truth applies to rabbits, too. Feed your rabbit a healthy and complete diet, and he'll be a healthy, happy-go-lucky bunny.

Providing a healthy diet for your bunny is much more involved than just dumping a cup of pellets in his food bowl every day. Rabbits need variety in their diet, just like humans do, and with just a little effort, you can provide all the vitamins, minerals, fiber, and food energy that your rabbit needs.

## Supplying Your Bunny with Belly Timber

Before you start feeding your rabbit, knowing that your rabbit is a *herbivore* is important. *Herbivores* eat only plants. Because rabbits are herbivores, everything they eat consists of plant material. So don't give your bunny a steak. Not only will his nose turn up at it, but also the smell of it will probably scare the heck out of him. To get the proper nutrients a rabbit needs, your pet depends on you for good, fresh foods. (Chapter 2 details more about a rabbit's body and helps you understand why a good diet is so important.) You need to understand some basic things about your bunny's biological needs:

- **Bunnies dig grazing in the grass.** In the wild, rabbits are grazers, which means they spend a significant amount of time roaming from plant to plant as they nibble. In nature, rabbits have a wide variety of plants at their disposal and are thus able to get all the nutrients that they need from them. Domestic rabbits, though, have no choice in the matter of diet. They depend on their owners to provide them with variety of nutritious foods — grass hay, vegetables, quality pelleted feed, and some fruits.

- **Water is vital to life.** Water makes up a substantial portion of the mammalian body, and rabbits are no exception. Rabbits drink a little over a quarter cup of water per pound of rabbit per day. This amount can be more if the temperature is warm or the rabbit is exercising, and less if the rabbit is eating a lot of water-containing foods, like vegetables and fruits. Without water, rabbits die quickly. Not only is water itself essential to keeping the vital organs working properly, but it also aids digestion and keeps the rabbit's body cool in hot weather.

  Rabbits must have *fresh* water at their disposal at all times. You should replace the water in their water bottles with fresh water every single day, without exception. Providing your rabbit with bottled or filtered water is all the better. Rabbits, like humans, can do without the impurities present in most tap water.

- **Gradual change is better.** The digestive system of a rabbit is unlike that of a human or even a dog or cat. Rabbits depend on a variety of intestinal bacteria to break down their food. When dietary changes are made too quickly (like giving your bunny a pile of strawberries or switching to a "gourmet" pellet), this intestinal balance is thrown off, making the rabbit sick. When adding new foods to your bunny's diet, do so one food at a time, one piece at a time, so that you're able to monitor any negative changes in her stools (diarrhea). A good rule is to try a new food for three days before adding another to the mix.

# Hay Every Day Keeps the Doctor Away

Knowing the general rules of rabbit nutrition is a good start, but the details are most important. To keep your rabbit healthy, you need to provide the right blend of fresh foods and fiber.

When you look at the rabbit's gastrointestinal tract (see Chapter 2), you can see that having a high-fiber diet makes everything move more smoothly; fiber is essential in producing *cecotropes,* which are the nutrient-rich droppings your rabbit needs to eat. The good news is you can provide fiber easily by feeding grass hay. In fact, being the grazers they are, rabbits should have grass hay available to them all the time. You can put it in a hay rack (see Chapter 5) or in a box inside the cage or exercise area. When the supply runs low, keep replacing it.

In addition to the fiber, grass hays are rich in other essential nutrients. Several types of grass hay exist: timothy, oat, brome, Bermuda, and mixed orchard grass. Any is fine. In fact, mixing them is a gourmet treat. Alfalfa, though, is one type of hay to avoid using; it's too high in calories and protein.

You can purchase hay at a pet store or feed store. Make sure that the hay smells fresh and isn't damp or moldy. Some stores leave hay sitting for a long time, so find out how long it's been around (the fresher, the better). Try to buy only as much as you'll use for about a two-month period and keep it dry. Store hay in a dry location out of the sun, in a container that is not air-tight (so no garbage cans). Don't store hay in sealed plastic bags; sealing in hay's natural moisture content can cause mold to grow.

When purchasing hay, look for the *grass hays,* which are light brown-green and grass-like. *Alfalfa hay,* which should only be fed to bunnies younger than six months, is dark green with more tough stems. Grass hay isn't readily available in some areas, but you can order it online. The Appendix gives Web sites worth checking out in this arena.

Depending on the availability of hay where you live, you may be offered a choice between first- and second-cut hay. Be prepared with the facts:

- **First-cut hay:** Tends to be coarser and stalky, like straw. This high-fiber cut is better for your bunny, but not as tasty as some rabbits would like.
- **Second cut hay:** Dark green, finer, and more grass-like than first-cut hay. This cut is lower in fiber, which makes it the second choice as far as nutrition. Rabbits, like humans, make many of their food choices based on taste, not nutrition (like choosing the chocolate chip muffin over the bran muffin); as far as taste goes, second-cut would be voted "best tasting" by many rabbits.

Sticking to first-cut timothy hay is probably the best choice for your bunny's health, but some rabbit's will outright refuse the stuff. In this case, less fiber is better than no fiber, just as long as your finicky bunny has hay for munching.

For those of you with allergies, use *timothy hay cubes* (avoid alfalfa hay cubes). Although loose hay is preferred, these compressed cubes are the next best thing. (Processed cubes have fiber but in short lengths, which aren't as effective in the rabbit gut as loose hay). If your rabbit eats cubes instead of loose hay, getting a high-fiber pelleted food is especially important. (See the upcoming section "Making the Most of Pellets.") If you can't find timothy hay cubes in your area, you can get them from Web sites listed in the Appendix.

Wild rabbits eat plenty of fresh foods and your domestic rabbit should, too. Greens and fruit aren't only important to your rabbit's health, but they're also tasty treats that he'll undoubtedly enjoy.

# Going Green

Green vegetables, particularly the leafy type, are the most important fresh food for your rabbit, and he should have at least three kinds on a daily basis. Root veggies are also good. On a daily basis, give your rabbit at least 1 cup of greens for every 3 pounds of weight.

For example, a 6 pound rabbit should get 2 cups of greens every day.

When adding new veggies to your rabbit's diet, do so gradually, one at a time, so you can keep track of which, if any, don't agree with your rabbit's tummy (soft stools or diarrhea). Most rabbit veterinarians suggest varying the vegetables offered, though they stress the point that at least three kinds be given each day. Choose from the following:

- Alfalfa sprouts
- Basil
- Beet greens
- Bok Choy
- Broccoli
- Brussels sprouts
- Carrot tops (with some carrots, for good measure)
- Celery
- Chard
- Chicory
- Cilantro
- Clover (too much can cause soft stools, so feed in moderation)
- Collard greens
- Dandelion flowers and greens (without pesticides)
- Endive
- Green peppers
- Kale
- Lettuce, dark leaf (romaine is best; iceberg lettuce is low in nutrients)
- Mint
- Mustard greens
- Parsley

- Pea pods (the flat, green edible kind)
- Radish tops
- Spinach
- Watercress
- Wheat grass

You can offer your rabbit other green leafy vegetables, too, to see whether she likes them. Remember that rabbits are all individuals, and you may find that your rabbit doesn't like some greens but particularly enjoys others. If you're not sure whether a plant is safe for your rabbit, take a look at the list of plants in Chapter 8 (or specific parts of plants) that rabbits should not eat.

Before you feed greens to your rabbit, wash them thoroughly and check for any rotten areas. Be sure to cut off those areas before offering the greens to your pet, or better yet, skip these rotted greens altogether. You can buy chopped and cleaned bags of mixed greens sold for people salad, but please — no salad dressing! When available, organic fresh foods are even better.

# Getting Fruity

Those who know and love bunnies can attest to the fact that many of them have a serious sweet tooth. Unfortunately, even the natural sugars in fruit can mean trouble for both rabbits and humans. Your best bet is to offer the following fruity delights sparingly and only as treats. (*Sparingly* means in tablespoons, not cups!)

- Apples (no seeds, please; they're toxic)
- Berries, such as strawberries, raspberries, and blueberries
- Peaches, pears, and plums
- Papayas
- Melons, such as watermelon, cantaloupe, and honeydew
- Orange slices (peeled)

Bananas, grapes, and raisins are especially sweet. Think of them as the "lollipops" of your bunny's diet — only on rare occasions. (The upcoming section "Giving Your Bunny Treats" discusses treats and portions in more detail.) As with all fresh produce, be sure to wash fruit thoroughly.

### Growing a garden

Rabbits love nothing more than to graze naturally. If you have a green thumb and want to give your rabbit a truly natural way for him to take in his daily nutrients, grow a bunny garden. Set aside a patch of your backyard and plant the seeds of some of the plants listed as good greens in this chapter. (Mint, parsley, basil, and leaf lettuces are easy to grow.) Use organic soil and avoid using pesticides or herbicides. When the plants mature, create a protective enclosure for your rabbit all around the garden and let him run loose among the plants daily, if possible.

Consider, too, that lawn grasses are similar to the different varieties of grass hay, just never allowed to mature. Left unmowed, a section of lawn grass becomes a veritable snacking meadow for rabbits. Be certain, of course, to ensure that the area is not treated with pesticides and is carefully supervised and protected from predators.

If you don't have a yard for planting, don't fret. Use a large tray that you can keep on your balcony, fire escape, or window sill as your garden. Try to find a south-facing area or any area that gets plenty of direct sun. Once your plants have grown to maturity in the tray, give your rabbit access to it for a while so that he can enjoy the fruits (and veggies) of your labor.

# Making the Most of Pellets

For years, pet rabbit owners have been giving their bunnies alfalfa-based, commercially produced rabbit *pellets.* These high-calorie nuggets of ground-up hay, grain, vitamins, and minerals were considered a staple in pet rabbit diets for a long time. The result, according to many rabbit experts, has been a plethora of obese and unhealthy pet bunnies (see Figure 6-1).

Readily available, alfalfa-based pellets are convenient, but newer information suggests that pellets aren't optimal for pet rabbits that are not growing or producing baby rabbits. Therefore, the latest recommendations for the pet rabbit are that any pellets you use should be timothy-based, and not alfalfa-based. Choose kinds that have 20 percent or greater fiber content.

## Picking pellets

Not all pellets are created equal. If you want a healthy, long-lived pet, search around for grass hay-based pellets, most of which are made from timothy. A few companies make this product, including Oxbow Animal Health, which is mentioned in the Appendix. You can also opt to leave pellets out of your rabbit's diet, as long as you provide a constant supply of grass hay and plenty of fresh foods. (Talk to your vet about specific amounts.)

**Figure 6-1:** Overweight? The top rabbit isn't; the bottom rabbit is.

When shopping for timothy-based pellets, you'll notice that the larger bags of feed are the better deal, money-wise. But don't be tempted to buy a huge bag that lasts for six months because the pellets will lose their nutritional value over time. Buy only what your rabbit can consume in a month's time and keep them out of sunlight in a cool, dry place to prevent mold. Like hay, pellets should be stored in a container that is not air-tight but that will keep out bugs and other pests.

## Determining the correct amount of pellets

The amount of pellets that your rabbit should eat depends on a few factors:

- **Babies (less than 3 months):** Up until 7 weeks of age, kits rely on their mother's milk for most of their nutritional needs. Access to alfalfa hay (which is okay for growing babies) and pellets should begin around 4 weeks. Try to avoid feeding alfalfa-based pellets to babies because it may make it more difficult to change them over to timothy-based pellets as adults. Wait until about 12 weeks to start introducing veggies, one at a time, in very small quantities (half an ounce).

- **Adolescents (5 to 12 months):** Up until 7 months, offer unlimited pellets and hay, making the transition from alfalfa to grass hay. Continue to introduce more vegetables and greens. At around 7 months, decrease pellets to ½ cup per 6 pounds of rabbit. Consider introducing a small amount of fruit as a treat (less than 2 ounces per 6 pounds of rabbit).
- **Adult (1 year and older):** The amount of pellets you give your rabbit depends primarily on your rabbit's weight, his health, and what other foods he eats. Continue to offer unlimited grass and slowly increase veggies up to at least 2 cups per 6 pounds of body weight. For rabbits that get all the grass hay they want and fresh greens daily, ¼ cup to ½ cup of timothy pellets per 6 pounds of rabbit is a maximum. Decrease the amount of pellets if weight gain becomes an issue.
- **Seniors (6 years and older):** Unless the older rabbit has problems with weight, you can continue a normal adult diet.
- **Ill or underweight:** If your rabbit is underweight or suffering from an illness that prevents him from eating hay and green foods, your veterinarian may recommend that you increase the amount of pellets. In some situations, the concentrated nutrients in the pellets may be beneficial to regaining strength, particularly after a disease that causes unhealthy weight loss. In these cases, please follow your veterinarian's recommendations. (Chapter 9 talks more about illnesses and their signs.)
- **Overweight rabbits:** In many cases, problems with weight result from overfeeding of pellets. (See this chapter's "Coping with a chubby bunny" for more information.)
- **Households with hay allergies:** If you or some other person have hay allergies, you may have to leave loose hay out of the diet and rely on compressed hay cubes. In that case, continue feeding fresh foods as suggested, but offer the amount of timothy pellets in the amount recommended on the food bag for your pet's weight; modify as needed.

If your rabbit doesn't finish the pellets you provide him in a serving, throw them out before doling out the next serving. Don't pour the new pellets on top of the old ones and don't forget to wash out the bowl on a regular basis to reduce the likelihood of bacteria or mold.

One advantage of monitoring the amount of food your rabbit eats is that you're better able to notice when your rabbit's appetite decreases, which can often be a sign of illness. Catching problems early can make a big difference in diagnosing and treating health problems.

Our understanding of rabbit nutrition has changed a lot over the years. Rabbits meant for the meat and fur industry were fed pellets with high alfalfa and grain contents to maximize meat production and luxurious fur. Many breeders and rabbit show participants still feed rabbits this way and may advise you to do so, too. However, most nutritionists and veterinarians believe the track to good long-term health is to avoid alfalfa based foods (except for growing and pregnant rabbits) and eliminate grains altogether.

# Coping with a Chubby Bunny

A common problem vets see in pet rabbits is obesity. Rabbits who eat too many pellets and don't get enough exercise become dangerously overweight. (Refer to Figure 6-1 to see an obese rabbit). If your rabbit needs to slim down, you can help him by reducing his pellet intake or removing pellets altogether as long as he eats hay and greens instead. Restrict his diet to ⅛ to ¼ cup of pellets for every 5 pounds of body weight. You can still give him treats but limit them to greens only. He can have as much grass hay as he wants, but certainly stick to timothy hay, rather than the higher-calorie alfalfa hay.

Not sure how much your rabbit weighs? And you can't get him to sit still on the bathroom scale? Simply stand on your scale and make note of your weight. Then pick up your rabbit and get back on the scale while holding your pet. Make note of the new total weight. Finally, subtract your weight alone from the weight of you holding the rabbit. This number is your rabbit's weight.

# Giving Your Bunny Treats

You can feed the food in one sitting or throughout the day while training (Chapter 12, which covers training, offers tips on using treats as training rewards). With that in mind, some treats your rabbit may enjoy include

- Apple slices without seeds
- Cantaloupe
- Honeydew
- Kiwi
- Nectarines
- Peaches
- Pears
- Plums
- Strawberries
- Tomatoes (but not the vines or leaves — yes, tomatoes are fruit)
- Watermelon

Think outside the box when it comes to treats, especially if you're watching your bunny's figure. Dried apple twigs and branches are a much appreciated source of fun and fiber for rabbits. And don't overlook the value of a good old-fashioned petting session as a reward.

# Popping Pills

You may be wondering if you need to give your rabbit liquid or chewable vitamins and minerals in addition to her regular meal. If your pet is getting a balanced diet with grass hay and fresh foods at its core, you don't need to provide vitamin or mineral supplements. The rabbit makes his very own nutritional supplements in the form of cecotropes (see Chapter 2).

The exceptions to this rule are when your rabbit is pregnant, nursing, recovering from an illness, or undergoing extreme stress. In these situations, check with a veterinarian first to see whether you need to use supplements.

When it comes to vitamins and minerals, you *can* have too much of a good thing. Over-supplementing certain vitamins and minerals can cause toxicity or severe illness.

Remember that if you have a pet bunny, you don't have to do much more than give her unlimited grass hay, plenty of fresh foods, limited amounts of high-quality pellets, and an ample supply of water. But if you have a female rabbit *(doe)* who is expecting a litter of baby rabbits *(kits)* or nursing her young, you need to do a bit more to get her safely through her pregnancy and nursing. Your veterinarian can offer guidance in such situations.

# Forbidding Foods

Avoid foods high in carbohydrates (starches and sugars, for example). Many commercial treat foods contain high levels of starch and fat. Although a rabbit can eat small amounts without ill effect, he'll start craving these foods. (Sound like a person?). Obesity and serious GI disease are just two of the resulting problems if his cravings are indulged. It's always easier to prevent than to treat a disease.

Think it's cute to feed your begging bunny some crackers, a nibble of your pasta, or a snack of cereal? Think again.

Please avoid these foods at all cost:

- Beans (any kind)
- Breads
- Cereals
- Chocolate
- Corn
- Nuts
- Oats
- Peas
- Potatoes
- Refined sugar
- Seeds
- Wheat (and any other grains)

Don't let your bunny munch out of the cat or dog food bowl. Cat and dog food are much too high in protein and carbohydrates for your rabbit. If he eats too much of these foods, the results can be fatal.

# Chapter 7

# Cleaning Behind Those Great Big Ears and More

### In This Chapter

- Having the right tools on hand
- Going through the list of grooming possibilities
- Brushing out loose hair
- Cutting nails and cleaning ears

Much like cats, rabbits are fastidious about their own bodies. They're constantly grooming themselves, making sure that every little hair is perfectly in place. For that reason, shorthaired rabbits seldom need our help in the grooming department. However, weekly grooming is still a great idea because it

- Encourages social bonding with your pet
- Encourages a thorough examination to help detect abnormalities
- Reduces the amount of hair shed into the environment and into your house

Unlike cats, however, rabbits aren't able to cope with (by vomiting) the excess hair that accumulate in their systems, leaving them prone to serious digestive issues. Fortunately, a weekly brushing is usually all it takes for your bunny to stay on the right track.

Cleaning your rabbit's cage regularly can also help your rabbit stay clean and healthy. A clean cage translates into a clean rabbit. Despite their self-grooming skill, however, rabbits need a little help from their human friends in this regard. As a bunny owner, you should provide regular grooming for your pet. This chapter shows you how to keep your rabbit's cage and coat in tip-top shape.

# Stocking Your Grooming Toolshed

Grooming your rabbit includes brushing, combing, clipping toenails, and examining your pet's entire body to make sure that all is as it should be. The grooming process will probably take about an hour a week, depending on your rabbit's coat. (Longer coats require more care.)

To properly groom your rabbit, you need the right tools at your disposal.

- **Pin brush:** A small pin brush, made for cat grooming, works great for rabbits. Pin brushes are made up of straight metal pins attached to a rubber base, and they're great at trapping loose hair within the coat. Pin brushes cost anywhere from a couple of dollars to $8, depending on the quality of the brush and where you live. The less expensive brushes do the job well, so don't feel compelled to spend a lot.
- **Flea comb:** A regular-size flea comb is a good tool. (Chapter 3 helps you determine which breed has short and which has long hair.) A flea comb smoothes out the coat, traps loose hairs, and helps you find out whether fleas are a problem for your rabbit. Flea combs trap fleas in their metal teeth. They also lift flea feces from the coat, which is an indicator that fleas are present. They're also good for removing *mats* (tangle of hair, often with undercoat) from all types of rabbit coats. (See "Running Down the Grooming Checklist," later in this chapter, for more about checking for fleas.) Flea combs usually don't cost more than $3.
- **Wide-tooth comb:** Useful on rabbits with long coats, wide-tooth pet combs separate the hairs and prevent matting. You can use this tool after using the pin brush.
- **Bristle brush:** After you brush and comb your rabbit's coat, the bristle brush works as a finishing tool. Bristle brushes have soft nylon or hair bristles, and you can use them to give the coat a once over after you use the pin brush. The bristle brush picks up any remaining loose hairs and leaves your rabbit with a shiny coat, which is especially important if you're grooming your rabbit for a show.
- **Mat splitter or mat rake:** Use these specially designed bladed tools on longhaired rabbits when mats are too severe to be removed by brushing or combing.
- **Toenail clippers:** Guillotine-type nail clippers designed for small dogs and cats work best on rabbit toenails. These clippers are small and sharp and are less likely to split the nail than a human nail clipper.
- **Flashlight:** For those who have bunnies with dark nails, a small flashlight will help you see where to clip nails.

- **Styptic powder:** In case a nail is cut too short, styptic powder tends to halt bleeding. It has an indefinite shelf life if kept dry. Although styptic powder is the preferred astringent, you can use flour or cornstarch in a pinch. What may work best is plain old direct pressure — simply put some pressure on the nail bed with a clean cloth for 1 to 2 minutes.
- **Cotton swabs:** Soft cotton-tipped swabs are handy for ears and eyes that may need tending; also good for applying styptic powder to nails.

You can purchase these items at a pet-supply store, through a mail-order catalog, or over the Internet. The Appendix lists several helpful resources.

# Handling with Care

Rabbits are incredibly cute, and everyone wants to hold them. The problem is that most rabbits aren't terribly thrilled about being held. Can you blame them? Their primary means of defense is being able to run away when they're in danger. When all four of their feet are suspended off the ground, they have no way to escape should something scare them. Further, when a predator captures a rabbit in the wild, that predator picks the rabbit up and carries it off. Given this reality, it's not hard to understand why being lifted and carried may be a scary sensation for a rabbit.

## Taking proper precautions

As a child, Audrey volunteered to be a rabbit carrier at her local 4-H club rabbit show. The rabbits flailed their paws against her as she carried them from their cages to the judge's podium. By the end of the day, her stomach was completely covered with scratches. Rabbit toenails can be sharp, and when a bunny becomes insecure and starts to struggle, human skin usually pays the price. To prevent your stomach and arms from being torn to bits when you handle your rabbit, take the following precautions:

- **Trim your rabbit's nails.** If you keep your rabbit's toenails trimmed, you're less likely to be scratched should your pet struggle when you're carrying him.
- **Train your rabbit.** By slowly acclimating your rabbit to the sensation of being carried, you reduce the likelihood that he'll start to flail when you're holding him.
- **Wear safe clothes.** Never carry a rabbit while your arms or torso is uncovered. If your rabbit panics, you'll find out first hand just how painful rabbit scratches can be.
- **Monitor children.** Kids love to carry their bunnies, but if they don't do it right, they can end up covered in scratches. Rabbits have powerful hind legs, and the scratches that result from kicking while being held can be deep and painful. Prevent younger kids from carrying rabbits (especially large ones), and teach older kids the proper way to do it.

So does that mean that you can never pick up your rabbit? Of course not (although you should only carry him when you need to move him from one place to another). But it does mean that you need to use patience, sensitivity, and the right handling techniques to reduce or eliminate fear in your rabbit.

Before you attempt to start carrying your rabbit around, you need to gain your pet's trust. If your rabbit is a baby, you're in luck. If you start the handling process when your rabbit is young, your pet can grow up to be more comfortable being handled. If you have an adult rabbit that you're just getting to know, you need to do a bit more work to win your bunny's trust, especially if your new pet was mishandled in the past.

Building trust is a time commitment, but taking 15 minutes a day to work through the following numbered steps may speed the process. (This chapter's "Need a lift?" sidebar offers an alternative method.)

1. **Sit on the floor with your rabbit or place your rabbit on a table.**

   Cover the table with a blanket to protect its surface and to secure the rabbit's footing.

2. **Get him used to the feel of your hands.**

   Pet your rabbit and talk to him while you do it. Then try giving him some treats. (See Chapter 6 for more on feeding treats.)

   Continue to pet your rabbit until you see that he's starting to trust you. (See Chapter 11 for information about how to read your rabbit's body language.) Signs of trust are when your rabbit

   - Approaches you on his own for touching (anytime)
   - Puts his paws on you
   - Shows relaxed body language during these 15-minute sessions

3. **Place your rabbit against your body.**

   While the bunny is on the table or on the floor, gently move him toward you. Keeping his feet on the ground, restrain him against your chest or legs. If you want, you can gently hold him by the *scruff* (the loose skin on the back of his neck) with one hand while pressing his hindquarters against you with the other hand.

   Your rabbit may struggle at first if she isn't used to being restrained. Use a calm voice and patience to show her that she's safe despite the fact that you're restraining her. If your rabbit starts to panic and struggles wildly, let him go. Start over again with the trust-building sessions until he seems comfortable with your touch and then try the gentle restraint again. After your bunny seems comfortable being gently restrained against your body, you can get him used to being lifted.

4. **Slowly place one hand under your pet's chest, just behind its front legs.**

   Make sure that you're in a quiet place where you won't be disturbed. Work from the table or floor area where you've been conducting your trust-building sessions because your rabbit feels safe here.

5. **Slide your other hand underneath the rabbit's rump to lift him.**

   Always support the hind quarters to prevent injury to the spine. The most common injury is due to improper handling.

6. **Lift upward with the hand that's on the rabbit's chest and support the rabbit's body weight with the other hand.**

7. **Pull the rabbit's body toward you as you lift, pointing the rabbit's head toward the back of your elbow.**

8. **Slide your hand out from under the rabbit's chest as you press his forequarters against your side.**

   The idea is to carry the rabbit under your arm as you would carry a football, as shown in Figure 7-1.

**Figure 7-1:** Touchdown! Holding your bunny like this will help him feel more secure.

If your rabbit begins to struggle, hold him more securely against you. If he starts flailing, place him gently back on the table or the floor. Don't drop your rabbit; you can seriously injure him.

After your rabbit is comfortable with you, hold him this way for several minutes and increase the time that you spend handling him.

9. **When you can comfortably hold him in this position for at least 5 minutes, you can start moving around with him tucked under your arm.**

   Be prepared — your rabbit may get scared when he feels you moving. If he starts to struggle, stop and let him get comfortable again before you begin to walk again.

Your veterinarian may have cause to place your rabbit on his back for examination of some kind, but please avoid putting your rabbit in this position unless it's absolutely necessary. Rabbits may become extremely frightened when they're placed on their backs and restrained. They may cease to struggle, but the current thinking is that's only out of terror, not relaxation. Try to work with your rabbit by keeping his feet on solid ground. She'll appreciate you for it!

# Running Down the Grooming Checklist

Grooming sessions provide an opportunity to examine your rabbit thoroughly for certain health problems. Catching these problems early increases the likelihood of being able to cure your pet. Chapters 9 and 10 tell you more about these diseases and what to look for.

When going over your bunny with a brush, make sure that you mentally run through this grooming checklist:

- **Look for parasites.** Rabbits are just as susceptible to these pests as dogs and cats are, especially if they live or play outdoors. When grooming, keep an eye out for fleas and ticks. Ticks appear as dark round protrusions about ⅛ to ¼ inch. Fleas are small, dark, and difficult to see. However, their feces *(flea dirt)* are readily visible, especially on a light-colored rabbit. They appear as small, dark flecks on the skin along the rabbit's back, neck, and especially rump. If you find parasites on your pet, contact your vet for information on how to safely rid your rabbit of these pests. Your vet can provide you with rabbit-safe products that can do the job. (You can find more parasite and vet talk in Chapter 9.)
- **Seek out lumps and sores.** As you go over your rabbit with a brush or comb, look out for any lumps or open sores on your pet's body. (The more familiar you become with your rabbit's body, the more you'll be able to notice such problems.) Lumps shouldn't be ignored. Scabs, sores, and crusty areas can be a sign of parasites or a bacterial infection.

Sores on the feet and hocks can be the result of a damp or dirty environment and improper flooring.

- **Check eyes, ears, and teeth.** Examine your rabbit's eyes up close to make sure that no discharge or swelling is present. Ears should be looked at for signs of parasites or bacterial infection, especially in lop-eared breeds (see Chapter 3). There's more ear talk in this chapter's "Cleaning Your Bunny's Ears." Teeth? Be sure your bunny's chompers are on the straight and narrow (see Chapter 9).
- **Feel along the jaw line for any lumps.** The sides should be symmetrical. Any obvious lumps or lack of symmetry should be examined by a vet.

## Bypassing the Bath

Unlike dogs, rabbits don't need regular bathing. In fact, you're better off not bathing a rabbit at all. The bath stresses them terribly and exposes them to injury because they'll struggle. In short, skip the bath.

If your rabbit needs help keeping clean on occasion, you can do some spot cleaning. If your bunny stepped in something sticky or irritating to the skin, remove it right away. Pet-supply stores sell waterless shampoos, which you can spray directly onto your pet's coat. Simply saturate the area with the waterless shampoo product and follow the directions on the label.

### Need a lift?

The best type of lift for a rabbit is one that makes him feel secure. You may choose to use a lift described in this chapter or a modified version of either — as long as it's safe for you and your rabbit.

1. **Kneel down and slide one hand down the rabbit's side while petting her head with your other hand.**
2. **Slide the arm at your rabbit's side under his chest and move your petting hand down under to support his hindquarters, as in this figure.**
3. **Scoop him closely to you and hold firmly, not tightly. Be certain to support your rabbit's hind end and keep him from slipping out of your arms.**
4. **Stand up slowly, keeping your rabbit close to you.**

   Hug the rabbit if he starts to struggle. Don't drop him, especially from a standing position.
5. **To put your rabbit down, old him close until you're back in a kneeling position and then carefully let him go on the floor.**

All of this will take time and practice. Consider a small treat to reward your rabbit and help her relax a bit when you put her down.

When you're dealing with a slightly soiled bunny, a dry bath approach is best whenever possible. Use a cornstarch-based baby powder that doesn't contain talc (which has been linked to cancer). Place the bunny in your lap on a bunched towel so that he feels secure and apply the cornstarch to the soiled areas, working the powder into the fur. As the cornstarch coats the soiled areas, you can gently brush away the debris.

Your bunny's hind end may become extremely soiled or wet if he develops soft stools or is wet with urine. Your vet should diagnose the cause of this problem, but it's up to you to clean your rabbit and protect his sensitive skin. In these cases, a dry bath may not be sufficient. Follow these steps to properly wash your bun's bottom:

1. **Fill two containers or a double sink with 2 to 3 inches of lukewarm water.**
2. **Dip the rabbit's rear end in the water.**

   Do not submerge the entire rabbit!
3. **Use a wash cloth, soft brush, or your hand to loosen the material.**
4. **Take the rabbit out of the water, apply a very small amount of shampoo (suitable for cats; don't use baby shampoo), and thoroughly massage the area with your hands.**
5. **Dip him into the clean water of the other container and rinse off the soap and debris.**
6. **Towel dry him, getting as much water out as possible.**

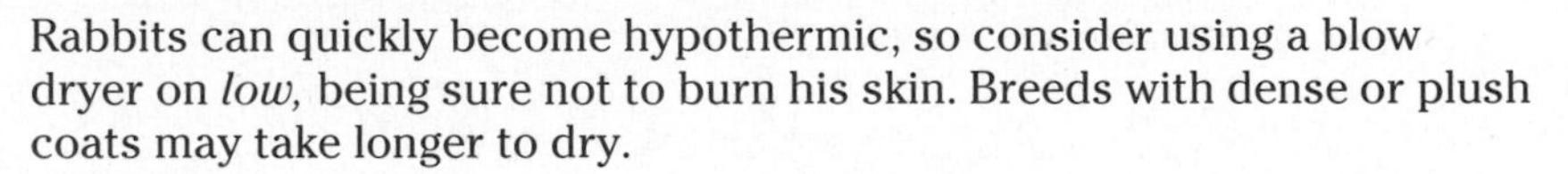

   Rabbits can quickly become hypothermic, so consider using a blow dryer on *low,* being sure not to burn his skin. Breeds with dense or plush coats may take longer to dry.
7. **Put him in a cage (in a warm room) with towels to continue to absorb water.**

   He'll finish grooming himself.

If you need to repeat or rinse more, you can let the rabbit take a break on some towels, change the water, and rinse again.

Removing matted feces and urine can be incredibly difficult if it has accumulated, causing the skin underneath to become very sore and irritated. In fact, the skin may even tear if you try too hard to remove this material. You may need to have a veterinarian give your sedated rabbit a thorough cleaning. You can ask the vet to clip the hair at this time so that future cleaning won't be as difficult. If in doubt, have a vet check it out! In many cases like this, a vet is a better choice than a groomer, who may not be experienced in the finer points of rabbit care.

# Breaking Out the Brush

Rabbits are good at brushing their own coats and using their tongues to clean their fur and smooth it down. Rabbits left to do their own grooming are also notorious for leaving loose hairs around. If you have an indoor rabbit who hops around the carpet and on the furniture, shedding will become a nuisance.

The way to help remedy this loose hair situation is to brush your rabbit regularly. Brushing reduces the loose fur around the house, helps prevent intestinal blockages caused by ingested hair, and also gives you an opportunity to examine your pet closely for lumps, bumps, and other health problems. (See Chapter 9 for more on health issues.) Grooming time also provides a great opportunity for bonding with your pet.

You want to make grooming a pleasant experience for your rabbit, so brush your pet gently to avoid causing him any discomfort or pain. Rabbits have sensitive skin, and your bunny will come to dislike grooming time if you're too rough with him. Likewise, when you handle your rabbit for toenail clipping or any other grooming procedure, be patient and gentle.

## Brushing short to medium coats

If your rabbit has a short to medium coat typical of most rabbit breeds, you need to set aside an hour a week for grooming.

Rex rabbit breeds have ultra short coats, so you need to take extra care when you brush him because you don't want to damage the skin. Rex rabbits, in fact, need very infrequent brushing.

To brush a short to medium coat rabbit:

1. **Find a comfortable place to sit while grooming your pet.**
2. **Assemble your grooming tools within reach.**

   See the section "Stocking Your Grooming Toolshed," earlier in this chapter.
3. **Hold your bunny securely in your lap.**

   Stabilizing your bunny against your body will help prevent him from struggling and hurting himself.
4. **Brush your rabbit with the pin brush, moving in the direction that the coat grows to minimize breakage of the hair.**

If you notice many loose hairs in your brush after a few swipes on his coat and it's spring or fall, your rabbit may be molting. (See the "A time to shed, a time to brush" sidebar, later in this chapter.)

Don't brush his face, feet, ears, or tail. Stay away from these areas because they don't have a lot of hair. When brushing your rabbit, be sure to be gentle and talk to your pet in a quiet voice to reassure him. If he's reluctant to be brushed, try offering him some healthy treats to nibble on while you're brushing. The treats will distract him and help him associate grooming time with something pleasant.

5. **Go through your rabbit's coat with your flea comb.**

   Check for fleas that may get caught in the comb. Check also for black specs on the teeth of the comb, which may be flea feces. If you're unsure, place these specs on a paper towel and place a drop of water on them. If the wet area of the towel turns red, your rabbit has fleas. If you're still not certain if your rabbit has fleas, ask your veterinarian to make a diagnosis.

6. **Comb out any hair matting.**

   Flea combs work well for this task.

7. **Give your rabbit the once over with the bristle brush if you have one.**

   This brush picks up any loose hairs you missed and helps give the coat a nice shine.

## Brushing long coats

If you have an Angora, Jersey Wooley, or other longhair rabbit breed (see Chapter 3), you need to brush your pet on a daily basis, regardless of the season. These rabbits are extremely prone to hair matting. The hair is not only long but fine textured.

To brush a longhaired rabbit:

1. **Find a comfortable place to sit while you're grooming your pet.**
2. **Assemble your grooming tools within reach.**

   See "Stocking Your Grooming Toolshed."

3. **Situate your rabbit comfortably in your lap.**
4. **Start with your pin brush.**

5. **Part sections of your rabbit's coat and brush from the area where the hair attaches to the skin outward, in the direction the hair is growing.**

   Be sure to loosen any areas that appear to be matting. If you do this every day, you'll eventually weed out all the mats, and your rabbit's coat won't have a problem. Flea combs can be great for getting out mats if you have enough space between the mat and the skin to get the comb started.

6. **Move on to the wide-tooth comb and bristle brush.**

   Gently comb in the direction that hair grows with both of these tools. Start with the wide-tooth comb and finish up with the bristle brush. Then move on to ear cleaning and toenail clipping.

If you aren't comfortable caring for your longhair rabbit's coat yourself or simply don't have time, you can take your rabbit to a professional groomer for grooming or shearing. Make certain that the groomer you go to regularly works on rabbits, because these delicate creatures need special handling to prevent them from getting injured during the grooming process.

Another option is to trim your longhair rabbit's fur yourself. Using a pair of sharp scissors, you can cut the hair back to a couple of inches in length so that it's easier to maintain (and easier on your bunny's tummy!). Don't cut your rabbit's fur all the way to the skin. Not only is this dangerous because you may accidentally cut your rabbit, but your rabbit does need to have some fur on his body. His coat acts as a natural insulator against heat and cold.

If you come across mats in your rabbit's fur, you can use a mat splitter or mat rake to gently break up the mats. Don't use scissors for this task because you risk snipping down to the skin. First try to remove matted fur with a flea comb or fine-toothed comb. Don't pull up on your rabbit's fur as you work on the mat because your rabbit's skin is very fragile. If the mats are severe, get help from your veterinarian. (A groomer is not likely to be skilled in the finer points of bunny grooming.)

# Clipping It Not Quite in the Bud

Rabbit toenails grow constantly, just like human fingernails, and so they need to be clipped regularly (about every 6 to 8 weeks). If you don't clip your rabbit's toenails, they'll become excessively long, and your pet will soon have trouble walking. He'll also be in danger of catching a long toenail on his cage wire or on your carpet and may possibly tear the nail right out of his paw.

## A time to shed, a time to brush

Rabbits shed like dogs and cats and seem to drop their fur most often during spring and fall. However, because rabbits are indoors under all kinds of lighting and temperature conditions, they can shed all year round. During the heaviest shedding times, brush your rabbit more often, especially on the rump area where the most loose fur seems to accumulate. (Some people find that the hair comes out simply by pulling at it with their fingers.) Should your rabbit ever shed to the point where bald patches appear, contact your veterinarian. This loss of hair may be a sign of hormonal abnormalities, parasites, or a disease.

Another good reason to keep your rabbit's nails trimmed is for your own protection. Whenever you handle your rabbit, you come into contact with those nails. Should your pet become insecure and start to kick and struggle, long nails may do a good amount of damage to your skin. (The section "Handling with Care" in this chapter provides details on the proper way to handle your rabbit.)

You can tell whether your rabbit's nails are too long because the nails extend beyond the edge of the fur on the rabbit's foot. If you're not sure, have your veterinarian take a look at your bunny's feet to let you know whether he needs a trim.

The good news is that you don't need to clip your rabbit's toenails every time you groom him. Simply evaluate the length of the nails whenever you sit down to groom him. If they're starting to get long, then it's time to get out the clippers.

Rabbits, like most pets, don't enjoy having their nails trimmed, so it's best for you to start clipping with the aid of another person. This helper, preferably an experienced person, is the one to hold your rabbit while you do the actual nail clipping. Sources for experienced people are rabbit breeders, other experienced rabbit owners (find through rabbit organizations), veterinary staff, pet stores, and groomers that care for rabbits.

To clip your rabbit's nails:

1. **Have your helper position the rabbit on her lap with the rabbit's rear resting against the helper's lower abdomen.**

   Make sure that both you and the handler are wearing long-sleeved shirts of heavy material because the potential for getting scratched is high with this grooming procedure. The helper should have a secure grip on the bunny without hurting her.

If your bunny tends to struggle no matter what you do, try wrapping her in a towel first, gently exposing the nails you want to clip.

2. **Gently grasp one of the rabbit's front legs.**
3. **Turn the leg so the *dewclaw* (the nail on the inside of the foot) is visible.**
4. **Examine the nail to determine where the quick is.**

   The *quick* is the vein that extends from the toe to nearly the tip of the nail. It appears as a dark line in the nail. You want to clip the part of the nail that does *not* contain the quick (about ⅛ inch before the quick), as cutting the quick makes the nail bleed. If you're having trouble locating the quick or have a rabbit with black nails, get a flashlight and shine it through the backside of the nail toward you. The vein will become visible.

   In the event that you should accidentally cut into your rabbit's vein, making the nail bleed, don't panic. Just dab a bit of styptic powder (available at drug stores) onto the nail, and the bleeding will stop.

5. **Cut the tip of the nail off, as shown in Figure 7-2, repeating for each of the five nails on each of the rabbit's front feet.**

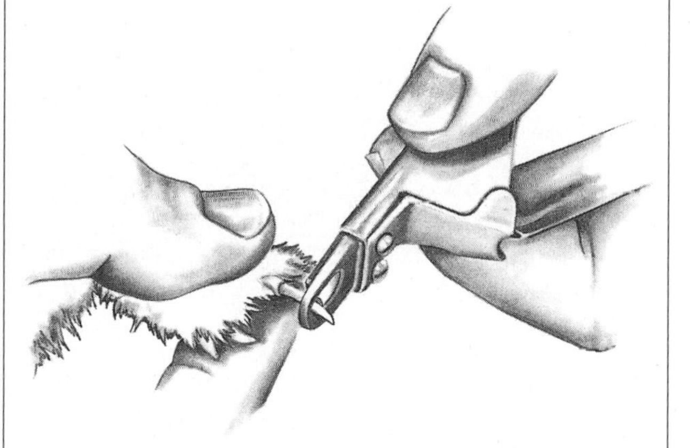

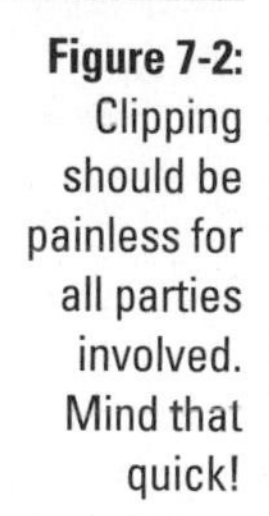

**Figure 7-2:** Clipping should be painless for all parties involved. Mind that quick!

6. **Relax for a while.**
7. **Have your helper hold the rabbit again, so you can start working on the hind nails.**

   This time, your helper should grasp the rabbit in the way described earlier in this chapter and shown in Figure 7-1. This will make the back paws accessible to you. Make certain that your rabbit is comfortable in the position that she's placed. Otherwise, she'll struggle and make clipping her nails impossible.

8. **Proceed with the back nails in the same way that you did with the front.**

   You may find that the back nails are a bit tougher to cut than the front because they're thicker. So be prepared to use a little more force to clip those hind nails. It's important to note that rear legs are more prone to fracture during struggling if you pull the hind leg sideways rather than straight back.

If clipping nails sounds too overwhelming to you as a first-time rabbit owner, you can always take your rabbit to the veterinarian, groomer, or experienced rabbit owner for nail clipping. Ask your vet to show you how to do the nail clipping so that you don't have to have it done at the vet's office, which can be a hassle and expensive, too.

# Cleaning Your Bunny's Ears

A rabbit's ears are his great showpiece, so you want to help him keep them clean. You can check them for cleanliness during your bunny's regular grooming time, as long as you're checking the ears at least once a week. (Don't worry; your lop ear won't get hurt if you check him out because his ears are soft and floppy.)

Whenever you groom your rabbit, thoroughly check his ears for waxy build-up, dirt, or a foul smell. If you see debris in your rabbit's ears, gently lift it out with a cotton-tipped swab or cotton ball. You can also ask your veterinarian for a solution that you can use to wipe the ears clean. If wax buildup is a problem, be careful not to push the wax into the ear canal. Wax actually has a protective purpose, so don't routinely remove it from a rabbit's ears. And *never* stick cotton swabs down into the ear canal.

You should do fine managing minor cases of dirt and wax. However, redness or a crusty discharge in the ear can indicate an ear mite infestation (see Chapter 9), which means you should consult your veterinarian.

# Chapter 8

# Making Fitness and Fresh Air Fun for Your Bunny

## In This Chapter

- Focusing on fitness
- Exercising your companion rabbit
- Exploring indoor options
- Providing a safe outdoor environment

If you want to keep your rabbit healthy and happy, you need to provide her with a lifestyle that includes plenty of exercise. Depending on where you live, this exercise routine may include some time outdoors, which requires that you take care of some safety precautions. This chapter can help you find out the best way to safely provide your rabbit with opportunities to exercise — both in the comfort of your home "gym" or in the great outdoors.

## Fitness Matters

Lack of exercise contributes to a long list of preventable health problems in domestic rabbits. By taking a look at the wild rabbit's lifestyle, you can easily see how a companion rabbit's health can suffer when he doesn't get the exercise he needs.

### Wild at heart

A wild rabbit may hop, jump, and skip through about 2 acres of land each day, looking for large amounts of high-fiber food (and, sometimes, mates). At times, he may have to escape from the grasp of predators and will use his powerful back legs to run and leap. This wild creature is not likely to thrive in a small cage, deprived of exercise and doomed to a life of boredom.

Many health problems are linked to obesity, and they're serious, chronic, and even fatal. The extra weight puts pressure on a rabbit's heart and joints and can lead to a host of health issues. Such conditions can be painful, decrease a rabbit's quality of life, and ultimately reduce a rabbit's lifespan.

Here are some common problems caused by lack of exercise:

- **Obesity:** The two most common causes of bunny obesity are a diet too high in calories and lack of exercise. Just like humans, when a rabbit sits around all day eating, he isn't going to burn many calories. Those extra pounds not only stress the cardiovascular system, but can result in inflammation of the foot and lack of energy. Excess weight can also cause the growth of folds of fat in the *dewlap* (roll of skin under the chin) or around the rectal area, which can interfere with healthy grooming habits, leading to a soiled bunny and even skin disease. That excess weight can also prevent your bun from eating his nutrient-rich cecotropes, resulting in nutritional deficiencies. You can start with a healthy diet, but a combination of diet and exercise is necessary to cure — or, better yet, prevent — obesity.
- **Pododermatitis (sore hock):** Although foot problems can develop because of damp flooring, an overweight rabbit is also prone to the inflammation and ulcerations associated with pododermatitis because the excessive weight results in wear on the footpads. On top of that, a chubby bunny may have trouble cleaning himself, leaving urine and stool on the hindquarters and feet, which can lead to inflammatory skin disease.
- **Gastrointestinal and urinary function:** A rabbit deprived of opportunities to exercise may develop problems maintaining normal elimination habits, which can lead to concentrated ("sludgy") urine or gastrointestinal shutdown. Rabbits that have an exercise routine will urinate and defecate frequently — a good thing for urinary and digestive systems.
- **Poor bone density:** Like humans, rabbits who don't get enough exercise can develop osteoporosis, a thinning of the bone. A rabbit with osteoporosis is likely to have a spine or other bones that can break easily when the rabbit is handled or jumps off a high surface. Doctors recommend that humans perform regular weight-bearing exercises to prevent osteoporosis. The same is true for your rabbit: Daily exercise is necessary to keep your rabbit's bones healthy and strong.
- **Poor muscle tone:** If your rabbit doesn't exercise, his muscles will be underdeveloped and weak, which can lead to a general inability to move properly. Think about your rabbit's most important muscle — his heart. If his heart muscle is weak, he will be less able to tolerate stressful situations. If you take an out-of-shape rabbit with a weak heart, like those who sit in a cage day after day, and then let her out and force her to run around the room, she may faint — or even die of cardiac failure.

- **Behavioral problems:** The boredom that comes with being confined to a cage without exercise can be linked to a number of negative behaviors observed in rabbits: aggression, obsessive grooming, lethargy, and obsessive chewing (of the bars of the cage, for example). In many of these cases, a bit of freedom and exercise can provide the very outlet needed to improve and even eliminate those behaviors (see Chapter 13). The results: happier and healthier rabbits!

# Keeping Your Rabbit Fit

Your bunny needs exercise and plenty of it. In fact, caged rabbits need at least three to four hours a day, every day, of free time outside the cage for exercise. You can satisfy this need indoors or out, as long as your rabbit has room and safe activities to keep her moving.

Some things to keep in mind as you focus on your bunny's fitness plan:

- It's best to offer exercise when a rabbit is naturally most active; for most house bunnies, this means early to mid-morning and/or late afternoon and evening.
- Try to be consistent with your rabbit's exercise schedule so that you establish a routine (better for both of you!).
- Whether indoors or out, be sure to rabbit-proof the exercise area. (See Chapter 5 for indoor rabbit-proofing and this chapter's "Rabbit-Proofing Your Yard" for outdoor precautions).
- Inspire your rabbit to move and play by giving her things to chew on, dig into, climb on, crawl under, and hop on and around. (See Chapter 14 for more on play tactics.)

## Indoors

For those who can't (or choose not to) take their rabbit's fitness routine outdoors, an indoor home gym or recreation room is a fine option.

After you designate which areas of your home will be accessible to your bunny and have securely rabbit-proofed these rooms (see Chapter 5) or set up a rabbit pen with moveable panels, you can give your rabbit permission to roam, under your supervision. When you first turn your bunny loose in "her" room, she'll hop about and investigate for several days. She'll scour the place and leave her scent on objects by rubbing her chin on them. (Don't worry; the scent isn't discernible to the human nose.) Eventually, though, the novelty of

the new room wears off, and bunny gets bored. To encourage her to do more than just sit in a corner and stare at you, you need to get active.

Some tips on getting your bunny to exercise:

- **Play with him.** If you've bonded with your rabbit, you'll be amazed at how easily he can learn to play with you. When playing with your rabbit, let the rabbit initiate the play. (See Chapter 14 for more details on playing with your rabbit.)
- **Teach him tricks.** A rabbit isn't going to fetch your slippers or rescue lost children, but you can show him some basic tricks and behaviors that result in food rewards. (See Chapter 12 for details on how to teach your rabbit tricks.)
- **Give him toys.** If your bunny needs motivation to exercise, now is the time to pull out those toys that you bought for your rabbit at the pet-supply store. Toss him one toy at a time until you find the one that strikes his fancy. Don't forget the homemade stuff, too. A cardboard box, a toilet paper roll, and even an empty plastic soda bottle can prove terribly exciting to your rabbit. (See Chapter 14 for information on toys for your rabbit.)
- **Provide company.** If you have more than one rabbit, and they all get along, put them together for exercise playtime. Not only can they get plenty of exercise, but you'll also laugh your head off watching them. But make sure that you provide them with several "hide" areas (at least as many as the number of rabbits), such as simple overturned cardboard boxes with a hole cut in the side, in case a spat breaks out. If the rabbit has nowhere to hide or escape and another one is being aggressive, a serious injury may result. (See Chapter 2 on the pros and cons of adopting multiple rabbits.)

Keep in mind that you should place your litter box somewhere in the area during these exercise sessions so that your rabbit can use it during playtime. If you have more than one rabbit, you may need to put at least as many litter boxes out as the number of rabbits.

## Outdoors

Just because you have an indoor rabbit doesn't mean that you can't take him outside for exercise. Fresh-air fitness is a good idea if

- You have rabbit-friendly weather (not too hot, not too cold, and not too windy).
- You live in an area that has good air quality.

- You can provide an environment safe from predators and other threats (even theft).
- You can provide an area free from fertilizers and pesticides.
- Your rabbit seems to enjoy his outside time.

Fresh air is great for all creatures, including your bunny. Plus, you won't need to do as much work to encourage your rabbit to exercise outdoors. The sights, sounds, and smells of the great outdoors can keep your rabbit busy.

Of course, just as with your indoor rabbit areas, your outdoor areas must be equipped with the basics of good rabbit-proofing, as shown in Figure 8-1.

Select an area where you plan to exercise your rabbit outdoors, and check it out for safety. For details on what this involves, see the upcoming section "Rabbit-Proofing Your Yard."

**Figure 8-1:** Indoors to outdoors: Just make sure you rabbit-proof your yard.

No matter how safe your yard appears, *do not leave your bunny out there to do his thing.* You should stay with your bunny to be sure he's not getting into mischief and to make sure that he is safe in his outdoor environment — from the weather, predators, toxic plants, or even himself. Remember that just about every land-based predator on the planet considers the rabbit a potential meal. Although a few minutes of carefully supervised time to roam may be okay, an enclosed area is the best way to protect your rabbit from tragedy.

### Thinking about location, location, location

Whether you choose to go with a pen or a run, where you put your rabbit's exercise area is important. Rabbits have a prey animal physiology and psychology and shouldn't be exposed to constant havoc and noise, which causes excessive stress. Likewise, you want your rabbit's exercise area in a place where you can see it and where you can access it easily for cleaning and other chores.

To keep your rabbit's nerves at ease, avoid putting the exercise area in a place where too much activity takes place. For example, if your kids like to play basketball in the backyard, don't put your bunny in a place where the ball is likely to bang against the pen. Or if you have a motorcycle, don't put the pen where your rabbit can listen to the engine start up every day (a great sound to you, perhaps, but murder on a rabbit's sensitive ears). By using common sense, you can figure out the best spot in your yard from a rabbit's perspective.

On the other hand, you don't want to tuck your rabbit's exercise area away in a part of the yard where you can't easily see him. Locating the pen where you can see him from your back window or door is ideal. Not only can this location enable you to keep an eye on your rabbit, but it will also afford you the pleasure of seeing your bunny's activities when he doesn't know that you're watching.

No matter how secure you believe your rabbit's outdoor exercise area is, steer clear of nighttime fitness sessions and strolls. The sights and sounds of predators can scare your bunny to death, literally.

### Going the pen route

One way to create a secure outdoor exercise area is to use dog exercise fencing that comes in panels that can be connected together in many shapes. Ideally, an outdoor exercise pen should have a top (to keep predators out) and a bottom (to keep bunny in). One advantage of using these panels is that the pen is temporary, and you can relocate it when necessary. See the next section, however, for a more permanent exercise solution.

### Building a bunny run

If you like the idea of leaving your outdoor rabbit outside for an extended period of time, but yet don't have time to hang out and watch him, consider building your pet a *bunny run.* A bunny run is similar to a dog run, except it's not as tall.

When building a run for your bunny, keep these points in the forefront of your mind:

- The object is to build an enclosure that allows your rabbit time outdoors while still keeping him protected from predators. Don't skimp on the design or materials. The stronger and more well built your rabbit's run, the safer he is. However, even with these precautions, you still need to keep a close eye on him.
- To keep predators (hawks, raccoons, snakes, and so on.) out and bunnies in (don't forget what skilled diggers they are!), use chain link or 1-inch wire fencing with a top, bottom, and sides; a solid top will protect your bun from the sun. Covering the bottom with clean straw gives your rabbit something safe to dig and burrow into.
- The larger your run, the more exercise your rabbit gets. Make the run as big as you can.
- Provide your rabbit with shade. In fact, building the run in an area where shade covers at least half the cage all day is best. Rabbits are susceptible to overheating, and direct sun can be deadly in the summer. Include a dish of fresh water, too.
- Provide a hide box for your rabbit. Should something spook your bunny while he's in his run, he'll be grateful for a hide box where he can duck for cover.
- Put some toys and a chew block or two in your rabbit's run to help give him something to do when he's out roaming around. Consider a bit of fresh hay as well.
- Never keep your rabbit in his run after the sun goes down because predators are more likely to lurk at dusk or evening. Remember, even if a predator can't get his choppers on your bunny, the presence of a predator can literally scare a rabbit to death.
- Make sure that you're home when your bunny is in the run. Don't leave him in the run while you go off to work. If he gets into trouble (such as an encounter with a predator, gets a foot caught in the fencing, or whatever), you won't be around to help him.

## Motivating a lazy bunny

Not all rabbits will jump when given the opportunity to exercise. In particular, single bunnies need a little more motivation to exercise than do two rabbits. When you let your solo bunny out in the yard to play, he'll probably run around a bit and then settle down to do some grazing and investigating.

To encourage your pet to stretch his muscles, you should provide him with some toys that he can amuse himself with. Such toys may include

- A clean, empty bucket
- An empty paper towel roll
- An empty cardboard box
- Hard plastic balls (try large and small sizes to see which your pet prefers)
- A tube of some kind, big enough for your rabbit to hop through

You can also play with your rabbit yourself by letting him chase you or by dragging a toy on a string for him to chase. Refrain from chasing your rabbit yourself because the poor creature may think that you've gone into predator mode and will become terrified. (For more game ideas, see Chapter 14.)

## Taking care of outdoor chores

Even though your rabbit's pen, run, or exercise area is outside and beyond the reach of your nose, you still need to keep up with your cleaning. Any dirty rabbit area is a breeding ground for bacteria, parasites, and disease. Chapter 9 has much more information on health if you're interested (and you should be).

But don't fret. If your rabbit's outdoor digs are well designed, you shouldn't have too much trouble keeping them clean with minimum effort. Just use the clean-up schedule in Table 8-1 (modified, of course, depending on the amount of time your bunny is outside).

**Table 8-1 Outdoor Clean-Up Schedule**

| *Task* | *How Often* | *The Details* |
|---|---|---|
| Poop duty | Daily | Your rabbit's droppings can accumulate quickly and should be removed on a daily basis. If possible, set up a compost area in your yard for the waste material or designate a special covered trash can for your rabbit's waste. Keep a waste receptacle close by, along with a shovel, so that it's easy for you to scoop the waste out and into the can without too much effort. |

| Task | How Often | The Details |
|---|---|---|
| Food and water container cleaning | Daily | To help keep bacteria to a minimum, wash out your rabbit's outdoor food bowl and water bottle or bowl on a daily basis. Use biodegradable dish soap for your rabbit's health. These products are available in health-food stores, as well as in many supermarket chains. |
| Pen or run structure | Weekly | You need to thoroughly clean an outdoor pen or cage (nest boxes, too). Once you've safely returned your bunny to his indoor digs, get a pail that has 1 part bleach to 10 parts water. Use a sponge to wipe down all the surfaces of the pen and then scrub it with a bristle brush. This process helps kill bacteria and other organisms that are building up. Be certain the pen is completely dry before putting your rabbit back inside again. |

# Rabbit-Proofing Your Yard

One of the nicest moments for a rabbit is when he gets to roam about the yard, investigating all the sights and smells that surround him. Of course, in order for your rabbit to play outside safely, you have to make sure that your yard is safely enclosed and free from rabbit hazards. You also need to be sure that your yard is protected from your rabbit.

## Keeping Wolfie away

Unfortunately, all kinds of predators would like to make a meal out of your bunny; preventing that from happening is your job. Most people think that cats and dogs are the only creatures they have to worry about preying on their rabbits while they're outdoors, but this is not the case. Most cats find rabbits to be too big for hunting purposes (with the exception of the dwarf breeds, who are small enough for larger cats), and if your yard and pen are secure, a dog probably won't be able to break in.

Predators who can go after your rabbit while he's getting fresh air include raccoons, coyotes, foxes, mink, hawks, and weasels, to name a few. These critters often live in suburban and rural areas, and some of them are even found in urban sections of the country. All of them are capable of scaling walls and fences, subsequently gaining access to seemingly protected backyards.

If your pen or exercise run is secure, it's unlikely that one of these animals will be able to break in and grab hold of your rabbit. However, a predator doesn't have to make contact with a rabbit in order to hurt or even kill it. Because rabbits are so easily frightened, the mere presence of a predator can literally scare a rabbit to death. At the least, a rabbit could injure its back, legs, or face while leaping around trying to escape.

Another danger is from parasites in the feces of some predators, especially the raccoon. Cleaning up all the food in the cage before night falls, and preventing predators from entering or climbing on top of and defecating into the cage can prevent exposure.

When a pet lives outside, the danger from predators is inherent. That's one of the main reasons your rabbit lives indoors with you. However, you can take the following steps to limit the possibility that a predator can take your pet's life during those times he is outside:

- Limit your rabbit's outdoor time to daylight hours when you can supervise.
- Keep your rabbit's exercise area close to your house. The sound and smell of humans can discourage some predators from approaching.
- Surround the area with an additional fence enclosure. A chain link or even chicken wire enclosure with a roof can keep predators from being able to get close enough to the area to have access to your rabbit.
- Keep trash cans covered and avoid leaving pet food outside where the smell can attract predators to your yard.

## Protecting your rabbit

You should have a tall wall or solid fence around your yard, one that a rabbit can't jump over (5 feet high or higher), through, or around. Because rabbits are notorious diggers, make sure that your wall or fencing goes at least a foot into the ground.

Just as you did when you rabbit-proofed your house (see Chapter 5), look at your yard from your rabbit's point of view (literally!) to see any potential dangers. Figuring out what your rabbit sees can give you clues into the kinds of trouble he can get into. Look out for the following:

- Holes or gaps in fencing that are small enough for a rabbit to slip through
- Small nooks and crannies where your rabbit can get wedged

- Debris that may come toppling down on your rabbit should he climb over or under it
- Containers holding toxic materials such as paint cans, turpentine, and antifreeze
- Objects with sharp edges
- Pesticides and other toxic garden products (snail and slug bait are particularly dangerous)
- Poisonous plants (check this chapter's list, "Avoiding poisonous plants")

## Protecting your yard

If you do decide that's your yard is safe enough for your bunny to roam — supervised, of course — for a bit, you should think about protecting your yard from your bunny. Rabbits are pretty harmless in general, but they do have two good resources when it comes to doing damage: their teeth and their claws.

If you look around your yard, you'll probably notice objects that are vulnerable to gnawing and areas that are susceptible to digging. For example, your rabbit may love to sink his teeth into your really nice wooden deck. Your rabbit will probably want to dig a trench in your freshly planted vegetable garden and then snack on the veggies after they're ripe.

So how do you protect your outside goods from your rabbit? You have two simple choices:

- **Keep your rabbit in a properly enclosed area, such as a puppy pen or a rabbit run while he's outdoors.** Puppy pens create a nice temporary exercise area, are moveable (so waste material doesn't burn the yard and you can put it in shade or sun), and fold up when not needed. Pens are an inexpensive, viable option for exercising your rabbit and keeping him away from the things in the yard you want to protect. A rabbit run is a more permanent option. (For more on these options, see the section "Outdoors," earlier in this chapter.
- **Supervise him while he's roaming around outdoors.** Keep an eye on him and see what he gets into. If you see him starting to gnaw on your wood deck or furniture, cover those areas with bubble wrap or another heavy plastic. If your bunny starts digging in the garden, put a fence around the area so that he can't get into it. You may want to provide him with a big box of dirt or sand that he can dig through to his heart's content or let him have an area of soft ground to excavate.

## Avoiding poisonous plants

Rabbits love to graze on plants when they're spending time outdoors. Unfortunately, we don't know every single plant that can be poisonous to rabbits, or how much they would have to eat to be poisoned. Just to be safe, it's best to keep rabbits away from plants that are known to be toxic in general.

If you have any of these common plants in your yard, remove them or find a way to keep your rabbit from gaining access to them:

- Jack in the pulpit, *Arisaema spp.*
- Common milkweed, *Asclepias syriaca L.*
- Boxwood, *Buxus microphylla*
- Oriental bittersweet, *Celastrus orbiculatus Thunb.*
- Poison hemlock, *Conium maculatum*
- Lily of the valley, *Convallaria majalis*
- Toadstools, *Crepidotus spp.*
- Jimson weed, *Datura spp.*
- Delphinium, *Delphinium spp.*
- Foxglove, *Digitalis purpurea*
- English ivy, *Hedera helix*
- Mountain laurel, *Kalmia latifolia*
- Lantana, *Lantana camara L.*
- Lupine, *Lupinus spp.*
- Daffodil, *Narcissus spp.*
- Oleander, *Nerium oleander*
- Azalea, *Rhododendron spp.*
- Black-eyed Susan, *Rudbeckia hirta*
- Black locust, *Robinia pseudo-acacia*
- Buttercup, *Ranunculus spp.*
- Castor bean, *Ricinus communis*
- Sumac, *Rhus coriara*
- American elder, *Sambucus canadensis*
- Nightshade, *Solanum spp.*

- Bird of Paradise, *Strelitzia reginae*
- Yew, *Taxus spp.*
- Arrowgrass, *Triglochin maritime*

## Plants for safe snacking

Many outdoor plants make safe and healthy snacks for domestic rabbits. However, you need to familiarize yourself with any plant before feeding it to your rabbit. Please be cautious when offering new plants! The following list is simply a sampling of plants that are thought to be safe for domestic rabbits, but consult your veterinarian if you're unsure or your rabbit experiences any unusual negative effects.

Only offer your rabbit fresh or thoroughly dried samples of these plants — never frosted, wilted, or otherwise spoiled.

- Apple (*Malus domestica;* leaves, branches, fruit, but not seeds)
- Basil (*Ocimum basilicum*)
- Blackberry (*Rubus villosus**; leaves, stems, fruit)
- Chickweed (*Stellaria media*)
- Chicory, wild (*Cichorium intybus*)
- Clover, red (*Trifolium pretense*)
- Clover, white (*Trifolium repens*)
- Dandelion (*Taraxacum officinale;* leaves, stem, flower)
- Grape (*Vitus labrusca**; leaves and vines)
- Lemon balm (*Melissa officianalis*)
- Maple, silver (*Acer saccharinum;* leaves and branches)
- Maple, sugar (*Acer saccharum;* leaves and branches)
- Mint (*Mentha piperita**)
- Pear (*Pyrus communis**; leaves, branches, fruit, but not seeds)
- Raspberry (*Rubus strigosus**; leaves, stems, fruit)
- Strawberry (*Fragaria vesca**)
- Sunflower (*Helianthus annuus*)
- Willow (*Salix nigra**; leaves and branches)

* *Indicates that other varieties may also be safe*

# Chapter 9

# Nipping Common Health Problems in the Bud

### *In This Chapter*

- Finding the right vet
- Spaying and neutering
- Recognizing signs of pain
- Spotting symptoms of illness

You may not be surprised to discover that your rabbit, like all creatures, can easily become sick or injured if he's mishandled or improperly cared for. In fact, rabbits can get sick even if you take really good care of them. Of course, a rabbit who's well cared for is less likely to become ill, but it can happen. The key to keeping your rabbit healthy is to watch him closely for signs of illness because rabbits are good at hiding their illness — a trait that's frustrating for rabbit owners but valuable in the wild. Rabbits instinctively hide their illness so that predators are unable to detect their vulnerability.

Most illnesses are more successfully treated if they're caught early. Familiarize yourself with your rabbit's normal behavior so that you'll notice when something is wrong — before it's too late. While this chapter covers more of the common ailments that bug bunnies, Chapter 10 outlines many of the chronic health problems of rabbits, as well as those health problems that arise later in life. Chapter 17 covers ten signs that you need to take emergency action.

If your rabbit gets sick, taking him to a veterinarian who specializes in treating rabbits is vital. After you locate a good veterinarian, bring your rabbit in for annual checkups.

## Finding Dr. Doolittle

No matter what kind of pet you own, finding a good veterinarian is imperative. Unfortunately, finding a vet who treats rabbits may be harder than you think, so please find a vet *before* you have an emergency situation.

A small animal vet who treats only cats and dogs isn't a good bet when it comes to treating a rabbit because rabbits have a unique physiology that's very different from more common pets (see Chapter 1). In the world of veterinarian medicine, rabbits are considered *exotics,* and they're grouped together with rodents, reptiles, birds, and other less common pets. Most veterinarians who have a special interest in treating these kinds of animals advertise themselves as exotics practitioners. They not only have special training in this area, but also a certain level of experience.

Not only must your vet know rabbits inside and out, but she must also be good at what she does. Just as with any profession, the skills and attitudes of veterinarians differ from individual to individual. You need to find a vet who is good at handling rabbits, excellent at diagnosing them, and an ace at treatment. Finding someone who has a good bedside manner with human clients isn't a bad idea, either.

In most areas of the country very few veterinarians have specific training or extensive experience with exotic pets. For example, people who live in rural areas won't have the selection that city dwellers have. Therefore, you may have to deal with a small animal vet who's willing to work with you and learn about your pet.

So how do you find a veterinarian to treat your rabbit? You can use a number of different options:

- **Personal referrals.** Talk to other rabbit owners and find out which vets they use. Ask them what they like about each one and get details of the situations where they've used them. By listening to these stories, you can get a good sense of who each doctor is.
- **Rescue groups or shelters.** Talk to the knowledgeable folks at rescue groups and shelters or check the House Rabbit Society's online referral list (`www.rabbit.org/vets/vets.html`) for a state-by-state listing of veterinarians who practice veterinary medicine on rabbits.
- **Veterinarians.** Even if they don't treat rabbits themselves, vets often know of exotic vets that do. Talk to local vets (you can find them in the phone book or through a state association of veterinarians) to get recommendations.
- **Veterinary organizations.** Contact the Association of Exotic Mammal Veterinarians (AEMV), an organization dedicated to improving

medicine and surgery of the exotic companion mammals (www.aemv.org). In 2009, veterinarians will be able to apply for exotic companion mammal specialist status through the American Board of Veterinary Practitioners (www.abvp.com). Several other organizations are considering adding exotic companion mammals as a specialty, so in the not-too-distant future, rabbit owners will truly be able to look for boarded specialists for their pets.

- **Club referrals.** Contact a local rabbit breed club or 4-H club to get a referral to a local exotics veterinarian. Please note that many people who participate in clubs or breeding do not subscribe to a house rabbit philosophy, so their veterinary needs may differ from yours.

## Evaluating a vet

Once you find a vet or two that you think you might like to use, contact the office by telephone and ask the following questions:

- **How long have you been treating rabbits?** The answer should be at least two years, preferably longer.
- **How many rabbits are treated at the office each week?** Ask, too, about the number of rabbits that are spayed or neutered each week. This answer gives you a good idea whether a vet really has a sufficient amount of experience with rabbits.
- **What kind of special education or experience do you have treating rabbits?** You want a vet who has training in this area, or at least has a significant amount of experience to make up for lack of formal training. Continuing education courses and programs are a good sign that this vet is serious about treating rabbits.
- **Which antibiotics do you prescribe to rabbits?** Some antibiotics commonly given to cats and dogs can be fatal for rabbits. An experienced veterinarian will know not to use amoxicillin and most of the other "...cillin" drugs. Chapter 10 covers more on antibiotics.
- **Do you take after-hour emergencies?** If not, where are they sent? If your vet closes at 6 p.m. and can't be reached for emergencies that take place after hours, she most likely refers patients to a 24-hour emergency clinic. Ask questions about the clinic's experience with rabbits and visit it to make sure that it meets your requirements.
- **May I visit your clinic to look at your facilities?** The answer should be a resounding "Yes." Please respect the fact that an appointment may be necessary so as not to interfere with the services given to clients during the day.

Once you've narrowed your search, pay a visit to the clinic. While you're there, look for the following:

- **Clean environment:** A clinic should look and smell clean. The exam rooms and reception areas should be neat and tidy, and the personnel should be well groomed.
- **Friendly, knowledgeable staff:** The receptionist and technicians you meet should be nice, friendly, and willing and able to answer questions.
- **Skilled vet:** You probably won't get to see the vet in action until you make your first appointment. When you're there, observe how she handles your rabbit. The vet should be gentle but firm and patient. She should also be willing to answer your questions, admit when she doesn't know the answer to something, and be friendly and a good listener.
- **Affordable fees:** With veterinary care, you often get what you pay for. Don't expect to get great care for dirt-cheap prices. On the other hand, make sure that you can afford the services offered. Ask for a fee schedule, which should show what the clinic charges for examinations, lab fees, and spays and neuters.

## Being a good client

You want a veterinarian who's skilled and compassionate and will take excellent care of your rabbit. You can do a lot to make sure that you're a good client, too, by following these guidelines:

- If you're happy with your vet, be sure to stick with her. Don't jump around from clinic to clinic trying to save money.
- Pay your bills on time. If you're having trouble paying, be honest with your vet and try to work out a payment arrangement.
- Follow your vet's instructions thoroughly regarding your rabbit's health.
- Be honest with your vet about your rabbit's care and condition.
- Ask questions if you don't understand explanations, diagnosis, or treatment plans.
- If you have a complaint with the veterinary staff, bring it to the vet's attention first so that there's an opportunity to get it cleared up to your satisfaction.
- Never be afraid to get a second or even third opinion. A responsible veterinarian won't feel threatened if you seek other ideas.
- Be a proactive pet owner and do research as needed to help your pet. Bring any information to your veterinarian and discuss your findings.

## Going for an exam

Unlike dogs and cats, rabbits don't get annual inoculations (except in the U.K. with myxomatosis and hemorrhagic viral diseases; see Chapter 10). However,' taking your rabbit to the vet for an initial exam is an excellent idea, even if he appears healthy. The vet can check him to make sure that he's in good health and can discuss your rabbit's diet, plans for neutering, and other health-related issues.

The initial exam also gives you the opportunity to get to know your veterinarian, and gives the doctor a sense of who your rabbit is. If your pet gets sick and needs immediate care, the vet will already have information on file and have a good sense of how you're caring for your bunny.

Following that initial exam, annual exams are a good idea. These annual exams are invaluable in keeping ahead of disease problems and in communicating any changes in care. As they become *geriatric* (7 years of age and older), get an exam every 6 months.

# Spay It, Don't Spray It

Plenty of good reasons exist to *spay* your female rabbit (having her uterus and ovaries removed) or *neuter* your male rabbit (having his testicles removed), including improved behavior (see Chapters 12 and 13) and the elimination of the potential for more unwanted rabbits in the world (see Chapter 2). But one of the best reasons is for the health of your rabbit.

Spayed and neutered rabbits are less prone to a variety of diseases and tend to live considerably longer than rabbits who haven't been spayed or neutered. Male rabbits who haven't been neutered are also inclined to spray strong smelling urine around the house and get into other kinds of trouble. You'll be much happier with your male rabbit if you have him neutered.

Rabbits can be spayed or neutered as soon as they reach reproductive maturity: about 4 months of age or later. Females should be spayed before 2 years of age to lessen the chance of developing uterine cancer. (See this chapter's "Fighting female troubles" for more on that topic.) Both procedures are fairly routine in the hands of a veterinarian experienced with rabbits.

## Counting backwards from ten

If your bunny needs surgery or a certain diagnostic procedure requiring that he be anesthetized, you may be worried. Is it safe to put bunnies under anesthesia? Can their sensitive systems handle the chemicals required for surgery or diagnosis?

The answer to these questions is yes. In fact, other than the obvious need for anesthesia during surgery, it's often better to sedate the rabbit for stressful diagnostic procedures. Doing so eliminates your pet's fear or discomfort. A safe anesthetic gas (usually in combination with other injectable drugs to reduce anxiety and pain) is used for general anesthesia, which produces complete unconsciousness. If lighter sedation is needed, the vet can use a variety of injectable drugs. Sometimes a local anesthetic alone is all that's needed (for example, in eye exams or small skin biopsies).

If your bunny needs surgery for spaying or neutering or some other medical procedure, take your pet to a veterinarian with rabbit experience. The vet can determine the safest method of anesthesia to minimize discomfort and stress for your pet.

The cost for these procedures varies depending on many factors, including the area of the country in which you live and the age and health of your pet. The spay procedure takes considerably longer than a castration to perform and requires abdominal surgery; therefore, the cost for spaying a female may be two or more times the cost of neutering a male. Many veterinarians require presurgical laboratory work to make sure that your pet is in good health prior to the procedure. Please discuss with your vet any questions you may have. This one-time cost is well worth it, however, because a spayed or neutered rabbit lives a longer, healthier life.

# Playing Doctor

An annual trip to the vet is a good idea, but you can do a great deal for your rabbit's health on your own. Your rabbit is likely to live a much healthier life if you monitor her health every day and prepare yourself for any first aid emergencies that may arise.

Whether it's daily (during a petting session) or weekly (while you're brushing your bun), get in the habit of doing the following eight-point check, starting at the top:

- **Ears:** Look inside and out to see whether they're clean and smooth, without sores, bumps, flaking, or excessive wax build up.
- **Eyes:** Be certain eyes are clear, clean, and free of discharge.

- **Nose:** Look for a dry clean nose and listen for clear, regular breathing.
- **Mouth:** Check that your rabbit's teeth are aligned (growing straight) and not overgrown or broken. Make sure that she's not drooling.
- **Fur/skin:** Feel her body for unusual lumps, bruises, cuts, or sores.
- **Tootsies:** Make sure that her toes are all straight, with no signs of lumps or inflamed tissue. Bottoms of paws should be covered with fur; any visible skin should not look bright red or infected.
- **Nails:** Check that nails aren't too long. Those that are may tear off, bleed, and even become infected.
- **Genital area:** Take a peek at her privates to be sure that the area is clean and dry. (See Chapter 8 to find out how to spot clean if it isn't.)

## Fighting female troubles

Unspayed female rabbits can develop a variety of problems. The ailments listed here can happen before, during, or after a pregnancy and some occur even if you never breed your rabbit. Knowing how to recognize these problems increases your doe's chances of survival.

Keep in mind that spaying your doe eliminates the possibility of all these conditions developing in your rabbit.

- **False pregnancies:** Female rabbits are so geared toward pregnancy that those who aren't bred can act as if they're pregnant anyway. Even though she isn't carrying any new baby bunnies, milk production and other characteristics associated with pregnancy appear. The female may become aggressive as part of this condition.
- **Mammary gland disorders:** Nursing mother rabbits are prone to a number of problems that affect the *mammary glands,* or breast tissue. Each requires help from a veterinarian.
- **Pregnancy toxemia:** This condition occurs in the last few days of pregnancy or the first days after giving birth. Does with pregnancy toxemia can develop depression, weakness, seizures, and coma.
- **Endometritis and pyometra:** *Endometritis* is an inflammatory disease of the lining of the uterus, and *pyometra* is an accumulation of pus in the uterus accompanying the inflammation. With mild disease, there may be few signs; however, as the disease progresses, she may develop a distended abdomen, loss of appetite, and weakness.
- **Uterine adenocarcinoma:** *Uterine adenocarcinoma* is a form of cancer of the uterus and is the most common cancer seen in intact female rabbits. Although it's a slow-growing tumor, if left untreated, it can metastasize, or spread, through the body, attacking the lungs, liver, bones, skin, and other organs. Eventually, it can result in death.
- **Uterine aneurysm:** *Uterine aneurysm* is a noninfectious disease that results from the rupture of one or more large veins in the uterus. These veins can rupture and heal several times. The blood loss may be gradual or sudden. If the blood loss is excessive, the results can be fatal.

If you notice anything out of the ordinary, including any odd behavior, contact your veterinarian right away.

Though it may not be much fun, you should also keep track of what's coming out of your rabbit. Changes in urine and feces can signal serious health problems, so do the following each day:

- **Check your bunny's urine for unusual color, odor, or consistency.** Changesin urine or urination habits may be a sign of dietary changes or disease. (For more on this topic, see this chapter's "Urinary tract concerns.")
- **Check your rabbit's droppings and get an idea of what's normal.** Any changes in size and consistency can indicate a gastrointestinal problem. (See "Gastrointestinal problems," later in this chapter.)

## Assembling a first-aid kit

Although many ailments described here require a vet's attention, it's a great idea to have some basic medical supplies on hand in the event that your rabbit needs some minor medical attention. Store these items in a tool or tackle box, with your vet's phone number and address taped to the inside:

- Antibiotic ointment (be sure it's safe for animals; your vet may recommend Neosporin, the formula *without* pain relief)
- Thermometer (animal or pediatric rectal; normal is about 103 to 106°F) and lubricant, such as K-Y jelly.
- Stethoscope (for listening to intestinal sounds and the heart and lungs)
- Hydrogen peroxide for cleansing (use diluted)
- Cotton swabs and cotton balls
- Heating pad or hot water bottle for shock or hypothermia
- Styptic powder or cornstarch for bleeding nails
- Saline eye wash (to flush out foreign matter)
- Gauze bandages and sterile cotton pads for wounds
- Plastic medicine dropper
- Tweezers
- Scissors
- Towel for wrapping or securing your rabbit

## Identifying signs of pain

Chapter 11 talks in depth about your pet's body language and what he does when he's in the world of hurt. If you're unsure about whether your bunny needs vet care, use the following signs as a cue that you need to call a vet:

- Abnormal hunched appearance when sitting
- Alert but reluctant to move
- Moves slowly or with effort
- Depression/lethargy
- Limping
- Unusual or sudden aggression
- Loss or decrease in appetite or water consumption
- Tooth grinding
- Hiding when it's not usual behavior, facing the corner
- Shows no interest in the surroundings (loss of curiosity)
- Crying or grunting when moving/defecating/urinating or being handled/examined
- Coat is unkempt due to loss of interest in grooming
- Taking a long time to eat
- Dropping food out of the mouth

# Dealing with Bunny Ailments

Rabbits can develop a whole slew of diseases and conditions; some of the more common health problems are covered here. Chapter 10 addresses other health problems, such as infectious diseases and conditions related to aging.

If you know how to recognize rabbit ailments, you'll respond quickly, calling the vet and getting appropriate treatment. The more quickly that you respond, the better your chances of effectively eliminating any disease or discomfort that's afflicting your rabbit.

## Gastrointestinal problems

Rabbits are prone to a number of gastrointestinal (GI) tract problems. The most common underlying cause of these disorders is an inappropriate diet. However, various microorganisms like bacteria, protozoa, and viruses can play a role, too. In rare cases, some rabbits are born with a GI tract that doesn't function normally.

Since proper diet is so important for GI health, the best thing you can do to prevent disease of the GI tract is feed a healthy diet high in fiber and low in carbohydrates. By following the dietary suggestions in Chapter 6, you reduce the likelihood that your rabbit will develop digestive problems. In the event that your rabbit does feel under the weather as a result of digestive tract disease, you and your vet can hopefully step in and get her back to normal.

Diarrhea in rabbits is characterized by the excretion of large amounts of dark brown to blood-tinged stool in the absence of any normal stool. Diarrhea is a different condition than soft stools, which is a mixture of soft pudding-like stools mixed with normal stools. Diarrhea can be the result of several different diseases, but it's always an emergency signal and is a life-threatening situation. Seek veterinary attention immediately if you observe diarrhea in your rabbit.

### Soft stool

Soft pudding-like stools present along with normal round, dry stools are a sign of a disruption of the delicate balance in the rabbit's intestinal flora. This condition is not life-threatening, but needs to be treated before it progresses to a more severe disease.

Rabbits normally produce two types of droppings. One is the round hard stool you find in great profusion in your rabbit's cage, and the other is the nutrient-rich cecotrope produced from the cecum and is eaten directly by the rabbit to be digested. (See Chapter 1 for more information on rabbit GI physiology.)

Normally you never see the cecotropes and if, on occasion, you do, they should be soft but formed in small, oblong pellets. When there's a mild disruption to the normal flora of the cecum, the cecotropes come out unformed in mucous-coated blobs or pools of thick pudding-like stool. (Sounds appetizing, doesn't it?) This isn't true diarrhea because the rabbit can still produce the normal round droppings. These soft cecotropes get stuck to the rabbit's fur and are deposited to dry into an almost concrete-like substance in the cage and exercise areas. The rabbit can't eat the cecotropes because they have no form and these sticky clumps can eventually cause not only a cleaning headache, but an impaction of stool on the bunny's rear end.

The most common cause of soft cecotropes is a high-carbohydrate, low-fiber diet. Other, less common causes are cancer, internal abscesses, partial intestinal obstruction, and other systemic diseases, such as liver or kidney disease. It's best to have your rabbit examined by a veterinarian to make sure that there is no underlying disease. Because the majority of cases are caused by an inappropriate diet, all that's usually necessary for treatment is a switch to a high-fiber diet low in concentrated carbohydrates. See Chapter 6 for details on feeding your rabbit a healthy diet.

If a rabbit doesn't produce any stool for 24 hours, he's in need of immediate medical attention. The most common cause is a complete or partial obstruction to the GI tract or a complete shutdown of the GI tract caused by a chronic GI motility problem. These conditions are fatal within 48 hours if left untreated. Chapter 17 has more information on this topic, including symptoms that may accompany this lack of stools.

### Enteritis

The rabbit GI tract, particularly the cecum, contains a complex population of bacteria, protozoa, yeast, and other organisms that make it possible to digest high-fiber foods. Any change in this population can lead to a disruption of normal digestive ability and, in some cases, to life-threatening disease.

*Enteritis* is an infection or inflammation of the intestines and has a number of causes. Rabbits suffering from enteritis may have

- Stools ranging from occasional soft stools to outright diarrhea
- Bloated abdomen
- Teeth crunching
- Restlessness
- Lack of appetite
- Weight loss

By far, the most common cause of enteritis is feeding your pet the wrong diet, particularly one that is low in fiber and high in carbohydrates. (See Chapter 6 for what bunnies should eat.) Other causes include the use of antibiotics that are inappropriate for the rabbit, exposure to high levels of stress, and exposure to certain bacteria. (See Chapter 10 for more information.) Really, anything that causes a serious change in the normal population of healthy microorganisms in the rabbit's gut will allow "bad" bacteria to overgrow leading to disease. If your rabbit is showing any abnormalities in his stools, you should contact your veterinarian as soon as possible.

The most important thing you can do to safeguard your rabbit from enteritis is to feed a healthy high-fiber diet, as well as provide a clean, stress-free environment (see Chapters 5 and 6).

### Enterotoxemia

The most dangerous complication that happens because of disruption of the GI tract's normal bacteria is *enterotoxemia.* This condition occurs when bacteria that are normally present — and cause no trouble (such as *Clostridium* species or *E. coli)* — start to overgrow.

When these bacteria proliferate, they produce dangerous toxins absorbed into the blood stream, and they poison the rabbit. Enterotoxemia is seen most often in young weaning rabbits, but can be seen in any rabbit that has had a severe disruption of the normal GI tract flora due to the conditions covered in the "Enteritis" section, earlier in this chapter.

## Medicating your rabbit

If your bunny is diagnosed with an illness, chances are she'll need medication. (Be wary of antibiotics, as some are toxic to rabbits; see Chapter 10 for more on using antibiotics.) Medication may be in the form of a pill, liquid, or eye or eardrops. Ask your vet to show you how to administer the medication before you take your bunny home. Before you begin, take a deep breath and resolve to be patient. Rabbits can be uncooperative when being medicated, so be prepared.

Your rabbit may drink the liquid medicine out of a bowl. Today, most medications are offered in liquid form, eliminating the hassle of trying to disguise a pill:

The best way to restrain your rabbit is to

1. **Have the medication all measured out and ready to go.**
2. **Wrap her in a towel.**
3. **Stabilize the bunny against your body.**

   Keep your rabbit from struggling so much that she hurts herself.
4. **Talk to her in a soothing voice and try to help her calm down while you administer the medications.**

Your method of administering medicine to your rabbit will depend on the form of the medication.

Here are tips on how to give a variety of medications:

- **Liquid medication:** You can put liquids in a syringe (without the needle) and place it in the space between the incisors and the molars on the side of the mouth. Slowly inject the liquid, letting your bunny swallow it. Don't put the rabbit on her back because she may inhale the medication into her lungs if you do that.
- **Eyedrops or ointment:** You can pull down the lower lid of the eye and place the drops or ointment in the pocket between the eyeball and the lid. When the rabbit closes her eye, the medication spreads around the surface of the eyeball. Be careful not to touch the eye with the applicator.
- **Eardrops:** Simply place the medication into the rabbit's ears and then gently massage the base of the ear to get it worked down into the ear canal. Expect plenty of ear-shaking and scratching. (Having something cold and wet running down your ear canal feels weird!) Be sympathetic toward your bunny and be sure to help her wipe her face clean if the ear medication musses her fur.

Signs of enterotoxemia include

- Profuse diarrhea that's brown or bloody
- Loss of appetite
- Weakness
- Sudden death

If you suspect that your rabbit is suffering from enterotoxemia, contact your veterinarian right away because this condition is rapidly fatal if left untreated with medicine. It's better to prevent this serious disease altogether with a high-fiber diet.

## Urinary tract concerns

Rabbits are prone to a number of ailments that affect the bladder and kidneys. Each of these maladies is serious and requires immediate veterinary treatment. If you're doing a good job of monitoring what comes out of your rabbit, you may notice changes in your rabbit's urine that can signal problems in your rabbit's urinary tract or elsewhere.

### Seeing red: Colorful urine

Normal rabbit urine can be quite colorful and range from light yellow to a deep orange-red (a rusty color). This rainbow of colors could be scary if you didn't know it was normal. The colors are produced either by pigments that pass through the system from some food or from normal pigments called *porphyrins,* which are excreted by the bladder.

Be alert, however, when the urine is bright red. Bright red color or red streaks is usually an indication of blood coming either from the urinary tract or, in the case of an unspayed female, from the reproductive tract (see the earlier sidebar "Fighting female troubles"), and is definitely something to pay attention to. Sometimes it can be hard to differentiate red from the rusty (which is more orange) color of plant pigments. It is easy to tell the difference by having your veterinarian test a fresh urine sample. If you see red in your rabbit's urine, particularly if she strains to urinate or acts abnormal in any other way, seek veterinary attention as soon as possible.

### Cystitis

An infection of the urinary tract or bladder, *cystitis* is somewhat common in rabbits. Signs of the condition are the same as urolithiasis. (See the list in the upcoming "Urolithiasis" section.)

Because these symptoms are similar to that of urolithiasis, taking your rabbit to a veterinarian immediately for diagnosis is critical. Cystitis may be cured with long-term antibiotic treatment.

Rabbits who develop cystitis often have recurring bouts of the condition, so watch them closely for recurrences.

### Kidney disease

*Kidney disease* (also called *renal disease*) can occur, particularly in older rabbits. Kidney disease can be caused by bacterial infection, parasites, toxins, or cancer. See whether your rabbit has any of the following signs of kidney disease:

- Anemia (may be indicated by pale gum color)
- Depression
- Poor appetite
- Weight loss
- Excessive water consumption
- Excessive amounts of urine

Kidney disease is a serious condition. The sooner treatment takes place, the better your pet's chances for survival. If you see any of these signs, take her to a veterinarian right away.

### Urolithiasis

*Urolithiasis* is seen in rabbits. Rabbits, unlike dogs, cats, and humans, normally excrete any extra calcium from their diet through their urine, which can give normal rabbit urine a cloudy look. (Humans, dogs, and cats excrete extra calcium through the stool.)

Occasionally, rabbits can develop stones or *bladder sludge* (thick material not yet formed into stones). The causes can be many, including long-term inadequate water intake (leading to more concentrated urine), underlying bladder infection, and genetic predisposition. The high calcium level of some foods has often been blamed entirely for this disease, but this alone won't cause stones. Inadequate water intake can occur when the water isn't changed frequently, is frozen, or isn't easily accessible.

Rabbits suffering from urolithiasis show the following signs:

- Straining to urinate
- Frequent small amounts of urine produced, often outside of the normal toilet areas
- Small stones or blood present in the urine

- Depression
- Abdominal pain (hunched posture)

If your rabbit shows any of these signs, take her to your veterinarian immediately for diagnosis and treatment. Surgery may be necessary in the case of large stones. Sludge and small stones can often be flushed out of the bladder under anesthesia.

The best prevention for bladder stones is making sure that your rabbit

- Takes in sufficient amounts of water daily. Chapter 6 discusses suggested water quantities for rabbits.
- Eats a healthy diet including high-moisture fresh foods, which adds water to his system. Read Chapter 6 for recommendations for fresh foods.
- Has available water changed daily and that the bottle is working properly. That way, your pet doesn't have to work too hard to get a drink.
- Exercises. You can get ideas on exercising in Chapters 8 and 14.
- Has a clean toilet area. Cleanliness encourages urination, which keeps the bladder contents flushed. Rabbits that aren't exercised or have unclean toilet areas may tend to hold their urine for much longer periods of time.

## Abscesses

An *abscess* is a collection of pus surrounded by inflamed tissue, the whole mess is typically the result of a bacterial infection. Abscesses, which can occur almost anywhere on a rabbit, are common and, unfortunately, difficult to treat. Common causes include

- Bite or puncture wounds
- Systemic infections
- Dental infections

The pus found in rabbit abscesses is very thick, which makes drainage and treatment particularly difficult. Treatment will vary according to the location of the abscess. In many cases, complete surgical removal of the abscess is recommended; however, you must address the underlying cause of the abscess, or the abscess will return.

Although some rabbits can live with abscesses on their body for years, any unusual lump found on your rabbit should be checked by your vet. As with other health conditions, early treatment can increase the chance of a cure; in addition, lumps can also be tumors or cysts that require immediate removal.

## Dental disease

Dental disease is fairly common in pet rabbits. Nature designed your bunny to eat a variety of plant materials that includes some tough, abrasive material. In order to keep your rabbit's teeth from wearing down to the point where he can't eat, nature arranged it so that rabbit teeth are always growing.

If a rabbit's teeth are improperly aligned, the teeth won't wear down properly. The result is teeth that grow too long, making it difficult for the rabbit to chew (a condition known as *malocclusion,* which is shown in Figure 9-1). Either the *crown* (the top) of the tooth can overgrow or the *root* (bottom of the tooth under the gum line).

If the crown overgrows, sharp edges form, which can cause sores on the tongue and the inside of the mouth. If the root overgrows, it can cause deformities of the jaw bone, leading eventually to abscesses (read more on abscesses in this chapter). If the upper incisor roots grow too long, they can pinch off the tear duct so that tears can't flow. This situation leads to spilling of tears on the face and a chronically wet and matted facial fur.

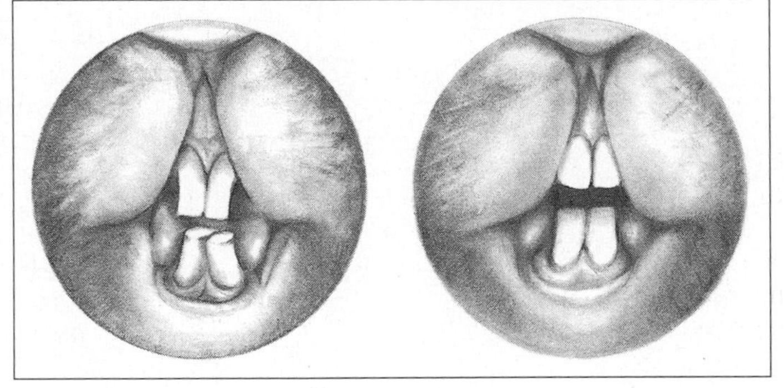

**Figure 9-1:** The rabbit on the left suffers from malocclusion. The choppers on the right are okay.

The exact causes of dental disease are still being debated. As in life, multiple causes are probably working together. The most commonly mentioned cause is inadequate wearing of the teeth due to a diet low in abrasive material (fiber), but other experts suspect early metabolic bone disease (a nutritional imbalance involving calcium) or bad genetics as well. Trauma to the mouth can be another cause of dental disease. Check your rabbit for the following signs of dental disease:

- Being picky about foods (particularly unable to eat pellets or hard vegetables)
- Bulging eye(s)
- Dropping food from the mouth

- Excessive salivation
- Loss of appetite
- Nasal discharge
- Tearing eyes
- Excessive teeth-grinding
- Lumps along the jaw or under the eye

If your rabbit has any of these signs, take him to a veterinarian immediately. Dental disease that's just starting may show no outward signs, so it's important that your veterinarian perform a thorough mouth exam at least once a year on even outwardly healthy pets; in fact, most dental disease is related to teeth other than the incisors. Early detection is key to treating dental disease in rabbits.

## Ear infections

Your rabbit's great big ears are prone to problems that include mites and infections. (For more on mites, see this chapter's upcoming "Banning pesky parasites.") Signs of infection include

- Head shaking
- Ear scratching and sensitivity
- Runny eyes

If you suspect a problem with your bunny's ears, have her examined by your vet; untreated ear infections can lead to head tilt, a more serious condition described later in this chapter. Lop ears, which create a warm, moist setting for bacterial growth, are particularly at risk for infection.

## Heatstroke

Your bunny is capable of tolerating cold much better than heat. Rabbits who become overheated are susceptible to heatstroke, which can be fatal. Temperatures of 80°Fahrenheit are dangerous to rabbits.

Rabbits on the verge of heatstroke lay in a stretched-out posture and pant, breathing rapidly and sometimes foaming at the mouth.

### How many teeth does my bunny have?

Take a guess. Most people will say rabbits have 4 incisors, but actually they have 6! Assuming all is well with your rabbit's dental health, her mouth should contain 12 upper cheek teeth and 10 lower cheek teeth, for a grand total of 28 teeth.

Heatstroke is an emergency situation. Before you transport your rabbit to the veterinarian, take measures to bring his body temperature down.

1. **Get him out of the sun and into a cool place.**
2. **Put a cool, wet towel around his ears.**

   The wet towel around his ears cools the blood that's flowing through his ears. Then that blood circulates throughout the rest of his body, thus helping to lower overall body temperature.
3. **If he's conscious, offer him fresh water.**
4. **Rush him to the veterinarian for immediate treatment.**

   The vet will give the rabbit fluids intravenously and other medications.

## Head tilt

*Head tilt* (also called *wry neck* or *torticollis)* is a sign of any one of a number of problems, including inner ear disease or disease of the vestibular (balance) area of the brain, such as cancer, trauma, stroke, or parasitic infection.

If your rabbit is tilting his head to one side, take him to your veterinarian right away for a diagnosis. Your vet may be able to treat the problem, depending on the cause. The earlier head tilt is treated, the greater the chances for a cure, so address this condition as soon as you notice it.

If the condition is irreversible despite treatment and your pet is still active and eating well, you can opt to let your rabbit live with this condition. Many rabbit owners have found that their "tilted" rabbits are able to live relatively normal lives.

## Inflammation of the feet

*Pododermatitis* (also known as *sore hocks*) occurs when the area below the *hocks* (the joint closest to the paw on the hind leg) becomes inflamed and

© Isabelle Francais

ARBA recognizes nearly 50 rabbit breeds, each with its own unique personality, size, coat type, and color. Shown here is a Mini Lop. For a description of the different breeds, see Chapter 3.

The Californian and Himalayan are similar in appearance. These rabbits look much like a Siamese cat, with a white coat and black-tipped ears, nose, feet, and tail.

The Jersey Wooly is a breed best kept by those who have the time and patience required to care for its long fur.

A well-established breed, the Dutch rabbit is easily recognized by the band of white fur around its chest.

Velveteen rabbit: Rex rabbits are known for their fur, which looks and feels like plush velvet.

One of the less common breeds, the Dwarf Hotot's black eye bands give it a unique look.

Though the smaller lop breeds are often sought after by those with children, a larger breed is typically a better, sturdier choice for families with youngsters.

© Isabelle Francais

The Satin Angora is known for the sheen of its glossy coat; like the French Angora, the Satin Angora does not have wool on its head and front feet.

© Isabelle Francais

With its Dalmation-style good looks, the English Spot makes a wonderful companion.

© Isabelle Francais

Forever youthful, the Netherland Dwarf appeals to many people because of its diminutive size and babylike features.

A medium-sized rabbit, the Champagne d'Argent is appreciated for the silvery effect of the breed's fur.

The Rex rabbit comes in many color varieties, including white with black and brown spots.

Though its build more resembles the lean look of a wild hare, the chestnut-colored Belgian Hare is truly a domestic rabbit and can be kept as a companion.

Like the Jersey Wooly, the American Fuzzy Lop has a long coat that needs careful and regular grooming.

The Cinnamon rabbit's rich, russet brown color gives the breed much of its appeal.

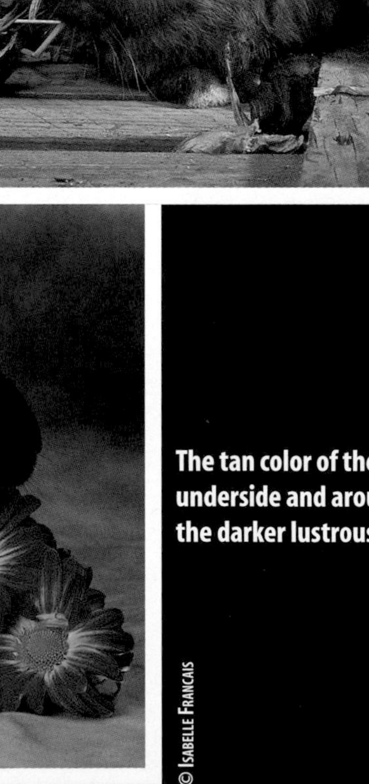



The tan color of the Tan breed, found on the rabbit's underside and around facial features, contrasts with the darker lustrous body color of the rabbit.

The short and stocky Havana can make a nice pet for an older child, thanks to its compact build. The Havana first appeared in chocolate, but also comes in blue and black varieties as well.

A favorite for rabbit shows, the laid-back and relaxed Flemish Giant is the largest breed of rabbit and weighs over 14 pounds. This popular rabbit's fur comes in steel gray, light gray, black, blue, white, sandy, and fawn.

Boasting a shiny coat, the Polish is a tiny bunny weighing only about 3 pounds. Commonly seen at rabbit shows, this breed comes in five color varieties: blue, black, chocolate, blue-eyed white, and ruby-eyed white.

True to its name, the Checkered Giant Black sports black spots and weighs in at a hefty 11 pounds or more.

Though bred for centuries for its soft wool, the English Angora makes a fine companion, as long as the caretaker has time for plenty of grooming.

The English Lop is all ears; according to the breed standard, the ears should measure 21 inches from tip to tip.

develops ulcers, often in conjunction with hair loss. A bacterial infection is usually present.

Obesity, a dirty, wet environment, or a lack of space within which to move around can set the stage for this condition. Your veterinarian can treat sore hocks with a wound cleanser and an antibiotic. You can also

- Keep the cage floor dry and clean. If your pet has an all-wire cage floor, provide an area off the wire to sit, like a box with shredded or flat newspaper in it (in addition to the litter box).
- Put your rabbit on a diet. Take a look at the nutritional guidelines offered in Chapter 6; in particular, read the section that coaches owners on how to cope with chubby bunnies.
- Provide more room and more exercise time for your rabbit. Cages that are too small can aggravate the problem. Chapter 8 talks about ways of bringing fresh air and exercise into your rabbit's life.

To avoid having to deal with this problem in the first place, keep your rabbit fit and healthy and provide him with a clean, good-size cage. (Chapter 5 offers more information on smart housing options.)

## Obesity

An obese rabbit is at increased risk to develop other health problems. It's vital to prevent this common condition.

You can keep a handle on your rabbit's weight by feeding him properly and weighing him regularly to make sure he's not gaining too much weight. (See Chapter 6 for information on proper diet and how to weigh your rabbit.) He'll be weighed at his annual veterinarian visit and your vet can tell you whether he's tipping the scales too far.

Some of the health problems that obesity can contribute to include

- Difficulty grooming
- Foot inflammation
- Inability to ingest *cecotropes,* rabbit-produced pellets that contain essential nutrients (see Chapter 1)
- Sluggish, unhealthy digestive tract
- Shortened life span
- Stress on the heart and vertebrae

Rabbits become obese the same way that people do — too many calories and not enough exercise. Among rabbits, excess calories often come from eating excessive amounts of alfalfa-based commercial rabbit pellets.

Rabbits who eat fresh foods and hay as a primary diet and get regular exercise are less likely to develop obesity. If your rabbit needs slimming down, talk to your vet about creating a new diet for your pet. (For more on diet and exercise, see Chapters 6 and 8, respectively.)

### Paralysis and hind limb weakness

Rabbits are prone to several conditions that can result in weakness or paralysis of the hind legs, including arthritis and fusing of the spinal vertebra, intervertebral disc disease, trauma, parasites, toxins, stroke, bacterial infections, cancer, and systemic disease.

Because the conditions that cause hind limb weakness or complete paralysis are so variable, you may see a variety of other abnormalities, such as loss of appetite, pain, or lethargy. However, any noticeable weakness of the hind quarters is abnormal even in the absence of other signs, and your pet should get veterinary attention as soon as possible. Some conditions are reversible if treated immediately.

If your rabbit has any of the aforementioned abnormalities, take him to the vet for an evaluation and treatment. Many diligent rabbit owners have been able to make life livable for paralyzed bunnies with special care and support. (If you're living with a paralyzed rabbit and need help, contact your local House Rabbit Society for information. See the Appendix for contact information.)

## Banning Pesky Parasites

Just like dogs and cats, rabbits can be bothered by *parasites* — organisms that feed off your rabbit's body — that can make them pretty darn miserable. Keeping those nasty parasites at bay is your job as a rabbit mom or dad.

### Intestinal parasites

Intestinal parasites include roundworms, pinworms, protozoa, and tapeworms. Signs of a heavy parasite infestation include

- Distended abdomen
- Poor coat condition (dry, unhealthy looking hair)

- Worms in the litter box or near the anus
- Loss of weight even though the pet is eating well

Your rabbit may have a light worm infestation without showing any obvious outward signs. Your veterinarian can diagnose intestinal worms in your pet by examining a stool sample. (You can get a sample by putting a few pieces of your rabbit's stool in a plastic bag.) Treatment consists of a deworming agent, administered orally or by injection to your rabbit.

To prevent your rabbit from becoming infested with intestinal parasites:

- Avoid letting your rabbit graze in areas where wild rabbits may have been, particularly where you see their droppings.
- Keep your bunny away from outdoor areas where dogs and stray cats may have defecated.

## Ear mites

Settling in the rabbit's ear canal, *ear mites* cause itching and a dark, crusty discharge. Frequent head-shaking and ear-scratching are common signs.

A veterinarian, examining the discharge from your rabbit's ears under a microscope, can diagnose ear mites. An injection or topical application of an antiparasitic drug can successfully treat ear mites. Infected rabbits need to be separated from other rabbits until the mites have been cleared up because ear mites are highly contagious between rabbits. Also, even though the mites that affect cats are different from rabbit ear mites, cats can carry the parasite that affects rabbits and pass it along to them. Left untreated, ear mites can lead to severe infections that can cause hearing loss.

## Fur mites

Fur mites are tiny spiderlike parasites *(Chelyletiella parasitovorax)* that can be seen with mild magnification. Also known as *walking dandruff,* fur mites can cause

- Clumps of hair to fall out
- Dry, flaky skin
- Red, crusty, and itchy patches of skin particularly along the spine and rump

Your veterinarian will examine a sample of the skin debris under the microscope. The treatment for this parasite can include topical or injectible antiparasitic medications as well as a thorough cleaning of the environment.

If the population of mites is low, signs of their presence may be nonexistent for a long period of time. (It can be for many months.) However, rabbits can still transmit the mites to other rabbits during this time. These mites can be transmitted to dogs and cats in the household as well (and back again). Treating all the mammal pets in the household as well as the environment is important because the mites can live off the pets in bedding, carpeting, and around cages for several days.

## Fleas

Yes, rabbits get fleas — the exact same fleas that drive your cat and dog crazy, too. In fact, if your indoor rabbit becomes infested with fleas, your dog or cat are most likely to have spread these parasites to your bunny.

To see whether your rabbit has fleas, observe your pet to see whether she's scratching herself a great deal. (Chapter 7 gives the lowdown on finding and getting fleas out of her hair.)

The best way to treat fleas is with a topical application (no flea dips, shampoos, or powders, please!) available from your veterinarian. Products applied once a month to your rabbit's skin are most effective, making flea reproduction impossible. All your other mammal pets need to be treated as well, including cats, dogs, and other rabbits.

Frontline, which is commonly used for dogs, should *never* be used on rabbits. Advantage, Program, and Revolution are considered safe flea treatments for rabbits if applied in conjunction with the advice of a veterinarian.

## Flies

Flies just annoy people, but they can be dangerous for your rabbit, especially an outdoor rabbit (another great reason to cohabitate with yours indoors). Some species of flies like to lay their eggs on the rectal area of a rabbit, especially if the area is moist and dirty. (See Chapter 7 for information on keeping your rabbit clean and well groomed.) Flies also like to plant their eggs on open sores anywhere on a rabbit's body. The resulting maggots burrow into the rabbit and feed on her flesh — disgusting (and painful), for sure.

You can keep flies from doing their dirty business on your rabbit by

- Making sure that both your rabbit and her outdoor digs (pen, run, and so on) are clean.
- Checking around your rabbit's rectal area and keeping it clean and dry. Keeping the rectal area clean is especially important if you have a long-hair rabbit because feces, trapped in the long wool, attract flies.

Contact your veterinarian immediately if you notice

- Fly eggs and/or maggots on your rabbit
- Matted fur
- Wet, irritated skin

To kill the fly larvae, your vet needs to treat your rabbit by removing the larvae and dead tissue from your rabbit. Your veterinarian then prescribes supportive treatments to help with healing.

One species of fly known as *Cuterebra* lays a single egg, often in the neck area where the skin is thinner. The egg hatches, and the single larva takes up residence under the skin in a snug little pocket where it continues to grow. Eventually, an oblong lump with a small hole becomes visible on the rabbit's skin; this is the larva's breathing hole. When the larva is mature, it enlarges the breathing hole, emerges, and drops to the ground. There it forms a pupa and hatches into an adult fly. Do not try to remove this larva by yourself because if it ruptures inside the sac, it can release dangerous toxins into the rabbit's system. Your vet can easily remove it with a minor surgical procedure.

## Encephalitozoonosis

*Encephalitozoon cuniculi* is a nasty protozoan parasite that can disable your bunny. *Encephalitozoonosis* is shed through the urine and can be passed along to other rabbits who come into contact with infected urine. This transmission most likely happens between a doe and her babies around the time of weaning. Mother rabbits can also pass the parasite along to their babies through the placenta.

This disease affects the brain, spinal cord, kidneys, heart, and possibly other organs of the rabbit. Its effects on the brain and spinal cord can cause the rabbit to develop

- Head tilt and clumsiness
- Inability to use the hind legs
- Wobbling when walking

Encephalitozoonosis is difficult to diagnose, and there is currently no cure. Usually, by the time the signs are present, the parasite has done its damage. Keeping infected rabbits away from healthy bunnies is important. The good news is that many rabbits exposed to this disease never develop any problems. Rabbits who are best able to keep disease at bay are those that are well cared for and stress-free.

## Baylisascaris

*Baylisascaris,* a roundworm transmitted through raccoon feces, is more likely to affect bunnies who spend time in outdoor areas frequented by raccoons. When the raccoon leaves its droppings, usually on logs, decks, and the like, they contain roundworm eggs. If your bunny is exposed to raccoon feces in the backyard or in contaminated hay, she can ingest the eggs, which then hatch into *larva* (baby roundworms). The larvae migrate to various areas of the rabbit's body, including the brain, where they cause inflammation and tissue damage.

The signs of infection with this parasite include

- Abdominal pain
- Blindness
- Head tilt
- Loss of muscle coordination
- Paralysis of one or both sides of the body
- Sudden lethargy
- Coma
- Sudden death

This disease is difficult to diagnose because it can mimic other diseases. Your vet can perform a variety of tests to try to pinpoint the problem. Some rabbits recover from mild cases, while others may have permanent neurological damage. Antiparasitic drugs are ineffective against this parasite. The best way to avoid this disease is to avoid areas that are visited by raccoons.

# Chapter 10

# Coping with Other Health Woes and Aging Issues

### In This Chapter

- Treating infections in rabbits
- Looking out for special needs and geriatric rabbits
- Knowing when to say goodbye
- Bringing home a new bundle of fur

If you're reading this book, you clearly care about your rabbit and want to do right by him. The healthcare guidelines offered in Chapter 9 prepare those who love and live with rabbits to spot, treat, and even prevent a host of common ailments. This chapter tackles infectious diseases, chronic health problems, and health issues associated with aging rabbits.

Rabbit rescue groups are filled with folks who care for rabbits with a whole range of health problems — whether from an injury, illness, a chronic condition, or aging. Their stories are plentiful and inspirational, and this chapter looks at the challenges and joys associated with caring for a special needs or disabled bunny.

When your rabbit is ready to pass on, you may suddenly have to make an incredibly difficult decision. Whether to keep your rabbit alive or euthanize your pet to spare her more suffering is one of the hardest decisions you will ever have to make. Whether their death is untimely or the result of old age, letting go of your rabbit so that you can go on to love again in their memory is important.

## Treating Infectious Diseases

The best defense against all diseases is a good, healthy immune system. Help your rabbit achieve this state of health with the proper environment (Chapter 5) and diet (Chapter 6).

This section talks about some of the diseases that can be transmitted from rabbit to rabbit. Several microorganisms (germs) can cause these diseases, which vary in severity and how well they respond to treatment:

- **Bacteria:** One-celled microorganisms that can often be killed with antibiotics.
- **Protozoa:** A single-celled microorganism that's the smallest form of animal life. The treatment for protozoal infections depends on what tissue in the rabbit's body they've invaded. Some tissues can be easily medicated, while others are nearly impossible to treat.
- **Fungi:** A multicellular organism that reproduces by budding or by spore production. Several kinds of medications treat fungal infections.

If your rabbit is diagnosed with an infectious disease, or you suspect that he may have one, be sure to

- Isolate him immediately from other rabbits.
- Disinfect everything with a solution that's nine parts water and one part bleach (especially before another rabbit uses his cage, food bowl, or other items).

## Respiratory infections

Rabbits can develop several different respiratory diseases that can affect the upper respiratory tract (nose, sinuses, trachea) and the lower respiratory tract (lower airways and lungs). The common term for upper respiratory infections is *snuffle,* which a number of different organisms can cause. Conditions that make a rabbit more susceptible include a dirty environment, particularly one that's wet, poor air circulation, and high humidity or heat. Many types of bacteria can cause respiratory disease in rabbits, but the two most common are *Bordetella bronchiseptica* and *Pasteurella multocid,* which may share symptoms. Rabbits may also develop other problems, such as heart disease or chest tumors, that can mimic some respiratory disease signs. The appearance of any of the following symptoms is a good reason to see a vet, who will want to perform tests to find out the organism involved and the level of seriousness:

- Sneezing and nasal discharge
- Matted fur on inside of the front legs (from wiping nasal discharge)
- Labored breathing
- Lethargy

- Loss of appetite
- Head tilt or head shaking

### Bordetellosis

The *Bordetella bronchiseptica* bacteria causes a condition known as *kennel cough* in dogs, but can also affect rabbits. It's transmitted through the air. The incidence of infection with this bacteria increases as the rabbit ages. Not only can this bacteria cause its own damage to the air passageways, including irritation to the nasal passages, bronchi, and lungs (pneumonia), but it can make it easier for other bacteria, such as *Pasteurella multocida,* to take hold.

Rabbits displaying signs of respiratory disease should get veterinary attention as soon as possible. Your vet may do a culture to determine the cause of the infection and a chest X-ray to see the extent of disease. Because bordetellosis is a highly contagious disease, your pet should be isolated from other rabbits. Guinea pigs in particular are susceptible to developing pneumonia from infections with *Bordetella,* so don't house them with rabbits. Also, if your pet dog is diagnosed with kennel cough, keep him far away from your bunnies until he's healed.

### Pasteurellosis

*Pasteurella multocida* is a bacteria found in the respiratory tract of many rabbits without any outward signs. There are many strains, some more prone to cause disease than others. In addition, this bacteria can take hold if the environmental conditions are poor or the rabbit's immune system is compromised. Usually it causes *upper respiratory disease* (infecting the nose, trachea, and bronchi), but it can on occasion cause ear infections, pneumonia, and abscesses in any area of the body. Like *Bordetella,* it's transmitted primarily by direct contact with infected objects and through the air when an infected rabbit coughs or sneezes.

Rabbits transmit the *Pasteurella* bacteria to each other via sneezing or direct contact, so keep affected rabbits away from the healthy ones. If you see your rabbit sneezing or coughing, contact your vet right away. As with bordetellosis, your vet may do a culture to determine the cause of the disease and an X-ray to determine its extent before devising a treatment plan.

## Ringworm

*Ringworm* is the common name for a disease caused by one of several fungi that can affect rabbits, people, cats, dogs, horses, and other animals. The disease is also known as *dermatophytosis.* Ringworm isn't a common disease in rabbits, but it can occur in young rabbits or those exposed to other animals with the disease. The disease is transmitted by contact with the fungi's spores, which can travel through the air and stay active in the environment for long periods. The common signs are

- Dry, crusty skin
- Itchiness
- Fur loss in a circular patches, usually on the head, feet, and legs

Some rabbits can recover from ringworm on their own, but the fungus stays in the environment to infect other rabbits, other pets, and even people. After your veterinary makes the diagnosis, your pet may be treated with both topical and oral medications, and you need to clean the environment thoroughly.

Disinfecting the rabbit's environment — cleaning the cage with a diluted bleach and water solution to remove hair and dander that may contain spores — is important, especially if your rabbit has ringworm.

## Myxomatosis

*Myxomatosis* is a disease caused by several strains of poxvirus. Insects serve as transmitters. This virus was spread intentionally in Europe during the 19th century to destroy large rabbit populations, which were considered vermin at the time.

The disease still exists in Europe today in both wild and domestic rabbits. In its most severe form, myxomatosis can be fatal. The United States tends to see a milder form of the disease, particularly along the California and Oregon coast. It's suspected that mosquitoes are the carriers in those areas. The version of myxomatosis seen most often in both wild and domestic rabbits in the United States is the appearance of skin tumors, particularly on the extremities. Occasionally, though, the more severe form can also be seen. The symptoms to look for are

- Fever
- Lethargy
- Discharge from eyes
- Swollen, red genitals
- Red, swollen, and watery eyes
- Facial swelling (occurs last)

A variety of different insects can transmit the disease. If you live in an area of Europe where the disease is found in wild rabbits, keep your pet rabbit indoors. If you live in a high-risk area, ask your veterinarian about the possibility of vaccinating your pet.

If your rabbit shows any signs of the disease, contact your veterinarian immediately. If your vet makes a diagnosis of myxomatosis, your vet will give your rabbit appropriate supportive care (primarily intravenous feeding and fluids) in the hopes that the bunny can fight off the virus on its own; in some cases, euthanasia may be recommended to prevent suffering and further spread of the disease.

## Tyzzer's disease

A bacteria called *Clostridium piliforme* causes *Tyzzer's disease.* Depression and profuse, watery diarrhea are symptoms of Tyzzer's. This disease can be fatal, particularly in rabbits that were recently weaned. Older rabbits with this illness may develop a chronic wasting disease, where the rabbit refuses to eat and slowly wastes away.

A low-fiber, high-carbohydrate diet, along with poor hygiene and stress, can predispose a rabbit to Tyzzer's disease. If your rabbit shows signs of depression and diarrhea, take him to a veterinarian right away. The most important part of treatment is a high-fiber, low-carbohydrate diet.

## Venereal disease

A *venereal disease* is one spread through sexual contact. Rabbits develop a form of syphilis caused by a bacteria, but it's not the same disease as seen in humans.

Rabbits transmit syphilis through breeding (another good reason to spay and neuter; see Chapter 9). If you do have a good reason to breed your rabbit, you need to take precautions to keep your rabbit from contracting syphilis: Inspect the genitals, lips, nose, chin, and eyelids of the rabbit with which you intend to breed your pet. Although an inspection won't guarantee that your rabbit won't come into contact with the disease, it certainly reduces your rabbit's chances.

Affected rabbits develop crusty sores on their genitals, lips, nose, chin, and eyelids. If your rabbit has been bred and develops these symptoms, contact your vet right away. Antibiotic treatment is recommended and usually works quickly to clear up the problem.

## Viral hemorrhagic disease

In 2000, the first case of *Viral Hemorrhagic Disease* (VHD) was diagnosed in rabbits in the United States. Since then, this deadly disease has been recorded in several areas of the country, prompting great fear among rabbit owners and breeders.

Caused by a *calici virus,* VHD affects 70 to 80 percent of rabbits exposed to it, and in rabbits that develop signs of the disease, it's 100 percent fatal. Oral contact with contaminated feces transmits the disease. VHD is also known as *Rabbit Hemorrhagic Disease* (RHD), *Rabbit Calicivirus* (RCV), and *Rabbit Calicivirus Disease* (RCD).

VHD affects major organs and causes severe hemorrhaging. The virus has a short *incubation* period (the amount of time an organism needs to become numerous enough to cause disease), and rabbits often die within a few days of exposure to the disease. The symptoms of VHD can include

- High fever
- Lethargy
- Loss of appetite
- Spasms
- Spontaneous bleeding from the mouth or rectum
- Sudden death

VHD is an insidious disease with no cure. However, a vaccine is available in areas of the world where the disease is endemic. The United States Department of Agriculture (USDA) is keeping close watch on the spread of VHD. If your rabbit shows VHD symptoms, rush him to a veterinarian immediately. Because VHD is a reportable disease, your veterinarian will contact the USDA.

The best prevention is to

- Keep your rabbit from coming into contact with other groups of domestic rabbits. (Keep a new rabbit separated for at least 30 days to ensure that he's healthy before you expose him to your other rabbits.)
- Avoid using grooming tools, cages, and other objects that strange rabbits have used.
- Wash your hands and clothes after handling rabbits at a show, shelter, or rabbitry.

The good news is that because death occurs so soon after the onset of the disease, rabbit owners are thus immediately alerted to its presence. If action is taken right away, then you can at least minimize the spread of the disease between rabbitries.

### *Encephalitozoon cuniculi*

A protozoan parasite, *Encephalitozoon cuniculi (E. cuniculi)* can cause a host of health problems in rabbits, among them kidney failure and liver failure, head tilt, loss of function in the legs, as well as other neurological problems. The parasite forms spores that are shed in urine, which the rabbit then inhales or ingests. Once inside, *E. cuniculi* travels through the body, affecting the kidney and other organs.

*E. cuniculi* is diagnosed by a blood test. Although a large number of rabbits throughout the United States test positive at some time during their life, few show signs of illness. (Those rabbits who do are typically ones whose health is already compromised.)

## Caring for Disabled and Special Needs Rabbits

There's no getting around the fact that caring for a special needs or disabled rabbit is a big commitment, but one with big rewards. Whether your rabbit has become disabled from age or illness, you love him all the same. But it's worth preparing yourself for the time, effort, and emotional commitment necessary to care for a rabbit with special needs. Every situation is different, so only you can evaluate yours; living with a partially paralyzed bunny is not the same as living with a bunny with dental issues that needs a special diet. Consider the following:

- Do you or someone in your family have the time to care for your disabled bunny?
- Is your rabbit in pain? Is she eating? Keep in mind that you've made this commitment for your rabbit and not yourself. Be realistic about what is best for your rabbit.

### Antibiotics are anti-bunny?

Antibiotics are one reason taking your bunny to a veterinarian who specializes in rabbits is so important. Some antibiotics commonly given to dogs and cats (like oral amoxicillin) can be fatal for rabbits. These drugs can kill off the healthy bacteria in a rabbit's GI tract as well as the bacteria causing disease. This disruption can lead to enteritis. However, many safe antibiotics can be used in rabbits orally, *topically* (on the skin), or by injection. An experienced veterinarian will know which type is safe to use.

Those that have made the choice to care for a special needs or disabled bunny will have to make certain modifications:

- **Home renovation:** If you're using a cage as part of your housing arrangement, think about getting rid of it altogether so that it's easier for your rabbit to move around.
- **Bedtime:** Be sure your rabbit has a comfortable bed that he can access. Add some layers of blankets or soft towels to make his bed extra plush and cozy.
- **Bunny business:** Make sure that your rabbit can still get into his litter box. If the sides are too high, consider cutting out an entrance on one side. If a litter box is out of the question, consider absorbent "puppy pads" or going the route of diapers; many caretakers find diapers can be useful. (Look for Web sites that offer advice on taking this approach.)
- **Sitting pretty:** Some disabled rabbits may have trouble keeping up with grooming. Lend a hand with extra brushing and take care to ensure that her hind end stays clean and tidy. (See Chapter 7 for more on the right way to groom and bathe a bunny.)
- **Pedicure time:** Keep up with your rabbit's nail clipping, and be sure that no sores have developed on the bottoms of your bun's feet.
- **Nourishment needs:** A special needs rabbit may require extra help with eating; some may even need the addition of a high-fiber liquid hay supplement, such as Critical Care, or syringe feeding. Monitor the amount of liquid your rabbit is taking in to be sure that he's properly hydrated.
- **Comfort level:** Keep a careful eye on your rabbit's comfort (see Chapter 9) to be sure that he's not in pain.
- **Keeping company:** A calm, older rabbit may provide an extra dose of what your special bunny needs: companionship and affection.
- **Support:** Ask for help from friends and family when you need it; check out some of the online support groups.

## Taking an alternative approach to treatment

More and more people are turning to alternative healthcare for themselves, and some believe such approaches can work equally well for rabbits. Though your vet may not be familiar with acupuncture and acupressure, chiropractic care, and herbal remedies, these treatments may complement conventional veterinary medicine. Many of these holistic approaches are reported to have few side effects. However, consult with your vet before embarking along an alternative path to treatment.

# Helping Bunny Live to a Ripe, Old Age

With the right care, your rabbit can live to be 10 years of age or even older. And of course, the better the care is that you give to your pet, the healthier he'll be in his old age. (See the rest of Part II for information on how to provide the best basic care for your pet.)

However, rabbits, just like people, start to develop some problems as they age. If you have a senior bunny in the house, watch out in particular for signs of the following:

- **Kidney disease:** Though not exclusively a problem associated with age, kidney disease occurs most often in older rabbits. Symptoms include weight loss, excessive water consumption, and excessive amounts of urine. (See Chapter 9 for more information.)
- **Arthritis:** Your older rabbit may develop arthritis, which can make it difficult to hop around and get onto his favorite spot on your Lazy Boy. Speak with your veterinarian to see whether medication to fight inflammation and pain is warranted.
- **Sore hocks:** Older buns, especially those who are obese or less mobile, are prone to calluses, sores, or even abscesses on their hocks (see Chapter 9).
- **Hind leg weakness:** An older rabbit may experience weakness in his legs, which can make getting up from a seated or reclining position more difficult.
- **Dental disease:** Dental disease includes incisor and/or molar malocclusion, tooth root abnormalities, and abscesses. (For more on abscesses and dental problems, see Chapter 9.)
- **Blindness:** Loss of vision can be caused by a number of reasons. Cataracts, for example, are a natural sign of aging, but glaucoma is a painful condition that should be treated. A veterinary exam is in order if you suspect changes in your rabbit's eyesight.
- **Deafness:** Many rabbit folks report loss of hearing in older rabbits. A deaf bunny needs no special care, but she will appreciate it if you approach her in a way that she can see you at a distance first so that she isn't startled.
- **Cancer:** Cancer can strike at any age, and older rabbits are not immune to this often devastating diagnosis. Aside from the preventable uterine cancer (see Chapter 9), rabbits fall victim to a number of other cancers, including lymphoma, which can develop anywhere in the body. Early detection, along with options that include surgery and chemotherapy, is critical.

Making some adaptations to his environment can make life easier for your older bunny:

- Be especially careful to give him a good, healthy diet (see Chapter 6).
- Cut down the side of his litter box to give him easier access.
- Lower his hay rack and water bottle.
- Provide him with plenty of soft places to sit; monitor hocks for calluses and see your veterinarian if hocks develop open wounds.
- Provide him with nonskid surfaces (carpet, sheepskin) to help him if he has trouble getting up.
- Make necessary modifications to make sure that your older rabbit is warm enough.
- Protect your blind or sight-impaired rabbit by keeping him in a safe living area.
- Reduce stress in his environment as much as you can.

# Saying Goodbye

The hardest part of having a rabbit in your life is saying goodbye when your pet's final moment comes. Rabbits have a way of hopping into your heart and then you feel a tremendous sense of loss when you no longer have your bunny to hug and hold.

If you're lucky, your beloved rabbit will live to a ripe old age and won't leave until it's truly her time to go. However, illness or injury may take a rabbit away from her human companions prematurely. If your rabbit is ill and struggling with illness and/or incapacity, you may be forced to consider euthanizing your rabbit. If so, then consider the following:

- Find out more about what euthanasia is and what it involves.
- Consider your rabbit's quality of life.
- Talk with your vet.

## Letting go: Euthanasia

Understanding exactly what euthanasia is can help you decide whether to take this route with your pet. Basically, *euthanasia* is the humane process of taking an animal's life. Veterinarians use a *barbiturate* (a drug that depresses the nervous system), which they inject in large quantities into a rabbit's bloodstream.

The drug ceases brain function almost immediately; thus, the rabbit loses consciousness, stops breathing, and her heartbeat ceases.

If you ever had a dog or cat euthanized, it may be helpful to know that the process is somewhat different for rabbits. For dogs and cats, a *catheter* (a needle that can be attached to a tube or syringe) is usually placed in the animal's vein while the dog or cat is still awake. The euthanasia solution is then administered. For rabbits and other small exotic pets, the catheter can't be placed unless the animal is heavily sedated. In rabbits that are sick or small, it can be difficult to place the catheter at all.

For this reason, veterinarians opt to sedate the rabbit first with a small injection in the muscle or with an *inhalant anesthesia* (an inhaled gas that sedates the rabbit). When the pet is no longer conscious, the euthanasia solution is administered via another injection. If the animal is sick or small, injecting the solution into the vein may not be possible. In these cases, the injection may have to be given directly into the heart or abdomen.

Although the thought of euthanasia can be upsetting, remember that the rabbit is already sedated and therefore can't feel anything. The rabbit isn't even aware of the injection. Rabbits feel no pain during the euthanasia process. From what scientists now know, rabbits don't experience fear when they're slipping away either, but instead, just a quiet sense of falling into a deep sleep.

If you find yourself in the position of asking a veterinarian to euthanize your rabbit, you can ask for sedation if the vet doesn't normally provide it. The sedative reduces any fear that your rabbit may have of being handled by the veterinarian and will result in a more peaceful euthanizing process.

Some people prefer the option of having their pet euthanized at home, particularly if it's difficult for them or their pet to travel. Check with your veterinarian to see whether he offers an at-home euthanasia service or call a veterinarian who specializes in house-call service.

### *Considering her quality of life*

If you find yourself struggling with this difficult decision, remember that euthanasia can be a great gift to a rabbit who is suffering and beyond help. Without you to make the decision to let your rabbit go painlessly, your rabbit would suffer needlessly.

Think about your rabbit's quality of life and whether it's fair to keep her alive in her condition. Do you think that she'd welcome a peaceful, quiet death?

Consider the following questions to help determine your rabbit's quality of life:

- Is she able to move around comfortably?
- Does she still enjoy eating?

- Can she comfortably relieve herself?
- Does she respond to you when you try to interact with her, or does she seem tired or withdrawn?
- Can she still take part in the activities that she enjoys?
- Does she experience more pleasure than pain in her life?

If your answer is no to a number of these questions, you have to come to terms with the fact that your bunny's quality of life isn't what it used to be.

Making the decision to euthanize a pet is extremely difficult. After you do, you'll probably experience all kinds of unpleasant emotions and plenty of doubt, too. You can read more about emotions and how to deal with them in the "Grieving is Good for You" section, later in this chapter. Most people aren't often in the position of making life and death decisions and having to decide to have their rabbit euthanized.

### Asking a pro

When it comes to making a decision about whether to put down your ailing rabbit, your veterinarian is a valuable resource. She can give you a good idea of how much pain your rabbit is experiencing and what the likelihood of curing or managing your rabbit's condition may be. After hearing your vet's opinion, you're then able to make an educated decision about how to handle your pet's future.

If you're uncertain about the medical aspects of the decision, getting a second opinion from another veterinarian is also helpful. You can get a second opinion from a vet in the same practice or in another clinic.

## Should you stay?

When you make the decision to euthanize your rabbit (whether you take him to the vet or the vet comes to your home), your vet may ask you whether you'd like to stay with your pet during the process. Choosing whether to be with your pet in her final hour is a personal decision, and one that only you can make. If your rabbit is sedated (which is highly recommended), your bunny won't even know that you're present. However, being at your pet's side at his final moment may provide you with comfort.

However, if you feel that you can't handle being present when your rabbit dies, you aren't obligated to stay nor do you need to feel guilty about leaving the room. Remembering to take care of your own feelings is important when you're in this situation. Do what feels right for you.

The decision is ultimately yours; do whatever makes you the most comfortable in the long run. Don't let anyone push you into a decision that you don't feel right about or that you aren't ready to make. Take a few days to think it over before you decide. Don't feel that you have to make a rush to judgment. If your pet is uncomfortable, ask your vet for suggestions on how to make her more comfortable, including using pain medication.

In the event that your decision needs to be made immediately, take a few minutes to sit by yourself and think about the situation or talk to a supportive loved one or friend. Feeling right about your decision is important, even if it has to be made sooner than you'd like.

### Finding a place of rest

Everyone has different feelings about how to handle the remains of their beloved rabbit. Planning what you'll do with your pet's remains well in advance is a good idea so that you don't have to make this sometimes difficult decision when you're feeling badly about just having lost your pet.

You have several options when it comes to dealing with your bunny's remains:

- **Individual burial:** You probably heard of pet cemeteries and may have even seen one as you're driving. For a fee of several hundred dollars, your bunny may be interred at a pet cemetery. A headstone or grave marker is usually included in the fee. By giving your pet a marked grave, you can visit your bunny whenever you like.
- **Communal burial:** Most pet cemeteries provide the option of a communal burial, which is more affordable. With this method, your rabbit is interred with other pets (sometimes cremated) at the pet cemetery in an unmarked grave.
- **Individual cremation:** Some rabbit owners choose the option of individual cremation. Then they place their bunny's cremated remains in a container for burial or in an urn that they keep at home. Keeping your pet's ashes at home is less expensive than a burial.
- **Group cremation:** For a lesser fee, your rabbit may be cremated with other deceased pets and buried in a communal grave at the cemetery.
- **Disposal by a veterinarian:** All vets offer to dispose of your pet's body after euthanasia. Depending on the clinic, group cremation or other means of disposal are used.
- **Burial at home:** If your county or municipality allows it, you can bury your rabbit at home on your property. Consult your local zoning laws before you take this route to make sure that burying your pet on your own property is legal where you live.

### Postmortems

It's unpleasant to think about your bunny undergoing a *postmortem examination* (also known as *necropsy*, it's an internal examination of the organs and tissue performed by a veterinarian after the rabbit has died). However, if you lose your beloved rabbit to illness or you don't know the cause, think about having your vet perform a postmortem.

The reason for this is simple: By helping your veterinarian learn about the problem that took your rabbit, you're contributing to your veterinarian's knowledge of rabbit medicine. This information can help your vet successfully treat other rabbits in the future and may actually save lives. In addition, if you have other rabbits in the household, you can find out whether the condition that caused the death puts your other rabbits at risk. Chapter 14 offers more information about how to deal with a rabbit's loss.

## Grieving is good for you

People who haven't loved and lost a rabbit are often shocked at how devastated they feel when their bunny dies. They hadn't imagined they could feel such grief over an animal. Many people who have lost pets say that the level of their sadness matches feelings they had when they lost a family member or loved one. The intense grief that someone may feel at the loss of a pet doesn't diminish the value of the beloved family member but instead makes a rabbit owner realize just how much attachment she had for her rabbit.

Your thinking processes won't be rational while you're grieving the loss of your pet. If you had your rabbit euthanized, you may feel as if you did something terrible; if she died naturally, you may feel as if you *let* her go. All those who grieve go through stages.

### All of grief is a stage

When you lose someone you love, whether you lose a loved one or a pet, you experience a number of emotions. Grieving is a process with several distinct stages:

- **Denial:** "I can't believe it."
- **Bargaining:** "If I had only done this or that, she'd have lived."
- **Anger:** "This is so unfair!"
- **Depression:** "I'm never going to have a pet again. No more pets."
- **Acceptance:** "I did the right thing. It was her time to go, and I loved my rabbit while she was here."

These feelings can come in any order, at any time, and can often repeat themselves in a period of an hour, a day, or a week. You may also feel other sentiments. The grieving process is unique to each person and there is no "right" way to grieve. It's important to

- Understand that these emotions and more are part of the normal grieving process.
- Be aware of why you're feeling these things.
- Talk to someone who's sympathetic. The Appendix in this book has grief resources.
- Know that in time, if you allow yourself to go through this process, the intensity of the emotions and pain lessen, and you'll enjoy life again. Avoiding and ignoring your feelings won't stop the process, but only delay it and make recovering more difficult.

### Finding support

Sometimes, finding a sympathetic ear when you're grieving the loss of your pet is difficult. People who don't care much for rabbits or who never had a pet tell you to just "Get over it," or "Go buy a new one," or ask you "What's the big deal?"

At this time of grieving, try surrounding yourself with other like-minded people who understand what you're going through. Limit your discussions of sadness over your pet's loss to friends and family members who can relate to what you're feeling. Keep in mind that everyone grieves differently. Don't expect members of your family to act and feel the same way that you do over your rabbit's death.

If you can't find anyone sympathetic to talk to, help is available. Over the past several years, a number of veterinary schools have set up grief counseling hotlines for rabbit lovers and other pet owners who have lost a beloved animal. (See the Appendix for a listing of these hotlines.) Make use of these services and contact other rabbit owner groups. They'll help you work through the grieving process and help you recover from your loss. Local pet-loss support groups meet regularly in many areas. Your veterinarian can provide information on local groups.

## Bonding with a new bunny

Just after losing your rabbit, the last thing you want to do is get another. The pain is too strong. You need time to heal.

After going through the initial loss, some people find that opening their home to a new rabbit can help with healing. Doing so is scary because it feels like you're setting yourself up for more pain in the future. However, if you're ready for this step, providing a good home to a rabbit in need can return your thoughts to the joys of rabbit companionship again. The affection that you shared with your first rabbit was so wonderful, that you're anxious to feel that warmth again — this time with your new bunny.

If you feel like getting a new bunny, consider it. If not, don't feel obligated or pressured to get another rabbit or any other pet. The decision is purely yours. Your new rabbit won't be a replacement of your old pet but a new companion to enjoy. For some people, giving a home to a rabbit in need is a wonderful way to honor their deceased pet.

## In memory of Fluffy

One way of feeling better after losing a beloved rabbit is to honor your pet's memory. You can do this in any number of ways:

- **Make a donation.** One of the nicest ways to honor your rabbit's memory is to make a donation to a rabbit rescue group. You don't have to make a huge donation. An organization that works hard to provide homes to unwanted bunnies will appreciate the $5 or $10 that you sent. Contact your veterinarian, local animal shelter, or House Rabbit Society (see the Appendix for contact info) to locate a rabbit rescue group in your area. Be sure to include a note with your check, stating that the donation is in honor of your rabbit's memory.
- **Discuss your rabbit.** A number of Web sites are set up to help grieving pet owners talk about their feelings and honor their pet's memories with poems, essays, and photos. (See the Appendix and Chapter 19.)
- **Create something.** Writing your feelings about your rabbit on paper can help you work through the grief while also honoring your rabbit's memory. You don't have to show your words to anyone. They can be just for you and your rabbit, or you can choose to share them with other rabbit owners on the Internet or through a rabbit club. If you're artistic in some way, you may find it more comfortable to express your feelings through drawing, painting, sculpting, or through another type of art. Perhaps you'd like to paint a portrait of your deceased pet from a photograph. Consider making a photo album for your pet, too. A great way to honor your rabbit's memory and cope during the grieving process is to make a photo album.
- **Volunteer.** Rabbit rescue organizations need plenty of help. Consider donating your time, energy, or special services to one of these groups in your pet's honor. (See the Appendix for more information on volunteer rabbit groups.)
- **Adopt a bunny.** It may sound a bit strange at first, and it's certainly not for everyone, but a wonderful way to honor your rabbit's memory is to provide a home for a bunny in desperate need of love. Knowing that your rabbit's passing provided an opportunity for a rabbit who really needed a home can help you overcome your grief, putting your rabbit's life in a truly positive light.

# Part III

# Rabbit Psychology: Behavior and Training

"The funny thing about rabbits is how they communicate. Binky will always IM when he's hungry, but to know if he's sick, you have to read his blog."

## In this part . . .

When you know how to feed and house your bunny, you can take on more intricate parts of your relationship. In this part, you discover what your rabbit means when he acts a certain way — including what he's saying with his body language and noises. This part also covers ways of handling problematic behaviors, such as chewing and biting. Training can be a fun part of your life together and this part tells you how to approach it, step by step. Throughout this part, you get tips for ways of bonding with your bunny.

# Chapter 11

# Thinking Like a Rabbit

*In This Chapter*

- Communicating with your rabbit
- Discovering the rabbit mind
- Pairing rabbits with others

On the surface, rabbits may seem like simple creatures who just want to eat, sleep, and play, but they're actually much more complicated than that. You don't survive as a species for millions of years if you don't have much going for you besides the basics.

Rabbits are excellent at reading humans' body language, communicating silently (and quite loudly), and figuring out what has changed and why. They're also experts at detecting danger. If you want to communicate effectively and live harmoniously with your domestic bunny, take heed of the following bunny wisdom.

## Making Sense of Body Language

Communication is the key to the success of any good relationship. You and your rabbit are no exception. Although your bunny may seem a bit quiet, she has many ways of communicating her needs.

The first step in communicating with your rabbit is being able to figure out what the heck he's trying to tell you. For the most part, rabbits speak with their bodies. They talk to each other and to you through their movements and postures.

To understand what your rabbit is saying to you, you need to pay close attention. Observe your pet in different situations to recognize the following:

- **Chinning:** "This is my turf." When your rabbit rubs his chin on the corners of furniture, on his nest box, or on your hand, he's marking his territory by *chinning*. The scent glands located on the underside of his face leave an odor detectable to other rabbits (*not* humans), letting them know that this territory belongs to the owner of the scent. Let your rabbit chin all he wants because it makes him feel safe.

- **Hopping, leaping, and racing:** "Whoopee! I'm happy!" Bunnies express pleasure this way with many variations and levels of difficulty.
- **Binky-ing:** "It's hard to describe how happy I am!" The *binky,* a high jump coupled with vigorous twists, is the unmistakable sign of a very happy rabbit.
- **Kicking:** "Let go!" or "What fun!" If you're holding your rabbit and he starts to kick violently, he's letting you know that you aren't holding him in a way that helps him feel secure. (Chapter 7 tells you how to hold your rabbit properly so that you can avoid this type of language.) You may also see your rabbit kick when playing. Kicking when playing is different than kicking when feeling insecure and basically means "Yippee, I'm having fun!"
- **Circling:** "I'm in the mood for love." A rabbit who circles your feet is in courting mode or may also be just trying to get your attention.
- **Flattening:** "I don't want you to see me." In the wild, rabbits are masters of camouflage. They can flatten their bodies and blend in with the brush to avoid being seen by predators. Pet rabbits flatten, too. If your rabbit gets nervous when being approached by someone he doesn't know or by another animal, he's likely to lower himself to the ground in a behavior called *flattening.* He holds his ears tightly against his head, and his eyes bulge out, as shown in Figure 11-1. In this position, your rabbit is trying to tell you that he's scared. Remove him from whatever situation is frightening him and let him know that everything is okay.

**Figure 11-1:** The squatter's on the top, the flattener on the bottom.

- **Squatting:** "I'm comfortable and secure." Flattening and squatting are polar opposites. Flattening expresses fear, whereas *squatting* expresses comfort. Rabbits who are squatting (also see Figure 11-1) have a distinctly more relaxed appearance. Their muscles don't appear to be tight, their ears aren't held tightly against their heads, and they have a relaxed expression.
- **Stretching out:** "Ah, what a life. . . ." A rabbit lying on his side with his legs extended is feeling relaxed and secure. A variation on this position is when a rabbit lays on his stomach with his legs stretched out behind him. And the ultimate in relaxation? The *flop,* when a rabbit sprawls on his back.
- **Ear shaking:** "Ick, I don't like that." If your rabbit gets a whiff or taste of something he doesn't like or if he wants you to leave him alone, he may give his ears a good shake to let you know what he's thinking. Ear shaking indicates that your rabbit isn't happy at the moment.

Frequent ear shaking can be a sign of a medical problem and should be assessed by a veterinarian. Chapters 9 and 10 detail other health problems and their potential signs.

- **Head butting:** "Hey!" A persistent rabbit will head-butt you when she wants something — petting, food, whatever.
- **Stomping:** "Warning" or, maybe, "I'm annoyed." If you saw the movie *Bambi,* you probably remember a little rabbit named Thumper, who got his name by repeatedly stamping his back leg on the ground. Thumper wasn't just displaying cartoon behavior. Real-life rabbits thump their hind legs on the ground to issue warnings, too. If you see your rabbit thumping, he's probably alerting you to danger or to something else that's going on.
- **Biting:** "I don't like what you're doing." A gentle nip is a rabbit's way of saying "Okay, I've had enough." A bite is different (and you'll be able to tell when you get your first real chomp) and is usually the result of fear or anger. Unless the biting is chronic and painful, give your rabbit a break from whatever you're doing. (Chapter 13 gives training tips.)
- **Sitting up tall:** "I'm curious," or "Is there trouble afoot?" An inquisitive rabbit will rear up on her hind end to look around. A frightened rabbit, on the other hand, may rear up and prepare to bite.
- **Licking:** "I love you." If your rabbit kisses you in the form of a lick on the hand or face, he's telling you that he loves you. Rabbits usually reserve this show of affection for each other, but special humans are also graced with rabbit kisses on a none-too-infrequent basis.

# Interpreting Rabbit Sounds

Although rabbits primarily communicate with body language, they also have the ability to make sounds. You may hear your rabbit make some of the following sounds:

- **Purring:** Like a cat, a rabbit purrs when content. Unlike the feline purr, however, the rabbit purr comes not from the throat but from the teeth.
- **Humming:** "I'm in the mood for love." You're likely to hear this sound mainly from those male rabbits that are still sexually intact.
- **Clucking:** This sound is the rabbit version of "Oh, that was yummy!" A rabbit cluck sounds sort of like the cluck of a chicken, but very faint.
- **Whimpering:** Rabbits who want to be left alone sometimes whimper in hopes that you won't pick them up. Pregnant females are especially likely to make this sound.

- **Tooth grinding:** You may hear two types of tooth grinding:
    - **Loud grinding:** He's in pain. Get your rabbit to a vet right away.
    - **Soft grinding:** He's expressing happiness.
- **Hissing:** Your rabbit may make this sound in response to another rabbit. Hissing is an aggressive sound that basically sends the message "Take another step, and you're toast!"
- **Snorting and growling:** An angry rabbit snorts and/or growls at whoever has made him mad. In most cases, this behavior is reserved for other rabbits that are perceived as a threat of some kind. A bite or charge usually follows the sounds of snorting and growling, so if it's directed at you, get out of the way!
- **Screaming:** You never want to hear this sound. When a rabbit is truly terrified for its life, it lets out a scream that is almost humanlike.

# Preying for Safety

Of course, it helps to put rabbit body language and vocalization into context. Exactly how do rabbits think? What goes on in those fuzzy little heads?

When trying to understand rabbit psychology, you need to realize that rabbits are prey (versus predatory) animals. They're close to the bottom of the food chain, so they basically exist to provide meals for other animals. Their lot in life of being a primary dinner source for other animals has made a significant impact on the rabbit's collective personality.

Imagine that you're always being hunted. Everyone wants to make a meal out of you. Does this idea make you a bit paranoid? We would think so. Now think about how rabbits must see the world. Although they somehow manage to enjoy life, they're always waiting for some big scary creature to make a play for them. The result? A very wary creature with quick reflexes and a strong propensity to run first and ask questions later.

If you want to live with a rabbit, you need to realize how much the prey mentality factors into her personality. Rabbits are surprisingly happy-go-lucky, despite their lot in life, but they're always on the lookout.

Don't assume that just because your rabbit is cuddling with you one minute that he won't suddenly be afraid of you the next. If you've ever watched nature documentaries on TV, you've no doubt noticed that zebra herds will calmly graze within close vicinity to a lounging pride of lions. The zebra seem to have no fear of the lions because the lions aren't acting like predators at that moment. But the minute the lions start making quick, aggressive movements, the zebra heads go up, and the herd heads out.

It's the same thing with your rabbit. Human companions must work hard not to be mistaken for predators. If you're calm and friendly, your rabbit sees you as friend. If you're loud and making fast, aggressive moves, your rabbit becomes afraid of you, thinking that you've turned into a hungry predator.

# Showing Others Who's Boss

In this book, you see mentioned time and again the rabbit's penchant for being a social creature. In fact, without this aspect of the rabbit's disposition, rabbits wouldn't be the terrific pets you've grown to know and love.

When left to their own devices, rabbits live in complex social groups with a distinct hierarchy. A *king buck* and *queen doe* rule the colony's *warren* (a series of dens and tunnels) with a collective iron paw, and more submissive bunnies play different roles within the group. In the case of domesticated rabbits, these rules of hierarchy are applied to humans, fellow domesticated rabbits, and even other household pets. An example of a dominant and submissive rabbit is shown in Figure 11-2. And just as within the world of wild rabbits, different bunny personalities exist in captivity that determine which rabbits will be king and queen and which will be subjects.

To understand this relationship, think about human beings. Some people are naturally more assertive than others. Some are natural leaders, but others prefer to follow. Individual personalities ultimately determine where a person ends up in life, and the same goes for rabbits. The tougher, more assertive rabbits rise to the top of the pecking order, while the ones with meeker personalities take a more subservient role.

**Figure 11-2:** The dominant stance is shown in the rabbit on top; the submissive rabbit is the one on the bottom.

It won't take you long to figure out what kind of rabbit personality you're dealing with. If you have a rabbit who's on the bossy side, always nipping at you to get out of the way or pushing your other pets around, you have a bunny who would probably be the king of the warren had he been born a wild rabbit instead of a domestic one. On the other hand, if you have a quiet, gentle soul who complies easily, never gets aggressive, and seems a bit on the timid side, you have a rabbit who'd happily let others rule were he a wild rabbit living in the social hierarchy of a colony.

Either type of rabbit — and all those in between — have much to offer. Assertive rabbits can be entertaining to live with, but the softer personality types surely steal your heart.

# Coexisting Peacefully: Ensuring a Happy Homecoming

When the time comes to bring your bunny home, take care to make the experience as stress free as possible:

- **Ticket to ride.** Most rabbits do fine during short car trips, but it's not likely to be your rabbit's favorite activity. Chapter 16 outlines ways of creating a secure and comfortable carriage ride for your rabbit.
- **Digging in.** Make your rabbit feel welcome and relaxed by being prepared for his arrival ahead of time, with cage and supplies set up, rabbit-proofing complete, and food ready to go. Put his cage in a quiet spot; he'll probably appreciate some alone time in his nest box. Try not to startle your rabbit with any sudden movements or loud noises and certainly wait

a while before bringing other pets around. (See the upcoming section "Meeting Fido and Fluffy.") Chapter 2 covers how to introduce a new rabbit to your home's current rabbit residents.

- **Meeting the family.** Talk to other members of your household (the humans, that is!) about what will be happening and how your rabbit is likely to feel. In particular, caution children about giving the rabbit time to get used to his new home. This chapter covers introducing new bunnies to children in the upcoming section "Combining Children and Rabbits.").

Your rabbit is dealing with a big change. Be patient and give him time to adjust; the process often takes a week or more. Be calm but friendly, and your companion will soon give you signs that she's settling in.

# Gaining Your Rabbit's Trust

Because of their natural prey instinct, trust can be hard to come by in a rabbit. If you want your rabbit to see you as a friend and not a foe, you need to act more like a rabbit than a predator. (See the earlier section "Preying for Safety.") Getting into your rabbit's mind and viewing the world from his perspective can help you become more "rabbit-like." To gain your rabbit's trust, convince him that you have no intention of turning him into a meal.

To help gain and deepen your rabbit's trust in you, have patience and take the following steps:

- **Speak softly.** When you're around your rabbit, talk in a quiet, gentle voice. You can talk and coo to your bunny all you like, but do it at a low volume in a soft and nonmenacing way.
- **Move slowly.** Quick, jerky movements are the movements of hungry predators. Move slowly and deliberately when you're around your rabbit. And whatever you do, don't chase your rabbit. If your bunny is being resistant about being caught, try luring him to you with a favorite treat. If you run after your rabbit, you'll suddenly seem like a predator with something unpleasant on your mind.
- **Feed at the right times.** Rabbits tend to prefer eating in the early morning hours and at dusk because they're the safest times to avoid predators. By giving your rabbit his main meals at these times of the day, you help cater to his instinctual need to eat at a safe time, which makes for a more generally relaxed rabbit. (Chapter 6 talks about food.)
- **Never use harsh discipline.** Rabbits don't understand harsh discipline, and bunnies interpret any kind of yelling or striking to be the maneuvers of an enemy. Use positive reinforcement to teach your rabbit how to behave. You can get help in Chapters 12 and 13.

# Meeting Fido and Fluffy

One of the neatest characteristics of rabbits is their propensity to get along with other pets. They're genetically programmed to find a way to live with others — even if those others are members of a different species.

Of course, the rabbit's status as a prey animal puts it in an awkward position when trying to get along with other domestic animals. When considering other pets, think about the same pairing in the wild. Would your canary take on your bunny? Probably not, so the two should be fine supervised at home. Same for hamsters and the like.

Parrots and ferrets, however, can be a challenge. Even though rabbits and these animals don't have a history of animosity toward each other, aggressive parrots should be kept away from rabbits, which isn't too difficult to do. Ferrets, on the other hand, are likely to want to make a meal out of a rabbit and so are best kept at a safe distance.

Although cats and rabbits have been on opposite sides of the chase for a long time, most cats and rabbits are virtually the same size, and no cat in its right mind would take on an average-size rabbit. Dogs are the greatest challenge because their wild relatives considered rabbits a prime source of food. In fact, if you research the history of dogs and rabbits, you can see that the dog and the rabbit have long had a strained relationship, as far back as the Ice Age. If you have a dog or a cat, take note of the tips in the following sections on determining whether your pets can get along.

## Dogs

If you have a dog and plan to get a rabbit, you need to take care. Most dogs have a strong instinct to chase and even kill rabbits, and some have gotten into the habit of running after wild rabbits in an attempt to annihilate them. If you're going to keep both of these species as pets, stay constantly aware of this inherent tension between the two creatures.

Think about your dog's

- **Personality:** Is your pooch a mellow old coach potato who's hard pressed to chase or get excited? Or is she a more active dog?
- **Age:** Older, calmer dogs usually do better with rabbits and are less likely to harass them. If your dog is young and you can reliably control her, it may work out, providing, of course, that you've set up a controlled, safe environment for such a meeting. But if your dog ignores you when you call her, you have a problem on your hands.

- **Breed:** Many terriers, some types of hounds, and a number of other breeds have been bred for hundreds of years to hunt rabbits. If your dog comes from one of these hunting breeds, one look at your new rabbit can trigger previously dormant hunting instincts in your dog. Unless you have a young puppy — preferably less than 6 months old — training your dog of a hunting-type breed not to harm the rabbit is going to be tough; breeds known for their hunting prowess include beagles, hounds, retrievers, and terriers, to name a few.

Before even attempting to introduce a rabbit to your household, take your dog to obedience training. Obedience training helps your dog listen to you and respect you as an authority. This recognition of you as the pack leader can enable you to show your dog *not* to harm a rabbit.

After you decide that your dog is controlled enough to officially meet your rabbit, and your rabbit has had time to get used to his new home, follow these steps to introduce the two:

1. **Put your dog on a leash and put someone the dog respects in control of the leash (an adult only).**
2. **Allow the dog to approach the rabbit's cage slowly, in a quiet manner.**

   If the dog starts to act up, correct him by saying "No" and quickly jerking the leash. Do this reprimand consistently.
3. **When the dog approaches the rabbit quietly, even for a moment, praise him with pats and verbal kudos.**

Your rabbit will probably be scared the first time that she sees your dog and is likely to hide in her nest box. Hiding is a good way for the rabbit to feel secure when the dog's around. If the dog is calm and nonthreatening, the rabbit will probably become braver, even curious. You know that the rabbit is curious if the bunny comes out of her nest box when the dog is around. When the rabbit seems comfortable with the dog and the dog is calm and quiet around the rabbit, you can assume that the two have reached a truce.

Don't assume that just because your dog seems disinterested in the rabbit that you can safely let the two loose together. Your dog can never be trusted with the rabbit. Don't take chances with your rabbit's life. Keep your dog and your rabbit separated by a cage or other barrier at all times. Some dogs, no matter how hard their owners try, can't avoid chasing a rabbit. Their predatory instincts are simply too strong. In these cases, you have to keep the dog permanently separated from the rabbit or find a safer home for your rabbit.

## Cats

Although dogs and rabbits are often a tricky combination, cats aren't usually a problem when it comes to cohabiting with a rabbit. Even though cats are predators and may be inclined to chase rabbits, they're less capable of doing damage. It's rare that a cat will be so aggressive toward a rabbit that the two can't be housemates, especially if the rabbit is a large one. On the flipside, some rabbits are so bossy that they make life miserable for kitties.

You can get a good sense of how your cat and rabbit behave toward each other when you introduce them. If your cat begins to stalk your rabbit and treats it like prey, don't allow the two together unless your cat is on a harness and leash, as shown in Figure 11-3. If your rabbit is the same size or larger than your cat, let the cat approach your rabbit and permit the rabbit to put the cat in his place. Your rabbit will probably try to bite and kick your cat, and you can be sure that your cat will never attempt to stalk the rabbit again.

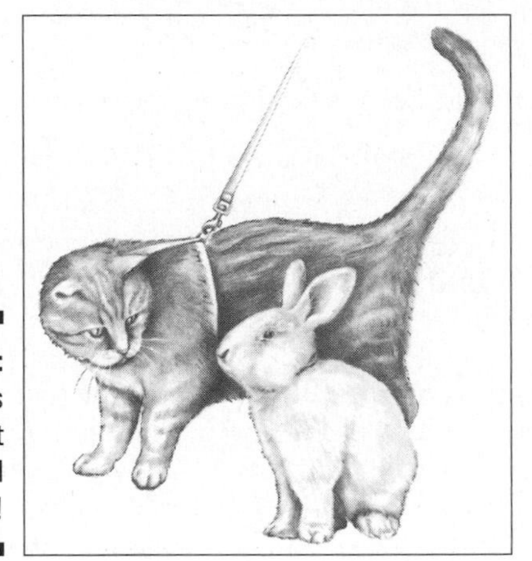

**Figure 11-3:** Harness that potential predator!

If you have one of the smaller breeds of rabbits or a baby bunny, take care if you have a cat who wants to stalk your rabbit. Make sure to keep the two separated at all times because your cat may actually be able to do some harm to a smaller bunny. (You can read more about breeds in Chapter 3.)

Follow these steps to safely introduce your cat and your rabbit:

1. **Trim your cat's claws using a nail clipper.**

   If your cat's nails are trimmed, he's less likely to be able to scratch your rabbit should he decide to take a swipe at your bunny. If you aren't sure how to do trim your cat's nails, see the nail trimming section in Chapter 7. Cat nails are trimmed essentially the same way as a rabbit's.

2. **Begin the introduction with the rabbit in her cage.**

   No need for the cat to wear a harness during this stage. Your cat and rabbit will probably stare at each other and seem nervous. That's because they are! Your rabbit may dive into the nest box, and your cat may arch his back and even hiss — all normal behavior.

3. **If your cat approaches the rabbit slowly and isn't aggressive, reward the kitty with praise and a treat.**

   If your cat hisses and runs away, ignore him. Eventually, your cat's curiosity will get the best of him, and he'll come back to take a closer look. In time, your cat will get used to the rabbit. Should he get too interested and stick his paw through the bars of the rabbit's cage, squirt the cat with a water pistol from a distance, which sends a message to your kitty that aggression toward the rabbit is not okay.

   When the cat and rabbit start to take each other's presence for granted, you can move to the next step: face-to-face introduction.

4. **Let your rabbit out of her cage in a rabbit-proof room.**

   See Chapter 5 for more on rabbit-proofing.

5. **Put your cat in a harness with a leash attached and let him be in the same room with the rabbit, while you're holding the leash.**

   Keep the cat in place and allow him to watch the rabbit hop around the room. When the rabbit hops, the cat may make moves toward her as if to chase her. Don't allow this. Instead, keep the cat still and let him watch the rabbit move around the room.

   If your rabbit behaves aggressively toward your cat, let your cat run away from the rabbit. If your cat feels cornered, it may attack in self-defense. If your rabbit continues to behave aggressively toward the cat, the cat finds out that he needs to stay away from the rabbit, which is fine. Your rabbit should be allowed to call the shots in this situation. In the unlikely event that your rabbit starts seeking out your cat just so that she can attack the poor feline, you can discipline your rabbit with a squirt of water to the body and a firm "No!"

6. **Repeat these sessions regularly until both your cat and your rabbit are comfortable with each other.**

   It will probably take time before the two start to ignore each other (or even become friends), but it's worth the effort.

## Combining Children and Rabbits

Children and bunnies are an adorable combination. The sight of a youngster cuddling a cute rabbit is almost too much to bear. But in order to keep both creatures safe in each other's company, parents need to be aware of potential problems.

Rabbits fascinate kids. Whether it's those giant ears or nonthreatening demeanor that attracts them, children tend to become obsessed with their bunnies. If you have a kid or two and a rabbit, your children will no doubt spend plenty of time with the rabbit, which is fine as long as you keep the following in mind:

- **Children must be taught how to handle a rabbit properly.** Carefully supervise any time children spend with your rabbit. Show the child how to pet a rabbit on the floor — gently, with the back of their hand — and teach them not to chase or harass a rabbit.
- **Set lifting limitations.** Young children shouldn't be permitted to lift a rabbit because both child and rabbit may get hurt in this situation. Older children (8 years and up) may lift smaller rabbits safely, as long as they're taught the proper technique (see Chapter 7).
- **Let your kids know that rabbits have sensitive ears and don't like loud noises.** Teach them to keep loud play to a minimum when they're in the vicinity of the rabbit. When kids are feeling rambunctious and want to scream and run around, they should do it outside or at least in a different room from where the rabbit is kept.
- **Rabbits need their quiet time.** Unlike most dogs, rabbits aren't always up for playing. Teach your kids to give the rabbit some space. If you need to, set aside a section of the day as the rabbit's quiet time when no one is allowed to bother him.
- **Children enjoy feeding time with rabbits in particular.** Let your children feed treats or dinner to your bunny, but show your children that they should sit quietly if they want to watch bunny dine. The rabbit shouldn't be touched or disturbed while eating.

# Chapter 12

# Putting Boxing Gloves on Your Rabbit: Training

*In This Chapter*

- Putting yourself into practice first
- Employing treat tactics
- Responding to your commands

Yes. You can train your rabbit, both for fun and to help you control some of his behaviors. Of course, you can't train them to sniff for drugs, guide the blind, or roll over on command, but you can train them to take actions that are appropriate for rabbits. For example, you can show a rabbit how to use a litter box, follow a few basic commands, and behave somewhat properly in the company of human companions. It's a matter of understanding your bunny — what he likes and dislikes, what motivates him, how to keep him interested — and going from there.

Although this chapter covers general training tactics, it focuses on positive behaviors ("tricks," if you consider sitting up a trick). Chapter 13 describes how to use training techniques to tackle common behavioral problems.

## Training Your Bunny the Right Way

No matter how bright your bunny is, though, he isn't going to get very far training himself. This is where you come in. As with many other companion animals, real training success depends on a great trainer.

Following these general rules is important when training a rabbit to respond to a command:

- **Take the time to bond.** Know that your rabbit trusts you before you attempt any kind of training. In other words, your rabbit must trust you before she'll be able to listen to you.

- **Train your rabbit in a quiet safe place.** Your bunny needs to be able to concentrate on you.
- **Be consistent.** Always use the same command; don't change or add words. If you want to teach your rabbit to jump up on the couch and want "hop up" to be your command, always use that phrase when you ask him to come up.
- **Use rewards.** Give your rabbit his reward immediately after he executes the command. The best rewards for rabbits are food treats. (See Chapter 6 for details on healthy food treats for rabbits.)
- **Be firm.** Don't give your bunny the treat if he doesn't follow the command. Doing so only encourages him to ignore you. Be firm, but not harsh.
- **Be kind.** Never use physical discipline with a rabbit. They're too fragile, and it only destroys the trust you've worked so hard to build.
- **Be patient.** If your bunny is having trouble catching on, figure out another way to teach him. Never use harsh words or punishment of any kind.
- **Go back to square one if you need to.** If you're having success with your rabbit's training but then hit an impasse, your rabbit needs a refresher course. Go back to square one and start the training process all over again.
- **Keep training sessions short.** Take no more than ten minutes at a time and always end on a positive note. In other words, stop right after your rabbit does it *right,* not after he does it wrong or gets tired or frustrated.

Training a rabbit can take as little as a few days or as long as several weeks, depending on the rabbit and what you're trying to teach him. Any rabbit that is old enough to interact with you is old enough to train. Even senior bunnies can learn new tricks.

# Giving a Command Performance

Training a rabbit is *not* like training a dog. Dogs are socialized to humans and are anxious to be accepted. Rabbits, on the other hand, hop to a different drummer. Even though rabbits are creatures that like company as well, they aren't as closely bonded to humans as dogs are, and obeying your every command is down low on their list of priorities. (When that fact of life becomes a real problem, refer to Chapter 13 for more behavioral information.)

When training, use short sessions of no more than five to ten minutes at a time; rabbits have short attention spans. Save one trick for each training session. In fact, it's a good idea to teach your rabbit one thing at a time so that he doesn't get confused. For example, once your rabbit knows to come on command, you can move on to jumping on command.

Using treats and praise, you can convince a rabbit to follow a few select commands and even perform a few cute behaviors to impress your friends.

## Training with treats

To inspire your rabbit during training, you need to understand what motivates her. Unlike dogs, these long-eared companions aren't naturally motivated to please their humans. Rabbits do, however, respond to particular incentives — food treats, mostly — and tasty treats typically play an important role in training. Keep the following in mind when using treats as a tactic in training:

- **Figure out your rabbit's favorite treats.** Chapter 6 talks in detail about smart food choices for rabbits, but remember that fresh greens and veggies, with occasional fruits, are the best options. Packaged gourmet rabbit treats have too many calories to offer in any quality or frequency. Check with your vet if you're not sure about a particular food.
- **Treats should be given immediately after your rabbit performs the requested action.** The goal is to associate the action with the reward.
- **Reward your bunny with treats until he consistently and correctly responds to the command.** Once your rabbit has mastered a skill, you can begin to wean him off the treats. The idea is to be able to give the command without having to use treats at all. Consider, too, the role of petting and toys as rewards.

  TIP: Wean your rabbit away from the treat gradually — one time, she gets the treat, the next time, she doesn't. Soon, all you'll have to do is say the command.
- **Never withhold food from your rabbit to make him hungry for training.** Fresh hay and clean water should always be available.
- **Don't overfeed your rabbit by using treats during training sessions!** The overuse of treats during training can lead to an overfed, perhaps overweight, bunny.

# Here, Fluffy: Coming when called

If you let your rabbit run in a large area of the house, you may want her to come when you call her name. Coming when called allows you to find your rabbit if she's hiding, and you're concerned for her welfare.

You can train rabbits to come when you call them, provided that you always give them a good reward when they do what you ask.

The best way to get a rabbit to come when you call him is to find out what his favorite treat is. Whether it's a piece of tomato or a chunk of melon, use this as your lure. (Chapter 6 gives you more ideas on what a good treat entails.)

To train your rabbit to come when called:

1. **Get down on the floor close to your rabbit.**
2. **Offer the treat.**
3. **Using your rabbit's name, say, "Come!"**

   Your rabbit will see or smell the treat and will come toward you to get it. She doesn't know that you called her because she hasn't figured out this part yet. However, if you repeat this routine over and over, she'll start to associate hearing you call her name and "Come!" with getting her favorite treat.
4. **After your bunny consistently comes to you from this close distance, start to work from farther away.**

   Instead of being so close, squat several feet away from your pet. Offer out the food and call your rabbit's name and "Come!"

Some rabbits catch on more quickly than others, but within a few weeks, your rabbit should come to you just about every time that you call her. You may even be able to get her to come to you from another room.

## Making like Van Halen: Jumping

Another fun behavior that you can drill is jumping up on a piece of upholstered furniture on command. (Unupholstered furniture can be too slippery!) Of course, that's if you *want* your rabbit on the couch. If you'd rather bunny keep all four paws on the floor, you may want to skip this one.

To train your bunny to jump up on the couch on command:

1. **Hold the treat on the couch when your rabbit is having her free time in the house and is hopping around on the floor.**
2. **When she approaches the couch, make sure that she sees the treat.**

   You can hold the treat in a spot where she can reach it just by standing on her hind legs with her front paws on the couch cushions.
3. **Using your rabbit's name, say, "Hop up!"**

   Or if you prefer, just pat the top of the couch with your other hand as a signal.

4. **Even though she's on her hind legs at the edge of the couch and hasn't jumped up on the couch, give her the treat so that she associates a treat with the couch.**
5. **When Fluffy responds to you without fail, hold the treat farther back onto the couch.**

   That way, your rabbit has to really reach to get the morsel.
6. **Repeat Steps 1 through 5.**

   Eventually, your rabbit will jump up on the couch to get the treat, provided it's not too high for her. If it is, you may want to skip this trick or provide a small stool for your rabbit to hop up on to make her way to the couch.

   Make sure that you've given the command just before your rabbit makes her attempt to get the morsel. You want her to associate hearing her name and "Hop up!" or a hand patting the couch with the action of coming on the couch and getting the treat.
7. **When your rabbit finally jumps up on the couch, gently praise her and scratch her on her favorite spot while letting her dine on her reward.**

Eventually, you can eliminate the treat because the command or a pat on the cushion should be enough to get your rabbit to join you on the couch.

Your rabbit can jump down alone. Helping her might be more detrimental!

## Working on the abs: Sitting up

Another good trick (and one that will impress visitors) is sitting up on command. This trick is pretty easy because rabbits naturally sit up on their hind legs all the time.

To teach your rabbit to sit up on command:

1. **When your rabbit has all four feet on the floor, put your hand above her head with the treat in your fingers.**
2. **Using your rabbit's name, say, "Sit up!"**
3. **When your rabbit rises up on her hind legs to get the treat, give her the treat along with some verbal praise.**

After your rabbit rises up consistently in response to your command, start eliminating the treats.

Depending on your rabbit, it can take anywhere from just a few training sessions to a couple of weeks before she's trained to sit up on command.

## Cozying up in his cage: Go in

You can train your rabbit to go into his cage or into his travel carrier on command. (If you want to train your rabbit to go into his travel carrier, make sure that he's already comfortable with being inside it. See Chapter 16 for details on how to make your rabbit feel okay about being in his travel carrier.) This trick can be handy because it will spare you the trouble of pursuing your bunny when you want to put him away for the night or in his carrier for a trip to the vet.

You should train for this behavior at times when you don't need to have your rabbit in his cage for a trip or bedtime, which allows for more flexibility in the training process.

To train your rabbit to go into his cage or carrier:

1. **Put your bunny close to the opening of his cage or travel carrier.**
2. **Say "Go in!" and lure your rabbit into the opening by placing his favorite treat inside the cage.**

   Make sure that your rabbit sees that you have put the treat inside.
3. **After your rabbit is inside the cage or carrier, give him the treat.**

After your rabbit gets the idea, you can place the treat in the carrier and then say "Go in!"

If your rabbit doesn't go in and retrieve the treat after you give the command, don't put him inside or give him a treat anyway. He needs to associate getting the treat with actually going into the cage or carrier.

## Taking a walk on the wild side

Do you have a bold bunny who likes to explore new places? Take your rabbit to a safe place, such as a friend's fenced backyard. You can walk your rabbit on a leash that's attached to a harness. A *harness* restrains the pet around the chest and shoulders, instead of by the neck, as a collar would. (Chapter 11 shows an example of such a harness..) A harness is a good way to take your rabbit outside while still having control over him.

When taking your bunny on a walk, keep these pointers in mind:

- Don't use a collar on a rabbit because your rabbit's neck can be seriously injured if your pet resists.

- Be careful about where you walk your rabbit. Dogs and disease are two serious dangers that rabbits can encounter in unprotected areas.
- Most rabbits are uncomfortable in strange surroundings and may not enjoy outings to new places.

### Adjusting to the harness

Before going for a walk, your rabbit first must get used to having his harness on.

Don't leave the harness on for long periods of time because a rabbit can chew it off, ingesting the pieces of leather, plastic, or metal belt buckle and causing intestinal obstructions.

To adjust your rabbit's harness:

1. **Buy a harness.**

   You can get a cat harness at your local pet-supply store or one especially made for a rabbit from a catalog or Internet retailer.

2. **Put the harness on the floor near your rabbit when he's hopping around.**

   Let your rabbit get used to seeing the harness.

3. **Place some treats around the harness to encourage him to get close to it.**

   This step helps him associate the harness with treats and to realize that the harness is harmless.

4. **Lay the harness gently on your rabbit's back to get him used to the feel of it.**

   You don't want to actually put it on him or buckle it at this point. The idea is to let him adjust to the weight of it on his back before you put it on him.

5. **When your rabbit seems comfortable having the harness on his body, buckle it on him and let him hop around the house under supervision.**

6. **After your rabbit seems at ease wearing the harness, snap a leash on to it and walk around the house with him.**

   If your rabbit panics when wearing the harness, go back to square one and start getting him used to it all over again. Don't leave the harness on when not using it, as the rabbit will probably chew it off.

### On the walkabout

When your rabbit is comfortably walking in his harness indoors, try taking him outside. Although you can let him explore your backyard or take him to a friend's house on lead, don't walk your rabbit around the neighborhood or anywhere unprotected by a fence.

After you have the leash on the harness, it's important to remember that

- Rabbits can't be taught to heel or do most of what leash-trained dogs do. Instead, your rabbit will hop around, and you'll basically follow.
- Be gentle with your rabbit while walking him. If you need to get from one place to another while he's on the leash, pick him up and carry him.
- Take care not to allow him to eat any unknown plants or walk through areas that may have been sprayed with pesticides or visited by dogs.

- Your pet is vulnerable when he's outside of his home. You need to keep a close watch for loose dogs who can attack your pet. (If you see a dog approaching your rabbit, pick your rabbit up and hope the dog doesn't try to snatch him out of your arms. Consider carrying pepper spray to protect your rabbit from an attacking dog.) Also, never leave your rabbit unattended or tied up because he could become tangled in his leash and might panic.

# Chapter 13

# Reckoning with a Bad Bunny

### *In This Chapter*

- Understanding your bunny's misbehavior
- Saying "No!" to biting, chewing, and fighting
- Changing your little devil into an angel

No pet is absolutely perfect, and rabbits don't wear wings either. Despite their innocent appearance, rabbits can be terribly naughty and nasty, but that doesn't mean that your "bad" bunny has to hold you hostage.

Though the word "No!" may have its place in training, in order to handle a bad bunny, you must first understand what's driving the bunny to do what she's doing and redirect her in a different direction. (For more on thinking like a rabbit, see Chapter 11.)

If you realize that your rabbit doesn't think or see the world the same way you do, being patient with him is easier. Then you can work on changing his behavior. For example, he doesn't recognize that certain objects have value or that urine smells bad to people. When your rabbit acts in a manner that you find offensive or unpleasant, he's only acting upon his rabbit instincts and learned behavior from living in a household. Many behaviors that owners classify as problem behaviors — chewing and digging, for example — are really quite normal and can be linked back to their wild ancestors' lifestyles.

Take the time to understand why your rabbit is misbehaving, have patience, and apply the knowledge you gain from this chapter. You may be surprised at how successfully you can turn your mischievous bunny into a real sweetheart.

## Just Say "No!"

By saying "No!" to your rabbit, you can train many rabbits to quit undesirable behaviors. Training your rabbit to respond to this verbal command is an invaluable part of managing negative behavior, especially if your rabbit is about to do something that may harm him. If your bunny is chewing on an electrical cord, stealing some of the cat's food, or getting into some other kind of trouble, you can say "No!" to get your pet to stop it immediately.

To train your rabbit to respond when you say "No!":

1. **Catch your rabbit in the act.**
2. **When you see your rabbit doing something he shouldn't, clap your hands loudly and say "No!"**

   The sound should startle him enough to stop the behavior.
3. **If your rabbit doesn't stop when you clap and say "No!", use a squirt gun or spray bottle to squirt water at him immediately afterward.**

   Aim for his body, *not* his head or face.
4. **Repeat these steps as necessary.**

Rabbits don't like being squirted with water, and after going through the preceding steps a few times, he'll start to catch on that "No!" is followed by a shower. Soon enough, you'll only have to say "No!" to get your rabbit to stop whatever he's doing. You can then retire the spray bottle or squirt gun.

# Taming Terrible Teenagers

Just about every species of mammal has its adolescent years, and rabbits are no exception. Like human teenagers, rabbit "teens," which are typically around 5 to 12 months, are coping with raging hormones, newfound independence, and moving from youth into adulthood. And just like human teenagers, rabbit adolescents feel the need to test their boundaries to see what they can do. They're trying to establish their social order within the group, and because humans are part of the "group," they're included in the aggressive, "testing" behavior. This behavior is normal and healthy.

Teenage bunnies tend to be mischievous, sassy, and even a bit hard to handle. Spaying or neutering before the behaviors become deeply entrenched can provide some measure of relief for the situation, as can a bucket load of patience. (Chapter 9 talks more about the benefits of spaying and neutering.) Just keep reminding yourself that like your child, your rabbit will indeed grow out of this phase. Some people even manage to find some humor along the way. You should also

- **Set the stage for success:** Take extra care with rabbit-proofing at this stage. The measures you took to protect your home and your older bunny from harm may not be enough for a rambunctious teen rabbit. Think, too, about changing or limiting where and when a teenager has his freedom (similar to allowing a human teen to drive to her grandmother's during the day but not to a party with her friends at night). For a rabbit, you may allow a lot of time in a cozy hallway and bathroom, but not so much time in the office, where the cords and books live!

- **Outsmart and reroute:** With any rabbit, but teenagers in particular, you're not likely to be able to stop a behavior like chewing or digging. Instead, figure out ways your rabbit can take care of these natural urges without wreaking havoc on the household. Giving him ten acceptable things to chew may be the trick to keeping him from chewing the two things that actually matter to you (your oak baseboards and antique wicker chair).

At all times, it's important to handle misbehaving bunnies properly during this period. Rough handling can cause irreparable damage to the bond you have with your pet.

# Coping with Aggressiveness

Not all rabbits are bossy, but more dominant bunnies behave this way toward human and rabbit companions. If your rabbit is an adolescent or hasn't been spayed or neutered, your pet may behave aggressively. Rabbits can demonstrate aggression in various ways — for example, lunging and biting, which are discussed later in this chapter.

Not all rabbits are inclined to get aggressive, some more dominant bunnies can start behaving this way toward human companions. An adolescent bunny or a bunny that hasn't been neutered or spayed can exhibit aggressive behavior. Most bossy bunnies are either

- **Adolescents finding their way in the hierarchy of the household (and trying out the dominance theme).** Read more on sassy rabbits in the section "Taming Terrible Teenagers," earlier in this chapter.
- **Established as dominant.** The top-dog status can happen when they've gone unchallenged during the establishment of dominance. In other words, people stopped handling the rabbit during his adolescent testing period, so the rabbit learns that he's at the top on the social heap.

You can gently show a bossy bunny that this behavior is unacceptable. (Not sure whether your bunny is being sweet or ornery? Check out Chapter 11 for rabbit body language information.)

# Biting the Hand That Feeds You — Literally

When a rabbit bites you, it hurts. Those incisors are designed to shear off pieces of tough plant material, and when they're directed at human skin, it's pretty darn painful, not to mention just plain upsetting.

Rabbit bites rarely break the skin, so you probably won't have to do much to your wound other than lament over it. If your rabbit does make you bleed, wash the area with plenty of water and soap and then check with your doctor to see whether further medical attention is needed.

Rabbits often bite when they're

- Defending their food
- Asserting dominance
- Protecting themselves

If your rabbit is a biter, you first need to figure out which of these situations you're dealing with. Then you can figure out how to solve the problem.

## Food aggression

In the wild, rabbits must compete with one another for food. Because bunnies live in large social groups, someone is always trying to snag the best patch of grass. The rabbit who is good at defending his food source is the one most likely to survive, especially in the wintertime when food is scarce.

If your rabbit gets nippy when you feed it, you have a rabbit with food aggression. Understanding this behavior is difficult for people because you're the one giving the rabbit the food in the first place. So why is he attacking you like you're going to take it away from him?

Actually, bunnies are pretty logical. From the bunny's perspective, food is present and so are you, and you may take it away if he doesn't defend it by biting your hand. Also, the fact that your hand places the food down and then moves away mimics the actions of another rabbit, who may come in closer to investigate a food source and then retreat.

Solving this problem can be tricky because in most cases, it's a product of your rabbit's inherent personality. However, you can try the following actions to thwart this inappropriate rabbit behavior:

- **Instead of placing your rabbit's food in the same place every time you feed him, place it somewhere else.** Relocating his bowl to different parts of his hutch, cage, or your home discourages your rabbit from viewing his food bowl as being within a specific part of his territory that needs defending.
- **Help your rabbit make the connection between the presence of your hand and the giving of a food item.** Feed him outside of his cage or hutch, holding onto a food object while your rabbit eats it. Use a carrot, piece of hay, or something long at first so that your hand isn't in close proximity to the bunny's teeth should he decide to nip you. After your rabbit is comfortable routinely eating from your hand, move the procedure to the inside of his cage or hutch and continue it.
- **Place food items all around your rabbit's cage or hutch so that he associates food with being all around — not just in the food bowl.** If you disperse food in this way, then your rabbit can't be quite so territorial about food that's spread out.

## Dominance

Rabbits are programmed to establish a hierarchy in social groups, and your domestic bunny is no exception. Just as with people, some rabbits are more aggressive and pushy than others.

If you have a rabbit who nips for no apparent reason, such as when you're watching TV, making dinner (ankles are the usual target), or simply moving around in his vicinity, you probably have a dominant biter.

The object of the dominant biter is to get you to move over, get out of the way, stop whatever you're doing, or get some food. Recognizing this motivation and refraining from rewarding the biter by giving him what he wants is important, because rewarding him just reinforces his biting behavior.

Try these approaches to help curb a dominant rabbit's nips:

- When the rabbit bites you, let out a screech. Then reach down and gently push your rabbit's head to the floor and hold it there for a couple of seconds. This action is rabbit speak for "I'm the dominant one here, not you." Hopefully, your rabbit will get the message over time and stop trying to push you around.
- If your rabbit nips you for food, don't give him any. Try screeching to discourage him and offer him food later on when he's being nice.
- If your rabbit keeps biting you and acting obnoxious, put him gently into his cage for a time out. He may soon discover that challenging you means his freedom is restricted, and he will cease and desist.

## Self-defense

Rabbits prefer to use running away as a means of self-protection, but in situations where they can't run, they resort to biting, lunging, snorting, or attacking (lashing out) with their front feet. If your rabbit bites you when you approach him or put your hand in his cage, he's most likely nipping you out of fear.

Consider taking the following actions to alleviate this problem:

- **Avoid approaching your rabbit from below eye level.** Placing your hand in front of your rabbit's face to make contact or reaching under his face to scratch his chin may be the problem.
- **Reach down into his cage through a top door.** If your rabbit bites you when you reach into his cage to remove him, he's reacting defensively to your approach. This reaction usually occurs if you reach in through a side door in the cage. Instead, reach down into the cage through an opening in the top door. Your rabbit is less likely to back into a corner and force you to approach from the front if you reach down to get him.
- **Back off from mother-to-be or nursing mother.** If you have a pregnant doe or one that's nursing a litter or experiencing *a false pregnancy* (a condition where the rabbit's hormones make her feel like she's pregnant, when in reality she's not), you can expect some maternal aggression on her part. Your rabbit is attempting to keep you away from her nest (before giving birth) or away from her young (after birth). Either way, try to cut her a little slack. This behavior is normal and shows that your rabbit is a good mother.

# Busting Loose: Kicking

Finding a rabbit owner who has never been kicked is hard — it sort of goes with the territory. Rabbits most often kick their owners while being held, and they do it because they're trying to escape. (Remember to always provide support to your pet's hindquarters and hold him against your body to provide the greatest amount of security.)

When your rabbit kicks you while you're carrying him, your pet isn't deliberately trying to hurt you. Kicking is a rabbit's way of flailing and trying to get his feet underneath him. If your rabbit is repeatedly kicking you when you're carrying him, you're not handling your pet correctly. See Chapter 7 and work on your bunny-carrying skills.

### Taming Bandit

Another example of how to deal with an aggressive rabbit comes from Marinell Harriman, an experienced house rabbit caregiver. In her book *House Rabbit Handbook: How to Live with an Urban Rabbit* (Drollery Press, 2005), she tells the story of a bunny named Bandit who was so dominant and aggressive that he attacked her whenever someone entered the room. Instead of punishing him, Harriman's approach was to give Bandit a rub down, brushing (which he loved), or scratching behind his ears. Eventually, Bandit's aggressive greetings became loving ones, and he would meet people with excitement and bunny kisses.

If your rabbit doesn't kick you but seems to be scratching the heck out of your child, then you need to work with your child to help foster his rabbit-carrying skills. Remember that young children aren't strong enough to handle most rabbits, so only allow your young children to interact with bunnies while all the rabbit's feet are squarely on the floor.

# Boxing Bunnies

Some aggressive rabbits may express their feelings by hitting and otherwise threatening, lunging, and growling at their rabbit and human companions alike. Doesn't sound like fun, right? Give your boxing bun an outlet for his aggression by providing him with toys that help let out steam. Think "punching bag for bunnies" and peruse the pet store for toys that you can hang, avoiding any plastic toys that he can chew apart and potentially ingest.

The following diversions may also help redirect your rabbit's propensity to hit:

- **Throwing:** Rabbits love throwing balls around; look for wire balls with bells in the center for extra excitement.
- **Nudging:** Some rabbits get a real kick out of playing with rubber playground balls, which are great for nudging and rolling around the house.
- **Batting:** A simple solution may be to hang a bell from a piece of cotton string (not a loop, which may catch a rabbit's head); some rabbits get a thrill out of hitting it with their noses.

Though it may take some trial and error, a bit of thought and patience may be all it takes to soothe your bunny's inner beast.

## I've got the TTOUCH

You won't find many training schools for rabbits out there, but if your rabbit has training and behavioral issues, you may find a method called Tellington-TTOUCH Training helpful. First developed for horses, this method is being used more frequently for rabbits. It has also been adapted for other companion animals.

TTOUCH employs a gentle, nonforceful way of helping your rabbit deal with whatever is troubling him. Using circular movements of the fingers and hands over the rabbit's body, as well as other related methods, TTOUCH practitioners help rabbits discover new ways to deal with problems. Issues, such as excessive fear and aggression, are addressed through this method.

To find out more about this type of training or to find a TTOUCH rabbit practitioner in your area who can help you, visit the TTOUCH Web site at `www.lindatellington-jones.com/ttouch.htm`.

# Chowing Down

Look at those choppers — rabbits are built for chewing. In the wild, rabbits chew branches, twigs, and leaves to help grind their teeth down. Without such items in your home, your rabbit will look for alternatives, mostly furniture, molding, books, carpeting, and cords, — you get the idea. Is this a bad bunny? Or just a bunny doing what he's supposed to do?

Wild rabbits chew on plant material that ranges from abrasive to soft. They don't chew on dead wood because it has little nutritional value. They do strip bark off young trees, however, but only because it has nutritional value in the living tissue. Both outdoor and indoor pets need to have exercise and healthy materials for their teeth. In domestic situations, however, the strong urge to chew can create huge problems for both the rabbit and his owner.

If you have an indoor rabbit who is making short work of your wooden furniture legs or electrical wires, you have a problem. Fortunately, you can easily solve this common problem. To begin, Chapter 5 has information about rabbit-proofing, protecting your property, and supervising your pet.

Although you can't (and shouldn't!) stop your rabbit from chewing, you can redirect her chewing urges. Consider the following:

- Whenever you see your bunny start to nibble on a forbidden item, quickly give her something else to chew, preferably something similar in taste and texture. Replacing the forbidden item with an acceptable chew toy is key.

- Provide your rabbit with a variety of different objects to chew: toilet paper rolls, cardboard boxes, phone books, wicker baskets, blocks of nontreated wood, and so on.
- Say "no" or clap your hands when you see your bunny chewing on something she shouldn't.

# Digging In

Pet rabbits love to dig, which goes back to their days as wild bunnies when they had to excavate their own homes. By digging their little hearts out, wild bunnies create their very own dens located safely underground.

Although your rabbit doesn't need to dig tunnels and warrens in which to retreat underground, her body doesn't know that. Unfortunately, when domestic bunnies get that urge to dig, it causes problems. Their owners get angry because the digging ruins the carpet, destroys the garden, and shreds the sofa. If your bunny is a merciless digger, causing damage and destroying your house and yard, you can take steps to rabbit-proof her surroundings, which is an essential part of the solution (see Chapter 5).

Rabbit-proofing will help but not prevent digging, however. Your next tactic is not to stop the digging but to provide your rabbit with acceptable digging alternatives:

- If a rabbit is determined to dig in a particular area, no matter what you do, cover a piece of board with carpet and put it in that favorite spot to protect the real carpet.
- Provide mats made from natural fibers, such as grass mats, which may satisfy the urge to dig and take your bunny's focus off the carpet.
- Sacrifice or buy a pillow or cushion for your digger.
- Fill wicker baskets or cardboard boxes with newspaper or shredded paper; cut holes in the boxes to create tunnels and make things more interesting.
- Make tunnels out of old carpet rolls or cardboard concrete forms; try stuffing newspapers in one end to give your bunny a mission: dig through that paper!
- Try a cat scratching post, ramp, or mat.
- If outside (in safe conditions, of course), let your rabbit dig in a protected designated section of garden or yard; a big pile of hay or a box of sand also work.

# Duking It Out

Rabbits have a reputation for being gentle and peace-loving creatures; so many new rabbit owners are shocked to find out that bunnies can be real hooligans when it comes to interacting with other rabbits.

Don't let your rabbits fight because it can result in serious injury. In situations where rabbits are closely confined and don't get along, they can even fight to the death.

Fighting is usually a problem in households where more than one rabbit resides. In single-bunny households, fighting is sometimes a problem between rabbits and other pets, although in most cases, the other pet backs down quickly and that's the end of it. If you have more than one rabbit and are encountering a number of bunny battle royales, you need to take a close look at the situation to figure out what's going on:

- **Sex:** If your rabbits aren't spayed or neutered and they're fighting, then the fact that they're not spayed or neutered may be the problem. Intact males, in particular, like to fight and may even try to castrate each other. Either have your rabbits altered or separate them. Two males that haven't been neutered will fight with each other. In many cases, females that haven't been spayed will also fight with each other.
- **Dominance:** Two dominant rabbits who refuse to back down to one another won't be able to live together peaceably. Keep these kinds of bunnies in separate cages and limit their exercise time together. Avoid feeding them while they're together because the presence of food can often trigger a fight.
- **Personality conflicts:** Rabbits who normally get along well sometimes get into fights with each other. Pay close attention to the circumstances that lead up to a fight and try to eliminate the situation in the future. A favorite toy, a certain treat, or attention from a special person can start a fight between bunny friends. If necessary:
  - Separate the rabbits when offering special things so that they won't fight over them.
  - Make sure that you have sufficient hide areas and litter boxes available when the rabbits are together. Have at least as many hide areas and litter boxes as you have rabbits. If space permits, one more space than the number of rabbits is preferred.
  - Establish extra feeding areas on opposite sides to avoid "discussion" at feeding time.
  - If all else fails, house the two opponents separately and give them individual free time. Although this approach will add to your workload, it may be best for the bunnies' well-being.

## Protecting their space and place

This penchant to brawl goes back to the rabbit's strong sense of territory and social hierarchy. In wild rabbit colonies, each bunny has to get along with the crowd yet also maintain his own space, territory, and place in the group.

Because rabbits aren't big on conversation, they claim their space and place through body language. Fighting is body language taken to the extreme. (For more on rabbit body language, see Chapter 11.)

# Pee Marks the Spot

Dogs and cats aren't the only critters who can urinate around the house and make a huge mess. Rabbits can be guilty of this atrocity, too. Just like dogs and cats, rabbits use their urine to mark their territory. When a rabbit urinates on something, such as your carpet or possibly even you, he's making a statement. In the case of an inanimate object, the statement is "This is part of my territory." If your rabbit is spraying you, he's claiming you as his mate!

You can take one significant step to eliminate the problem of inappropriate urinating: Spay or neuter your pet. The rabbits who are most guilty of this behavior are intact males, who are committing this act as a result of raging hormones. Females who haven't been spayed are also prone to the behavior of urine-marking for the same reason.

If you don't want to neuter or spay your rabbit because you plan to breed him, then you have to live with the urine-marking problem or keep your bunny from running loose in the house. Chapter 5 has information on how to clean up messes.

Other factors that contribute to inappropriate urination include

- **Not enough litter boxes:** You may not have enough litter boxes for the number of rabbits you have, or you may not have enough litter boxes for the space the rabbit is exercising in. If your rabbit has the run of the house, one box is not enough.
- **Medical problems:** If your rabbit was housetrained and is suddenly urinating outside his litter box (especially if he's going in multiple places with small amounts of urine), call the vet.
- **Behavioral factors:** For example, rabbits object to changes in the household and their caregiver's schedule, as well as the introduction of new animals or people. Rabbits urinate inappropriately in response to situations that are stressful to them for whatever reason. You need to address these problems.

Realize that rabbits, particularly intact males, urinate (spray) on vertical surfaces. Females can spray but usually do so to a lesser degree. Even if neutered, male rabbits tend to direct the urine outward instead of downward, urinating along a border, wall, or corner. In order to prevent inadvertent accidents in the litter box, make sure that the litter box is deep enough to have a side to confine the urine and put newspaper or plastic carpet protector under litter boxes that are outside the cage to catch any urine that goes over the edge for easy cleanup.

## Barbering

Do you have a rabbit who is pulling big chunks of fur from his coat? *Barbering* refers to hair pulling or hair chewing (not pulled out but chewed off). Rabbits can do barber themselves or each other. If you see barbering, it's not because your rabbit is pulling his hair out in frustration or trying to make a rabbit fur jacket for your next birthday.

Actually, one of several things is going on:

- Your female is pregnant, preparing to give birth, or suffering from a false pregnancy. Pulling fur from her body to line the nest she's preparing for her kits is normal, so if she's pregnant or thinks she is, it's not something you need to worry about.
- When two or more rabbits are pulling each other's fur, it's usually a sign of boredom or dominance behavior. The behavior may not stop until they're separated or given a larger space and more things to do
- Someone is sick. If your female is spayed or you have a male rabbit who is pulling fur, take your rabbit to the vet. Parasites, such as fleas and mites, as well as irritating skin disorders, or internal pain can motivate a rabbit to pull out its fur. (Chapters 9 and 10 offer more health information.)
- Barbering can also be the result of a poor diet that is low in fiber.

## Shaking in His Bunny Boots: Fearfulness

Being the owner of a nervous, fearful rabbit is frustrating. Although rabbits tend to be flighty in general because of their nature as prey animals, some rabbits never seem able to relax. No matter how comfortable you make their surroundings, they seem to hop around in constant fear.

Like people, rabbits are individuals, and some individuals are more nervous than others. Factors can include

- **Breed:** For more information on which breeds tend to be nervous, read Chapter 3. Smaller rabbits tend to be more high-strung than larger breeds.
- **Genetics:** Some rabbits come from genetic lines that are more fearful than others within their own breed.
- **Socialization:** Poor socialization as a youngster can make for a distracted adult.
- **Stress:** A stressful environment can put a rabbit on edge.

If you have a rabbit with a nervous personality, think about which of these preceding factors may come into play. If it's breed or genetics, you can't do much about it except create a calm, relaxing atmosphere for your pet. If your pet's environment is to blame for your rabbit's nervousness, the situation needs some reworking.

The following checklist can determine whether you can make improvements to your rabbit's environment:

- **Good climate:** Don't expose your bunny to temperature extremes, especially heat.
- **Privacy:** Your rabbit must have a nest box where he can go when he feels the need to hide from the world.
- **Proper diet:** Give your pet access to unlimited amounts of grass hay and fresh green foods daily.
- **Proper handling:** Your pet needs to be handled in a way that helps him feel secure; lift him only when necessary.
- **Protection from other pets:** Don't allow your dog or cat to bother or terrorize your rabbit.
- **Quiet surroundings:** Don't expose your bunny to repeated loud noises and activity.

# Part IV
# Enjoying Your Fun Bunny

"We filled his run with plenty of toys, but he seems to prefer the trampoline."

## In this part . . .

This part exposes all the fun stuff you can do with your rabbit: play, enjoy watching him romp around on his own, and make toys for him. You also discover the safest way to travel with your rabbit. A close-up look at rabbit shows and the new sport of rabbit-hopping helps you get even more involved with your pet, while discussions of rabbit rescue and organizations give you ideas for volunteer jobs and ways of socializing with other rabbit fans.

## Chapter 14

# Playing Around Isn't Just for Dogs

***In This Chapter***

- Choosing the best toys
- Playing interactive games
- Watching rabbits have fun

Whoever coined the phrase "Jump for joy" must've had rabbits in mind. Bunnies love to run, jump, and play probably as much or more than any other creature. Seeing a rabbit play is one of the most delightful scenes to watch.

Play is a natural behavior for rabbits, even in the wild. When a rabbit plays, he cavorts, running, leaping, and batting around inanimate objects. The amount of play any rabbit engages in depends on his personality (some are more playful than others) and the opportunities he has to play.

As a rabbit owner, you have a couple of options when it comes to appreciating your rabbit's propensity for play (and helping him get the daily exercise he needs). You can choose to share in your rabbit's playful moments by providing toys for your pet (some interactive), or you can sit back and delight in the rabbit's goofiness.

## Getting Playful with Toys

It comes as a surprise to many people that rabbits love to play with toys. People typically think of cats and dogs as being the only critters who like to bat a ball around or carry something in their mouths, but rabbits are right up there with animals who like to amuse themselves with a variety of inanimate objects.

Some common toys for rabbits include household items like empty toilet paper rolls, cardboard boxes, and plastic cups. Store-bought toys often enjoyed include items commonly sold for cats: small balls, catnip mice (rabbits don't get turned on by catnip, but they like the shape of the toy), and string-equipped toys you can drag around.

Of course, not every rabbit likes every toy. Rabbits are individuals, and while one toy may make one rabbit crazy, the same toy can bore another. Trial and error is key to discovering what your rabbit likes to play with. Donate the toys he doesn't like to an animal shelter or swap them with your rabbit-owning friends.

In the case of rabbits, toys are a great way to

- **Help your rabbit focus his energies.** House rabbits deprived of toys play with furniture, electrical cords, and other interesting items. (Although if you read Chapter 5, you can find out how to help prevent these catastrophes from occurring.) By providing your rabbit with suitable toys to play with, you help him to be a good, nondestructive member of the household. Toys, particularly wooden ones, help keep bunnies' teeth in check.
- **Encourage regular exercise and prevent boredom.** By providing your rabbit with a toy and space to play, you give him the opportunity to remain physically active and mentally alert. Whether they're for digging, chewing, climbing, hiding, running through tunnels, toys help initiate play and exercise. And, of course, exercise means a healthier rabbit who is less likely to develop problems, such as obesity, weak bones and muscles, and digestive maladies. (For more on these conditions, see Chapters 9 and 10).
- **Bond with your bunny.** While using toys to play with and even interact with your bunny, you enrich the relationship between you and your bunny and build trust in the heart of your rabbit. (Another great way to bond is through grooming, which is discussed in Chapter 7.)

## Keeping safety first

Whether you give your rabbit toys that are homemade, commercially made, or a combination of the two, safety is important. The following list tells you what to look out for:

- **Rabbits like to chew on just about everything.** Be certain that all products that you give your rabbit are nontoxic.
- **If you see your bunny chomping on a toy that's not meant to be chewed — a towel, rubber ball, a shoe, or stuffed sock — take the toy away.** Although most rabbits don't swallow nonfood items, it's best to watch carefully and remove anything the rabbit is appearing to ingest, including allegedly "rabbit-safe" toys.
- **Keep an eye out for toys with small parts that can be pulled or fall off and be easily swallowed.** Look out for string, plastic eyes, and other toy parts that can end up in your rabbit's stomach, causing a blockage.

- **Just because a product claims to be made for rabbits doesn't make it a good choice.** Consider, for example, an edible tiki hut made of straw and hay combined with some grains and molasses (two ingredients *not* in a rabbit-friendly diet). Instead, choose a 100 percent hay hut for your bunny's enjoyment.

## Going prefab

If you like shopping for your rabbit, then you'll enjoy going to the pet-supply store and buying toys for your pet. Keep in mind, however, that the most expensive toy you buy may also be the toy that is consistently ignored by your rabbit who is instead fascinated by the cardboard oatmeal canister.

TIP

See the following list of commercially made toys that rabbits often like:

- Assorted toys and bells made for parrots
- Hard plastic toys made for human babies
- *Sisal* (a type of rope) toys made for rabbits
- Small cat or dog houses made of cloth that look like tents
- Small plastic or wire balls with bells inside made for cats
- Straw or bamboo balls made for hamsters
- Stuffed socks made for cats
- Unfinished (no stain or lacquer applied) wicker, straw, or woven grass baskets of all sizes
- Unfinished wicker tunnels for rabbits
- Wooden chew toys made for rabbits or rodents

You can also search the Internet for rabbit toy manufacturers. See the Appendix for a list of online rabbit-supply retailers.

## Made from scratch

If your budget is tight, go the homemade route with your rabbit. Or if you're like most rabbit owners, you may want to combine homemade rabbit toys with store-bought items. (Keep in mind that rabbits can sometimes be destructive with their toys. Don't share anything with bunny that you don't want teeth marks in!)

Check out this listing of homemade toys that rabbits enjoy:

- Box of shredded white paper to encourage jumping and digging
- Cardboard box of any size (Make sure that all staples, tape, and other noncardboard items are off the box before the rabbit gets a hold of it.)
- Cardboard toilet paper and paper towel rolls
- Dried pine cones (Make sure that they're *untreated*. Some pine cones are sold painted or varnished.)
- Large PVC pipes for tunnels or large cardboard tubes
- Newspapers
- Oatmeal boxes with the ends cut off
- Old phone books (take off shiny covers)
- Paper cups (without coating and no Styrofoam)
- Paper grocery bags for shredding
- Metal lids from jars for flipping
- Soda can with a pebble inside (Be careful about any sharp edges.)
- Straw baskets (untreated and filled with straw for digging)
- Straw whisk broom
- Towels (for bunching and pulling, but be sure they're not being ingested)
- Tree branches for your rabbit to gnaw on and drag around (must be pesticide free and dried — apple and pear are appreciated (see the list of safe plants in Chapter 8).

# Tag! You're It! Playing Games

You can get interactive with your pet and make it a game for two. Rabbits have been known to initiate games of tag with humans, bat a ball, and chase toys dragged around in a circle. Start simple by getting down on the floor, offering your bunny kisses, and tossing a toy gently in her direction.

If you want to play interactive games with your rabbit, keep in mind that the game is best left up to the rabbit. Because of the rabbit's wary nature, chasing your pet isn't a good idea. A game of chase usually frightens a rabbit, who may suddenly feel like he's being preyed upon. However, if your rabbit starts to chase you, he wants you to leave the area, or he's prodding you for a game of tag. If your rabbit is in a playful mood and starts to chase after you, he's initiating a game of tag.

Table 14-1 describes games that you can play with your rabbit.

**Table 14-1 Rabbit Games: Fun for the Whole Family**

| *Game* | *How to Initiate* | *What Happens* | *Possible Concerns* |
|---|---|---|---|
| Towel drag-and-chase | Drag a towel across your rabbit's body and then in front on your rabbit. | Your rabbit may start to give chase! Drag the towel around the room with your rabbit chasing it or over and around your bunny as he tries to pounce on it. | Your rabbit may feel attacked. Be cautious and watch your rabbit's reaction. If he's fearful, he may become aggressive or spend more time hiding. |
| Hanging clothes | Hang some strips of newspaper or paper towel from a clothesline within your rabbit's reach. | Your pet may find it amusing to grab these items with his teeth or paws and tug on them. | |
| Hide and seek | Hide in a spot where your rabbit can easily find you. With a favorite treat in hand, call your bunny. When he discovers you, give him the treat. Then hide again with another treat. | It won't take long before you won't have to use the treat. Some rabbit owners have even discovered their bunnies will take turns hiding with them. | |
| Obstacle course | Use boxes, tubes, and other items to create a rabbit-size obstacle course. | Use your bunny's favorite treat to lure her around, over, and through the course. | |
| Tag | You don't initiate this game: He does, by chasing you. | Let him catch you and then sprint off again. | Avoid chasing and tagging the rabbit because this type of play frightens bunnies. |

*(continued)*

**Table 14-1 *(continued)***

| *Game* | *How to Initiate* | *What Happens* | *Possible Concerns* |
|---|---|---|---|
| Toy pull | Buy a cat toy attached to a string and a pole. Pull it around in front of your rabbit. | Your bunny may start to chase after it. You can pull this toy all around the house, with your rabbit in hot pursuit. | |
| Find the treat | Hide a couple of your rabbit's favorite treats in your pockets or elsewhere on your body and then give him a clue that the game involves food. | Once your bunny gets a whiff of what's going on let him play detective and find the treats. This game is good for bunnies who are timid or not yet trusting. | |

# Amusing Themselves

One of the greatest joys of rabbit ownership is watching your bunny play in a rabbit-proofed room or backyard. (See Chapters 5 and 8, respectively, for details on rabbit-proofing and outdoor exercise.) Rabbits can be incredibly silly and goofy, and their antics can leave you rolling on the floor laughing.

## Having a hoppy good time

If you have a rabbit who seems especially keen on hopping and maneuvering through obstacle courses, consider going pro. The sport of rabbit hopping is taking off in the United States (see Chapter 15).

Imagine you and your rabbit (with or without matching tracksuits) negotiating your way through the jumps and obstacles of a hopping course on your way to victory. Sound appealing? Check the Appendix for contact information for The Rabbit Hopping Organization of America.

Much like their wild ancestors, pet rabbits also like to play — with humans and with other animals. Rabbits have been known to play with dogs and cats, as well as with other rabbits. Solitary play is also a popular pastime of rabbits, who love to find ways to amuse themselves.

## Making like The Pointer Sisters: Jumping

Nature gave the rabbit strong hindquarters and leg muscles to escape from predators, but rabbits also use these assets for jumping in play. Playful rabbits can be seen leaping up in the air, springing forward, or even straight up for the sheer joy of it.

In the wild, jumping helps a rabbit change direction quickly when running from a predator. When a rabbit leaps, her body twists in the air and typically lands facing a different direction, usually a 180-degree turn.

When two rabbits play together, they often run together, one chasing the other. The bunny being pursued sometimes leaps into the air, twists around, lands, and takes off again. The goal of the pursuing rabbit is to switch directions just as fast as the bunny she's chasing.

## Tiny chariots of fire

Another defense mechanism that rabbits use for amusement when they feel safe and relaxed in their environment is running at top speed. This ability comes in handy for avoiding predators, but a speedy run is also a terrific way to have a good time, especially with other rabbits.

If you have a single rabbit, your bunny may simply run through the house or yard just for the fun of it. If you have more than one rabbit, running and chasing will be a favorite pastime among the two. (See Chapter 2 for the scoop on whether adopting two rabbits is a good idea.)

Watching your rabbit run playfully at full speed is loads of fun. The speed at which bunnies run is amazing. If you blink, you can literally miss your pet going by.

## A rabbit and her friends

In the wild, rabbits are playful creatures who love to engage their fellow rabbits in games. In his book *The Private Life of the Rabbit* (Buccaneer Books), R.M. Lockley writes about wild rabbits chasing each other, running in circles, jumping into the air, and rolling in the grass. In the situations Lockley observed, the only reason for this behavior appeared to be that the rabbits felt good and wanted to show it.

### Various and sundry other hijinks

When it comes to funny antics, rabbits have a slew of tricks up their proverbial sleeves, such as the following ones:

- **Binki:** A rabbit may hop quietly along and then suddenly leap straight up for no apparent reason and then land again. Then the bunny continues to mosey along as if nothing happened.
- **Digging:** Another favorite and funny pastime of rabbits is digging. Give a bunny a good box or corner of sand, fine gravel, or soft dirt, and watch it fly. You can buy bags of sandbox sand at home-improvement stores and nurseries (the plant kind of nursery, not the baby kind). (Giving your rabbit a box to dig in is also a good way to keep him from doing it to the carpet.)
- **Tunneling:** Rabbits love tunnels, and it's great fun to see your bunny go in one end of a box or tube and come out the other, over and over again. Some owners buy play tunnels meant for cats and hook them together with built-in snaps to create elaborate tunnel systems for a playful bunny.

# Chapter 15

# Getting Hoppy with Your House Rabbit

### In This Chapter

- Flocking together with other rabbit lovers
- Signing up to save bunnies
- Leaping into rabbit hopping
- Competing against other rabbits

Most people get enough joy from their rabbits by just having them as companions. If you're more laid-back or have little time to spare, you can have plenty of fun playing at home with your rabbit (see Chapter 14). But if you're the type of person who likes to really get involved with your pets and has the time and money, you may want to consider participating in any of one several activities available for rabbit owners.

Whether showing your rabbit, hopping alongside your pet, participating in a rabbit club, or rescuing homeless rabbits, you get much more from your relationship with your rabbit if you take advantage of some of what's out there for rabbits.

## Clubbing It

If you love rabbits, you want to be around other people who love rabbits, too. Being with other rabbit lovers is where rabbit clubs come in. You can find all kinds of rabbit clubs and groups, designed for various tastes:

### Regional rabbit clubs

People are much like rabbits. They like to be with their own kind. That's why regional rabbit clubs are growing in popularity. Geared toward rabbit owners who live within a specific geographical area, regional rabbit clubs are locally based. Not every city and town in the country has a regional rabbit club, of course, but plenty of them do. If you live in a place that doesn't have one, consider starting one.

In the United States, most rabbit clubs are geared toward adults who are showing purebred rabbits, but some groups do include pet owner and youth programs. By joining a regional rabbit club, you can attend meetings and local shows, and you'll find out much more about caring for your rabbit. If you're interested in showing and breeding, you can gain invaluable knowledge on these subjects from fellow members.

To locate the regional rabbit club in your area, contact the American Rabbit Breeders Association, Inc. (ARBA). You can find links to ARBA chartered clubs on the group's Web site at `www.arba.net` or by asking your local rabbit veterinarian whether a regional club exists in your area. (If you're outside the United States, see the Appendix for contact information on international rabbit associations.)

## Signing up with the House Rabbit Society

If you want to devote your rabbit-oriented energies to helping bunnies in need, as well as helping to educate others about rabbit care, you may want to consider joining a local House Rabbit Society chapter. The House Rabbit Society is a national organization that works to improve the quality of life for rabbits everywhere. The members of local chapters host regular meetings, volunteer at shelters, house abandoned rabbits in foster homes, and set up booths at community events to promote responsible rabbit ownership.

For more information about the House Rabbit Society and similar groups, see Chapter 4 and the "Rescuing Rabbits" section, later in this chapter.

## Kid-friendly groups

So your daughter begged you for a rabbit, and now you're the one cleaning his litter box. Or maybe you bought the rabbit that your son wanted, and he just can't get enough of his pet. Either way, getting your child more involved is a good idea. Your best bets are

- **4-H:** By getting involved in a 4-H rabbit project, your child can find out about rabbit care and handling. She can also show her rabbit, even if the bunny isn't a purebred.

  Parents have plenty of opportunities to get involved with their child's 4-H rabbit project, too. Clubs are always looking for leaders, chaperones, and other volunteers. You should also help your child with the rabbit's daily maintenance. Find out more about 4-H in the "Taking the 4-H route" section, later in this chapter.

- **House Rabbit Society:** See '"Rescuing Rabbits," later in this chapter.
- **Local kid-focused groups:** 4-H programs are probably most prevalent, but be on the lookout for other clubs for rabbit- and pet-lovers alike.

# Rescuing Rabbits

If you want to go beyond being a responsible rabbit owner, you can get more involved by joining a local rabbit *rescue club,* a group devoted to the rescue and rehoming of unwanted rabbits. The problem of homeless rabbits is a serious one, and people who love rabbits are needed to volunteer at rescue organizations around the country. Chapter 4 offers more specific shelter and rescue group information, including why this problem exists and how each works from the adoption perspective.

Perhaps the most prominent rescue group is the House Rabbit Society, which has local chapters around the United States, each involved in rabbit rescue and welfare. By getting involved with a House Rabbit Society chapter or another rabbit rescue organization, you can do wonders to help rabbits in need. (You can find a list of House Rabbit Society local chapters and other rescue organizations in the Appendix.)

Among the type of volunteer opportunities available for rabbit lovers:

- Passing out fliers in front of pet stores about rabbits needing homes.
- Providing rabbit food to a rabbit foster home in your area.
- Providing a foster home for a rabbit. (See the "Halfway there: Fostering" section, later in this chapter, for more on this topic.)
- Start a local chapter of the House Rabbit Society if one doesn't exist already.

## Being proactive

Your heart aches for homeless bunnies, but what can you do about it? Plenty.

- **Consider adopting one from a shelter or a rabbit rescue group.** That is, when the time comes to acquire a rabbit, take in a homeless rabbit.
- **Be a responsible rabbit owner.** Being responsible means spaying or neutering your pet rabbit and refraining from breeding your pet if you don't plan to get involved with showing.

- **Educate fellow rabbit owners about the plight of homeless rabbits.** Encourage them to spay and neuter their pets and advise them not to breed their pets or turn them loose for a life of so-called freedom.

  Give them information on local rabbit organizations and the proper care of rabbits (available from the House Rabbit Society.) Be honest about the pros and cons of owning a rabbit when asked and have people read in advance about rabbits for pets . . . books like this one!.

- **Be an advocate for responsible rabbit ownership.** If you come across a friend or relative who is thinking about getting a rabbit, encourage them to consider their decision carefully. Owning a rabbit is a big commitment and shouldn't be taken lightly. Maybe you could loan this book to him.
- **When you meet someone who has just acquired a rabbit, offer to help with the new pet.** Provide the new pet owner with literature on how to properly feed and care for a rabbit and explain the importance of responsible ownership. Remind new rabbit owners that if they want to get rid of their pet, they should take it to a shelter or rabbit rescue group — *not* turn it loose to fend for itself.

## Halfway there: Fostering

If you have a big heart and want to help homeless rabbits, consider providing a foster home for a bunny in need. Foster homes for rabbits are halfway houses of sorts, providing homeless bunnies with a temporary place to live and adjust to normal life while a permanent home is sought.

As a foster parent to a rabbit, you keep the bunny until a home is found. You'll probably be asked to evaluate the rabbit's temperament and behavior, so people seeking to adopt a rabbit have a sense of what the bunny is like.

Instead of shelters, foster homes are used by a variety of rabbit rescue groups throughout the country. In the case of the House Rabbit Society, the organization has local chapters and a network of foster homes within each chapter. (You can find a list of HRS chapters in the Appendix.)

A call to your local chapter can start you on the road to becoming a foster parent. Providing a foster home for a rabbit is rewarding and really makes a difference for the animal. Of course, when you foster a rabbit, you may fall in love with the bunny and want to keep it. Many foster parents do.

# Rabbit Hopping

Some people think that showing rabbits is fun, but they haven't seen fun until they've gone rabbit hopping. What the heck is *rabbit hopping?* Similar to horse show jumping and dog agility, rabbit hopping is a competitive activity that involves both rabbit owners and their rabbits negotiating various obstacles on a course. (Rabbits wear harnesses and leashes.)

In the United States, the sport of rabbit hopping is managed by the Rabbit Hopping Organization of America, or RHOA. (See the Appendix for contact information.) According to rabbit owners who participate in this sport, the rabbits enjoy it as much as the owners. The obstacles are varied, but most of them are jumps. The following jumps are typically seen in the rabbit hopping arena:

- **Broad:** Two horizontal poles with a set of boards placed on the ground between them.
- **Pole:** Two horizontal poles with one or more raised vertical poles between them.
- **Water:** An obstacle consisting of a small body of water, usually with bushes on either side

For the safety of your rabbit, don't try these obstacles at home! Both you and your rabbit need training to participate safely in rabbit hopping. Get involved in the RHOA to safely learn this sport.

Horse show jumping was the inspiration for rabbit hopping, and many of the first rules and ideas for rabbit hopping came from horse show jumping. Rabbit hopping started in Sweden in the 1970s and quickly spread to other parts of Europe. The sport is popular in Norway and Denmark and is growing in Germany and the United States.

## Getting up to speed (and height)

Just as the hopping course has hurdles, so does the preparation process:

1. **Become a member of your national rabbit hopping organization.**

   In the United States, contact the RHOA. Outside the US? See the Appendix for rabbit-hopping organizations in your country. Not all countries have one of these groups.

2. **Train your rabbit.**

   Training for rabbit hopping involves careful work with the rabbit's safety and emotional well-being in mind — training must be positive and gentle. Basic training, including walking with a leash, is described in Chapter 12; you'll work up to using a structured groundwork technique, which shows you how to train your rabbit to negotiate a hopping course.

Conditioning, another important aspect of training, requires you to slowly build your rabbit up to the point where he has the physical agility and endurance to negotiate a rabbit-hopping course.

For help on training your rabbit for rabbit hopping, contact the local chapter of your national rabbit hopping association. If you live in the United States, contact the RHOA.

3. **Become familiar with the rules.**

   Designed for the safety of the rabbit in large part, the rules for rabbit hopping are more complicated than you may think, involving close to 150 guidelines. A couple of basics:

   - Any rabbit over the age of 4 months can participate.
   - Rabbits must wear a harness and leash during the hopping competition.
   - Handlers must give rabbits enough room to move around the jumps if they're so inclined and jump freely through the course.

4. **Memorize the course in advance.**

   Walking through the course several times will help you remember the order of the obstacles when it's time to do your *run.* The obstacles tend to be laid out in a logical order — the obstacle you first see upon completing a step is usually the one you're supposed to take next.

## Taking the plunge

If rabbit hopping sounds like fun to you and you'd like to try it, contact your national rabbit-hopping association. (See the Appendix for contact information.) Because the sport is just getting started in the United States, not too many clubs have been created throughout the country. However, you can start your own rabbit-hopping club.

Membership in a rabbit-hopping organization usually includes a packet with rules and guidelines, detailed information on choosing the right rabbit for hopping, training information, directions to and descriptions of the hopping courses available, diagrams on how to build jumps, and judge's score sheets for hopping events.

## Putting on the sweatsuit: Training

Before you can participate in a rabbit-hopping event, you need to train your rabbit. Training involves careful work with the rabbit's safety and emotional well-being in mind. Remember that rabbits are timid creatures, and training must be positive and gentle! A structured ground work technique is used in training rabbits for this sport. Conditioning is another important aspect of training and requires that you slowly build your rabbit up to the point where he can negotiate a rabbit-hopping course.

For help on training your rabbit for rabbit hopping, contact the Rabbit Hopping Association of America. For the price of membership, the organization provides detailed information on how to train a rabbit for competition, along with other kinds of information on the sport of rabbit hopping.

# Showing Rabbits

Probably one of the oldest of all rabbit activities is the sport of *showing*. Although no bunny show parallels the Westminster Dog Show broadcast on TV every year, you can still take your rabbit in front of an American Rabbit Breeders Association judge for evaluation.

ARBA rabbit shows are basically bunny beauty contests. Rabbits are judged in categories according to their breed and are compared to their breed *standard,* a blueprint of the ideal rabbit of that breed, which describes what the rabbit's body should look like in great detail. Judges give points to each of the rabbit's body areas described in the standard.

To participate in the *conformation* part of ARBA rabbit shows (the part of showing where your rabbit is judged on his appearance as opposed to you being judged on your handling skills), you need a special show rabbit, one that you have purchased specifically for this reason.

Picking up the rabbit and looking over his physical qualities, judges examine the rabbit. A rabbit is *not* judged on the basis of his behavior — only his appearance. The rabbit exhibited in a given show within his breed class who most represents the breed standard that day is the rabbit who wins the blue ribbon.

Owners who show their rabbits are responsible for grooming the bunny before the show, transporting him to the event, and getting him to the judging arena in time for the rabbit's class.

You can show only unneutered and unspayed purebred rabbits in the beauty contest aspect of rabbit shows. (See Chapter 9 for information on problems relating to rabbits who aren't spayed or neutered.) Showmanship classes for youngsters that evaluate the child's *presentation* of a rabbit (the way the child presents the rabbit to the judge for evaluation) don't require an unspayed or unneutered purebred bunny.

## Considering pros and cons

Before you embark on a show career with your rabbit, consider the pros and cons of participating in this activity with your pet.

Pros:

- Showing your rabbit can be plenty of fun. You'll not only enjoy the excitement of the game, but you'll meet other rabbit owners and find yourself becoming part of a whole new world of rabbit lovers.
- You'll find out more about rabbits by showing them.

Cons:

- Showing puts plenty of pressure, both physical and emotional, on your rabbit because of extensive handling and transporting. He's also more likely to come in contact with a contagious disease from another rabbit at a show.
- For a rabbit to be shown at some events, he must be tattooed. (See this chapter's "Getting some ink: Tattooing.") Some rabbit owners don't like tattooing because a tattoo leaves a permanent mark on the rabbit's ear, and the tattooing process causes temporary pain to the rabbit.

## Attending your first show

What can you expect when you attend your first rabbit show? The experience can be a bit daunting if you don't know what's going on. However, if you have a sense of the process, you'll be less confused and intimidated, and you may actually have fun your first time around.

### Preparing

Before you even set foot at the show venue, prepare yourself and your rabbit in the following way:

- **Go to a show.** Before you enter your first show, attend a rabbit show as a spectator. Attending gives you a good idea of what to expect, and knowing what to expect can make the difference between a nervous rookie and a confident pro. Arrive at the show in the morning and spend the entire day walking around and watching how things work. Don't forget to ask questions if you don't understand what you're seeing. Rabbit people are a friendly lot, and most are happy to answer questions.
- **Study the breed standard.** Before you even select your first show rabbit, familiarize yourself with your rabbit's breed standard. Write to ARBA or visit the organization's Web site to order a copy of *Standard of*

*Perfection* — a booklet that contains descriptions of all ARBA-recognized breeds of rabbits. Judges use these breed standards to evaluate rabbits that come before them at shows. After you study the standard, take a good look at your rabbit to get a sense of how much your bunny exemplifies the breed's standard. You can even ask another expert in your rabbit's breed for an opinion.

- **Have your rabbit tattooed.** Before you show your rabbit, you must have someone place a permanent tattoo in his left ear that will be registered with ARBA. (See the "Getting some ink: Tattooing" section, later in this chapter.)
- **Groom your rabbit.** The quality of your rabbit's coat has a strong impact on the judge's decision at a rabbit show. The judge wants to see a coat that's proper for the breed (according to the breed standard) and that looks healthy and well cared for. (Chapter 7 has details on grooming your rabbit, and Chapter 3 can tell you more about rabbit coats.)

- **Condition your rabbit.** Rabbit show judges not only look for rabbits with good fur but also in good "flesh." The term *flesh* refers to the rabbit's overall body condition. Rabbits who are underfed or poorly fed won't be in good flesh, and a judge is likely to mark down your show rabbit. (See Chapter 6 for details on how to properly feed your rabbit.)
- **Psyche up your rabbit.** No, you don't need to teach your rabbit to meditate before he goes into the competition ring, but you do need to get him ready for the way that the judge will handle him. Practice handling him the way the judge will.

  Judges usually pose a rabbit in his *proper position,* the designated proper position each breed must be shown in. The judge then turns the rabbit over on his back to check the teeth, toenails, and straightness of legs, eye color, and tail. The rabbit is returned to his proper pose and checked for *body conformation* (the way your rabbit is put together) and condition of the flesh and fur.

  Keep in mind that not all rabbit breeds are posed the same way, so determine the proper posing for the breed that you're showing by studying the breed standard and watching the judging of your breed while at a show. Spend about 10 to 15 minutes a day practicing posing with your rabbit and remember to be patient with your pet.

### Making your checklist

Glance at this checklist the night before the show and make sure that everything is packed before you head out:

- **Entry forms and judge's card:** Pack your filled-out entry cards (which you picked up at another show) and judge's comments cards, assuming that you've done this ahead of time. (If you didn't, don't worry. You can get the forms and fill them out when you get to the show.) Figure 15-1 shows a judge's card.

- **Pedigree:** If you plan to register your rabbit at the show, bring your rabbit's three-generation *pedigree* (your rabbit's genealogy) with you.
- **Rabbit eats:** Your bunny needs food and familiar water during the time he's at the show. Bring chopped-up vegetables, hay, and timothy pellets, if he eats them. Use a cooler to keep the produce fresh and bring a bottle of water from home.
- **Grooming tools:** Don't forget to bring a brush for last-minute fur brushing. (For more about these tools, see Chapter 7.)
- **Disinfectant:** Bring a hand disinfectant to clean your hands after handling rabbits other than you own. You can also buy disinfectant wipes to wipe off a table or other items touched by another rabbit. These products are alcohol based and should contain 60 to 70 percent alcohol to be effective. You may also want to bring a spray disinfectant and paper towels to clean up any accidents your pet may have outside of his cage.

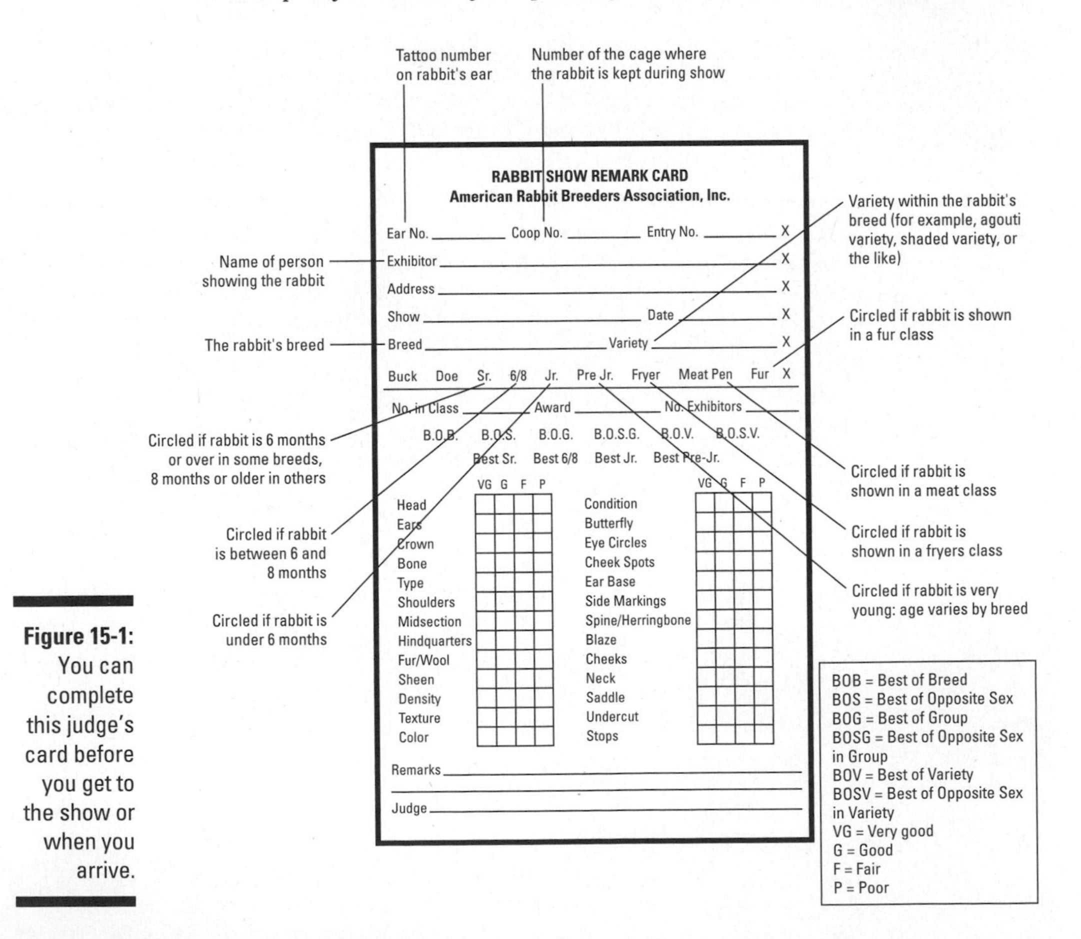


**Figure 15-1:** You can complete this judge's card before you get to the show or when you arrive.

- **Clothing and shoes:** Consider bringing a smock or another shirt that you can put on over your regular clothes if you're going to handle rabbits other than your own. Remove that shirt before going back and handling your rabbit to minimize the spread of disease. If rabbits are allowed to run around the floor at the show, consider wearing washable shoes that you can remove before you return home.

- **Your other stuff:** Bring directions to the show, a chair to sit on, something to drink, your lunch, and whatever else you may need. (If you had to travel far to get to the show, bring your overnight bag. See Chapter 16 for information on how to pack your rabbit's suitcase, too.) Remember, most of your day is spent waiting for your rabbit to be judged, so you want to be comfortable.

- **Your good sportsmanship:** Win or lose, remember to always be a good sport. Be polite to the judge and to the other exhibitors. And have fun!

### The big day

On the day of the show, you have a number of responsibilities. Following these guidelines can help you feel more confident and may even improve your chances of winning:

1. **Travel well.**

   You need to get your rabbit to the show, and you'll probably do so by way of automobile. Believe it or not, the way that you transport your rabbit that day can make a big difference in how well you do at the show because rabbits are easily stressed.

   You can help reduce the chance of a stressed-out rabbit by

   Keeping your rabbit in a secure, comfortable carrier that contains your rabbit's favorite bedding.

   Making sure that water and food are available to your rabbit at all times during the trip.

   Padding under the carrier to reduce the bumpiness of the ride for your rabbit. (Chapter 16 has in-depth traveling information.)

   Showgrounds and parking areas are usually well marked with large signs that say "This way to rabbit show!" Be prepared to pay for parking, although it depends on the venue.

2. **Check in with the show secretary.**

   There you also

   - Pay for your entries (for each class your rabbit enters, usually a fairly small fee per class).

- Fill out entry cards (your rabbit's name and breed, your name and address, and so on) and *show remarks cards* (the card that the judge writes her comments on after judging your rabbit) if you haven't already done this at home.

3. **Register.**

   If you haven't already registered your rabbit with ARBA and you want to do so, you can do it if you have time before your first class. Take the rabbit to the registrar seated at an ARBA table at the show. Show your three-generation pedigree to the registrar. (See the "The ARBA Way" section, later in this chapter, for more on how such shows are organized and what's required.)

4. **Find the judging.**

   Locate the table where your breed is being judged and pick a place close by to set up your rabbit's carrying cage and your chair. Be sure to find a shady spot if the show is being held outdoors because direct sun and heat can hurt your rabbit.

5. **Pay attention.**

   You'll soon find yourself visiting with other rabbit owners and getting distracted looking at all the cute bunnies. Pay attention to when your class is called so that you don't miss your turn at the judging table.

## Taking the 4-H route

If your kids are interested in rabbit activities, you may want to join a 4-H club in your area. 4-H is an organization created to help children learn about how to care for and exhibit livestock.

To obtain information on a local 4-H rabbit project, contact your local Cooperative Extension Office listed in your local telephone book under County Government. For general information about 4-H, contact the National 4-H Council listed in the Appendix.

4-H is open to children from age 9 through 19, and sometimes younger, depending on the individual club. Typical 4-H rabbit projects feature hands-on work with rabbits. Children are taught how to feed, care for, handle, groom, and show their rabbits, and they often bring their rabbits to meetings.

Volunteers, usually parents whose children have been involved with the program for some time, run 4-H clubs. Individual 4-H projects, such as rabbits, have leaders as well. These people are usually parents and are often breeders or former breeders who have spent a substantial amount of time showing rabbits.

Shows specifically for 4-H rabbit owners are held around the country and follow the rules and breed standards established by ARBA. Typically, 4-H members exhibit their rabbits at county fairs because 4-H often has a strong presence at these events.

4-H fairs usually occur in the summer, when heat stroke is common in warmer parts of the country. To keep rabbits cool, some owners will provide frozen water bottles (a 2-liter soda bottle works well) for their rabbits. Hot bunnies can curl up next to these bottles when temperatures get too high.

Aside from valuable hands-on experience, members of 4-H rabbit projects can also earn awards. Although actual awards and requirements vary from club to club, typical activities, such as displaying a winning rabbit-related project in the local 4-H fair or successfully exhibiting a rabbit at a show, can earn participants medals, ribbons, or certificates.

Don't get the impression that your kid can't participate in 4-H if she has a mixed breed rabbit. If your bunny isn't a purebred, your child can still show the animal in the 4-H showmanship class. In showmanship, the exhibitor presents the rabbit to a judge, demonstrating an understanding of rabbit care and anatomy as well as proper handling. Children are graded on their ability to present the animal properly and to understand their pet's overall health. The breed of the rabbit is irrelevant.

## No relation to the Swedish band: ARBA

When it comes to the big time in rabbit showing, the American Rabbit Breeders Association (ARBA) is the governing body. As the official organization for rabbit showing and registration in the United States, ARBA sponsors rabbit shows, put on by regional rabbit clubs, around the country. Rabbit fanciers, serious about showing, attend these shows, which are usually for all breeds of rabbits but are sometimes open only to one breed.

ARBA maintains a list of rules and regulations for rabbit shows, and each sanctioned show operates by these rules. Officiating the ARBA shows, judges evaluate the rabbits using the breed standards published by ARBA. Rabbits that are exhibited at ARBA shows may be registered with the organization, but registration isn't absolutely necessary.

Rabbits at ARBA shows are judged in classes organized by breed. Within the breed classification, rabbits are then divided up by age before they're judged. Awards are given to individual class winners, as well as the best of

- Breed
- Opposite Sex (given to the best rabbit of the opposite sex of the Best of Breed winner)

- Show
- Variety or Group

Class winners usually receive a ribbon; Best of Variety or Group, a *rosette* (a type of ribbon); Best of Breed, a trophy; and Best In Show, a large trophy. Small cash awards are also given to some of the winners.

When competing in ARBA shows, rabbits can also earn legs toward their Grand Championship. Three legs qualify a rabbit as a Grand Champion, which is a distinctive title in the rabbit world.

### Registering

Registering a rabbit isn't necessary in order to show it. However, many people choose to do so because having a registered rabbit assures that the animal's pedigree is true and that the rabbit meets all the requirements of its breed. (It's interesting to note that you don't need any solid proof that a rabbit is a purebred to show it. If the rabbit looks purebred, it's assumed that the rabbit is purebred.)

To register your rabbit in the purebred classification, your bunny needs a three-generation pedigree). An official ARBA registrar must examine your rabbit and determine whether your bunny is eligible for registration. The rabbit must be 6 months or older and meet the senior weight limits for its breed. It must also be free from disqualifications as defined by its breed standard.

### Getting some ink: Tattooing

If you've been to a rabbit show, you probably noticed that some rabbits have tattoos in their left ears. You may also see a registrar actually tattooing rabbits at the show.

For a rabbit to be shown, he must have an identifying number tattooed into its ear for many shows. The registrar tattoos the rabbit's registration number in his ear at the time of examination. Many breeders do their own tattooing, using a system of letters and numbers that they've created for their own record-keeping purposes.

The procedure is painful for a rabbit, so the most humane method is to have an experienced vet do the procedure using an anesthesia. However, some breeders and show registrars will apply tattoos. (Your rabbit doesn't need to be entered in the show for you to have his number tattooed at the event.)

# Chapter 16

# Hitting the Road with Your Rabbit

## In This Chapter

- Finding a smart and loving bunny caretaker
- Taking the first car ride home
- Going out into the wild blue yonder with Fluffy
- Making pet-friendly accommodations

You don't have to live with a rabbit for too long before you find yourself completely bonded with your pet. Pretty soon, you won't even want to leave your rabbit for extended lengths of time, even when you go on vacation! You'll think that maybe he'd enjoy seeing the Grand Canyon. You'll tell yourself that he's yearning for a look at Mount Rushmore, or maybe your aunt and uncle in Paris would like to meet him.

Well, don't let your affection carry you away. The truth is that rabbits aren't the greatest of travelers, and pleasure jaunts aren't necessary or even healthy for most bunnies. (Sorry, but you'll have share your travels with your rabbit by showing him your vacation slides.) The reason rabbits don't travel well is simple: They're easily prone to stress, and being exposed to new environments stresses them out. They prefer the safety and comfort of familiar surroundings. Also, rabbits who travel are at risk of being exposed to diseases and parasites — another reason why bunny is best off at home.

Take your rabbit only if the trip is absolutely necessary for him: trips to the veterinarian, relocations with you to a new home, and the like. This chapter helps you reduce your pet's stress and keep him safe and sound when there's just no getting around hitting the road together

## Keeping Him at Home

Because traveling with your rabbit is a last resort, your first resort is to keep your pet at home. Rabbits take great comfort in familiar surroundings, and leaving your rabbit in his usual place with a responsible person (either someone whom you trust or a pet sitter) who can come by once or twice a day is your best option. Although leaving your rabbit in your house is better, boarding is also an option if you absolutely can't find anyone to care for him. (See the section "Boarding your bunny," later in this chapter.)

The most crucial aspect of keeping your rabbit at home while you travel is finding the right person to care for your pet. Get someone who is responsible beyond question because your rabbit's life literally depends on this person while you're away. If you have a friend or neighbor who you trust implicitly with your rabbit, you can go this route. If the person you're considering is under the age of 12, make sure that a parent is overseeing your rabbit's care.

Consider your

- Boyfriend or girlfriend
- Friend or neighbor
- In-laws (no outlaws)
- Parents or adult children
- Spouse
- Trusted member of your rabbit club
- Vet technician (some do pet-sitting on the side)
- Professional pet sitter

## Preparing your pet sitter

After you hire someone to take care of your rabbit, you need to prepare your home and your pet for your absence:

- **Go over your rabbit's needs with the sitter.** Invite your sitter over for a visit before you're scheduled to leave. When she's there, give a run-through of all duties so that she can ask questions. This is also a good time for a rabbit handling and holding lesson. If it's someone you know well and she can't come before you leave, give specific instructions over the phone (or leave this book open to the page that talks about holding your rabbit!).
- **Create a how-to list of all the rabbit chores and dos and don'ts.** Even though you'll have verbally instructed your rabbit's caretaker on what she needs to do, it can't hurt to write it all down and leave it in a place where your sitter can see it. Also let the caretaker know what she should do — or shouldn't: Don't let the rabbit run loose throughout the house, do give her supervised exercise in a rabbit-proofed room, do be on the lookout for signs of illness (consult Chapter 9 of this book), and so on.

- **Stock up on supplies.** Make sure that your rabbit's caretaker has everything she needs to care for your rabbit properly and knows where you keep this stuff. Have a supply of hay on hand so that your caretaker won't need to scramble to find any and have fresh vegetables chopped up and portioned in bags, ready to go in the refrigerator. Make sure that you have enough litter for your rabbit's litter box if your bunny uses one and have plenty of fresh bedding on hand.
- **Make a list of foods.** If you're going to be gone for an extended period of time, your caretaker needs to go to the store to pick up fresh foods for your rabbit. Leave behind some cash or payment instructions for the caretaker, along with a list of foods that your rabbit can eat.
- **Instructions for veterinary care.** Post the phone number and address of your rabbit's veterinarian in a prominent place, with a 24-hour emergency clinic number and address alongside. Leave a signed note stating that you authorize the rabbit's caretaker to seek veterinary attention for your rabbit in your absence and provide a means for the caretaker to pay for veterinary care. (The simplest solution may be to call your vet's office and work out an arrangement in the event that your rabbit gets sick while you're away.)
- **Your contact information.** Leave phone numbers (here's where a cell phone is incredibly handy) and addresses where you can be reached while you're away. Also leave the number of a local friend who's willing to be responsible for your rabbit if you're unreachable.

## Going the professional pet-sitter route

Another route you can take is to hire a professional pet sitter. A *professional pet sitter* comes to your home to take care of your rabbit every day. That means she'll feed your rabbit, give her fresh water, let her out of her cage for supervised exercise, and clean up after her. If you have other pets, you can have the pet sitter care for these critters, too. (If you do have other pets, let your sitter know whether your rabbit can safely be with your other pets.)

To find a reputable pet sitter, get a referral from another rabbit owner or your veterinarian. If you're unable to get the name of a pet sitter in your area from either one of these sources, contact Pet Sitters International or the National Association of Pet Sitters, listed in the Appendix, for a listing of pet sitters near you. These organizations have standards that its members must meet. For example, they must be insured and bonded (see explanation in the following bulleted list), have experience caring for animals, and be able to provide references, to name just a few requirements.

Before you hire a pet sitter, you need to interview her and ask some important questions. Most pet sitters want to come to your home to meet you and your pet, and this is the time to pose the following questions:

- **What is your experience with rabbits? Have you cared for rabbits before?** If you can't find a sitter who has rabbit experience, then get one who interacts calmly with your pet and seems to have a natural feel for being around these sensitive pets.
- **How much do you charge to care for a rabbit? Do you charge per day, per visit?** These details can be important, especially if you'll be gone for an extended period of time.
- **How many times a day will you come see my rabbit? At what times of the day will you come? What services are available?** For example, in addition to feeding and giving fresh water, will the pet sitter sit with your rabbit during exercise time? Will the pet sitter groom your rabbit? How much extra does the pet sitter charge for these additional services?
- **May I see references?** Preferably get several from other rabbit owners. Call each one of these people to find out whether they were happy with the pet sitter's work. Ask whether the pet sitter is responsible, if she took good care of the animals in question, and whether the pet owner would recommend this pet sitter to others.
- **Are you bonded?** If a professional pet sitter is *bonded,* you, as the customer, are financially protected against theft of your property perpetrated by the pet sitter. In other words, if the pet sitter steals something from your house, you'll be reimbursed for it. Most professional pet sitters will also ask you to sign an agreement as to the services that will be rendered. A liability waiver may also be included in the agreement, holding the pet sitter free from certain responsibilities if anything happens to your pet or your home while the pet sitter is in charge. Read any agreement carefully before you sign it and make sure that you have no problem with the stipulations that the pet sitter has put forth.

## Boarding your bunny

Another option for your rabbit while you're away is boarding in a private home. Some people, for a fee, take in other people's pets for short-term boarding.

Home-boarding is preferable to placing your rabbit in a boarding kennel or a veterinarian's office, the kind that regularly services cats and dogs. Such places are generally not hospitable for rabbits because of the close proximity of all those barking dogs.

You can locate a rabbit-friendly boarding home through a rabbit club in your area. Contact the House Rabbit Society (see the Appendix for contact information) and ask for a reference to a House Rabbit Society chapter in your area. Your local club should be able to recommend someone in your area. In addition, contact your rabbit-experienced veterinarian's office; they often have a list of qualified people who can board your pet.

When choosing a private boarding situation, make sure that

- You visit the home before you commit to leaving your rabbit in the proprietor's care.
- The home is clean.
- The rabbit's quarters are secure, have all the comforts of home, and are safe from predators.
- You ask for references of other rabbit owners who have used the services of this home-boarder and call them. Find out whether they had a pleasant experience and whether their rabbits came back happy and healthy.

# Traveling with Your Rabbit

If you find that you absolutely have to travel with your rabbit, do it in a way that's safe and comfortable for your pet.

Options for rabbit travel are usually limited: Cars and airplanes are the vehicles in which rabbits are usually welcome. Whatever mode of transport you choose, the situation must be handled carefully to keep your bunny in good health — physical and mental — during the trip.

You also need to pack for your bunny. (I've yet to meet a rabbit who could close his own suitcase.) Packing the right items is vital to keeping bunny comfy while on the road. In addition, keep in mind these general dos and don'ts when it comes to bunny globe-trotting.

## Travel dos

Before taking your pet on a trip, bear the following tips in mind: These bits of advice can make the difference between smooth travel and a cumbersome ride.

- **Plan ahead.** Think about the circumstances of the journey and how to best make your rabbit comfortable. (See the upcoming section "Carrier comfy" in this chapter.) If you're flying with your pet, you need to contact the airline to make reservations for your rabbit. For overnight road trips, plan ahead by making reservations at pet-friendly hotels.

- **Get veterinarian information at your destination.** Before your trip, get the name and phone numbers of rabbit veterinarians in the towns where you'll be staying. If your rabbit gets sick, the last thing that you want to do is struggle to find a qualified veterinarian.
- **Consider the weather.** Think about how hot or cold it will be. Rabbits can tolerate cold much better than heat. If you're traveling by car during the summer, be sure your air conditioning is working. If you're traveling by plane, keep in mind that your rabbit may be exposed to extreme heat during loading and while in the cargo hold, and when it comes to rabbits, heat kills. A tip for potential hot-weather travel is to place a frozen water-filled plastic drink bottle in the carrier with the rabbit.
- **Get a temporary tattoo.** Using a nontoxic felt marker, write your telephone number in your rabbit's ears. This temporary ID will wear off but may come in handy.
- **Use a travel carrier.** Airline carriers, the best traveling case for a rabbit, come in different styles. (See what a travel carrier looks like in Figure 16-1.)

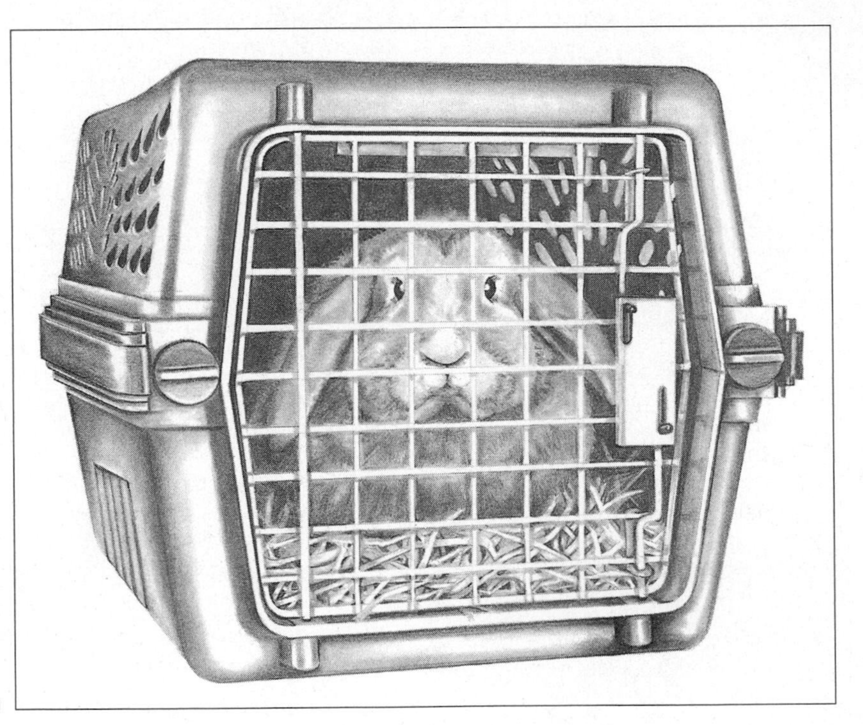

**Figure 16-1:** Snug and secure — but not necessarily happy — in this well-equipped carrier.

## Travel don'ts

Make sure that you do follow these "don'ts." Your rabbit and you will be far better off if you

- **Never leave your rabbit alone in a car, even for a few minutes.** A hot car is a death trap for a rabbit. Even if the windows are rolled down, the temperature in a sun-baked car can rise at a fast and deadly rate. Leaving a rabbit alone in a car (whatever the weather) can put the rabbit at risk for being stolen.
- **Don't skimp on a carrier.** Don't carry your bunny in a box or bag. Instead, use only travel crates or carriers designed for small animals. Plastic-and-wire airline crates are an excellent choice, although some owners prefer soft nylon carriers.
- **Don't fly.** Avoid taking your rabbit on airplane trips, if at all possible. Airplane trips should be reserved for relocation situations only. Most airlines don't allow rabbits to fly in the cabin of an airplane, which is the preferred way for a rabbit to fly. Rabbits who don't fly in the cabin are relegated to the cargo area, where they're exposed to life-threatening stressors, such as heat, barking dogs, and rough handling.

## Packing a mean bag

If you're planning an overnight trip, you need to pack a number of items for your traveling bunny. You need some of this stuff while you're en route (if your trip is longer than an hour or so) and some after you arrive.

You can put all this fun stuff in a plastic bag or a canvas tote. Or you can go all out and get your bunny his own Samsonite. If you travel often with your pet and have a little money to spend), you can purchase a nylon pet travel bag or knapsack at a pet supply store.

Here's what you need:

- **Food:** If you won't be traveling through an area where hay and fresh vegetables are readily available, you need to pack these items for your trip. Bring a cooler, fill it with ice and the fresh, washed food your rabbit needs. Bring hay in a plastic bag to help keep it fresh.
- **Water:** Don't upset your bunny's digestive system by giving him strange water. Pack some bottled water and give that to him on your trip.

- **Litter box and litter:** If your rabbit is trained to use the litter box, bring his litter box along. He'll take comfort in being able to use his familiar commode when nature calls.
- **Bedding:** Bring fresh bedding (whatever you use at home) for your rabbit if you're staying overnight. He needs his bedding changed every day. (See Chapter 5 for information on rabbit bedding.)
- **Chew items:** Your bunny takes comfort in gnawing on some favorite item while he's traveling.
- **A toy or two:** When your bunny gets to where he's going, help him acclimate to his new environment with a familiar toy.
- **Harness and leash:** Bring your rabbit's harness and leash with you so that you can take him out of the carrier when necessary and still have complete control over him. Chapter 12 tells you about the harness and how to use it.
- **Grooming tools:** If you'll be gone for a week or more, bring your rabbit's brush and nail clippers. If you have a longhaired rabbit, even an overnight trip requires that you groom your pet during your trip, so bring along your grooming tools. Chapter 7 tells you all about grooming and its required tools.
- **Rabbit vet's contact information at your destination:** If you planned ahead, you'll have this info ready when it's time to go.
- **Identification:** Equip your rabbit's carrier with an ID tag bearing your name, address, and cell-phone number. Include the phone number of your destination in case your rabbit becomes separated from you during the trip.
- **Paper towel rolls:** Use for cleanup of cage or hotel room if needed.
- **Carpet cleaner and white vinegar:** Use for cleaning in case of an accident.
- **First-aid kit.** Bring along your bunny's first-aid kit so that you'll be equipped should he become sick or injured. (See Chapter 9 for information on gathering the necessary first-aid supplies.)

Your rabbit's carrier is his home away from home, but you don't need to bring your pet's entire cage with you. Think of his carrier as his traveling cage.

## Carrier comfy

Before taking your rabbit on a trip, help him get used to his carrier. The more comfortable he feels in his travel carrier, the less stressed out he'll be when he travels. This whole process can take up to a month, so be sure to start way ahead of your scheduled departure time.

First off, make sure that you have a good carrier for your bunny. The best ones for rabbits are the small airline approved plastic-and-wire carriers normally used for cats. Rabbits find these cozy because they're enclosed, and the construction helps protect the four-legged occupants in the event of an accident. You can also opt for a soft nylon pet carrier bag, although it doesn't provide as much protection during car travel and rabbits can more easily chew through them.

Take the following steps to familiarize your rabbit with his carrier:

1. **During your bunny's exercise time, place the carrier in the area where he runs around.**

   Put some clean straw in the carrier, or your rabbit's sleeping blanket inside. Leave the door open and place some treats inside. After your rabbit eats the treats, add more goodies about half an hour later.

2. **After a few days of eating treats in his carrier, close the door while your rabbit is inside.**

   Keep the door shut for just a minute or two at a time and then let him come out if he wants to. Gradually increase the amount of time the door is closed until your rabbit is confined for at least half an hour.

   If your rabbit shows distress at being confined, you're moving too fast. Back up and start over by putting treats in the carrier and leaving the door open. Gradually begin to close the door for short periods of time until you work up to a comfortable confinement time for your rabbit.

3. **After your bunny is okay with being inside his carrier with the door closed, take him on some short car trips.**

   When he first feels the car moving, he may become distressed. If he does, have someone else drive while you sit in the backseat with him. Feed him some of his favorite treats through the carrier door and talk softly to him. Keep the trips short and gradually work up to longer car rides as he becomes more comfortable.

When your rabbit is completely comfortable confined to his carrier and traveling in the car, you're ready for your trip. Your carrier (or car) should be equipped with the items mentioned in "Packing a mean bag," earlier in this chapter.

## Bunny you can drive my car

If your rabbit is just taking a short trip to the vet, you'll mostly likely be traveling with him by car. That's a no-brainer unless, of course, you live in a big city and don't have a car, instead relying on public transportation. If that's the case, call a car service or hail a taxi for a ride to the vet. Avoid subways and buses with your rabbit if you can. The noise and commotion will scare him and are best avoided. (Check ahead before taking your rabbit on public transportation. Some cities don't allow pets on trains and buses, even if they are in a carrier.)

Another reason why you may be traveling by car with your rabbit is to move to a new home — an excellent reason to take your rabbit on a car trip. If you move, your rabbit moves with you.

Keep the following points in mind when traveling by car with your rabbit:

- **Keep your rabbit in a secured (safety belted or otherwise) carrier while in the car.** This is for your safety as well as the safety of your rabbit. In the event of an accident, your rabbit is safer in a carrier. Also, a loose rabbit can be distracting to a driver and can actually be the cause of an accident. Be sure to get your rabbit used to his carrier before taking him on a trip. (See the section "Carrier comfy," earlier in this chapter.)
- **Face your rabbit's carrier to the side instead of from front to back of the car.** This way, if you have a sudden stop or take off, your rabbit is less likely to be thrown forward into the carrier door, where he may break a tooth. A piece of carpet place in the carrier will help prevent your bunny from sliding.
- **Skip the scenery.** Your bunny will not enjoy seeing glimpses of the world speeding by. Cover his carrier with a towel so that he won't become panicked by the surrounding sights (kind of like blinders on a horse).
- **Protect your rabbit from heat.**
  - Use the air conditioner if you're driving in hot weather.
  - Make sure that your rabbit's carrier is not in direct sun. Move the carrier to the other side of the car's seat or put a towel over the area of the crate that's exposed to the sun. (Be sure to leave some open areas for ventilation.)
- **Provide healthy air.** If you get stuck in traffic, keep the windows rolled up and the air vent closed, preferably with the air conditioner turned on.
- **Take breaks on long trips.** If you're driving for a long time (more than a couple of hours), stop and give your rabbit a break. Park in the shade if the weather is hot and let him hop around inside your parked car, making sure that you block off any areas in the car where the rabbit can become wedged or hide. Be certain he has fresh water in his carrier and clean up any accidents that may have occurred while he was confined.

## Bunny's first trip home

Your bunny's first car trip may be the one he takes to your home. When that time comes, follow the car travel guidelines in this chapter and then consider the following tips to make the journey especially stress free:

- Have someone (or yourself) sit next to the bunny's travel carrier or cage, comforting her by speaking softly and using her name.
- Keep windows closed and radio off to eliminate scary noises.
- Go directly home! Do not take any detours along the way — not even to introduce your new companion to your mother.
- Drive carefully to avoid sudden stops or sharp turns that could throw your bunny off balance.

Once you arrive at home, your bunny will need a quiet place to relax and adjust to her surroundings; Chapter 11 offers more details on this important transition.

## Flying the unfriendly (for bunnies) skies

Traveling by plane is the least favorable way to get your rabbit from one place to another. Consider the following as you think about whether to subject your rabbit to a flight:

- Airports are places of crowds, long waits, and security checks—all of which are stressful to humans, let alone a trapped and terrified bunny.
- Very few airlines actually allow rabbits to travel in cabins; most require that rabbits fly in the plane's cargo hold (where checked bags are kept). There rabbits are exposed to noise, usually other animals, and great fluctuations in temperatures. There's also the risk of being exposed to heat if the plane gets trapped on the runway for an extended period of time.
- The rare airlines that do allow rabbits to fly in cabins require that carriers fit under passengers' seats (which is physically not possible with larger rabbits).

If your rabbit must fly by plane, certain precautions can help your pet survive the stress of the trip. Follow these guidelines if you're planning a plane ride for your pet:

- **Fly *with* your rabbit.** Avoid sending your rabbit alone on a plane. Without you on board, the rabbit has no one to watch out for him. If the plane gets trapped on the runway for hours on end, your rabbit could die of heat exhaustion.
- **Book a direct flight to reduce the amount of handling your rabbit has to endure.** A connecting flight increases the chances of circumstances going awry in your pet's journey. More than one dog or cat has been

incorrectly routed and ended up in the wrong city. Also, ask for your rabbit to be loaded last, after all the checked bags have been placed in the cargo hold. If your rabbit goes in last, he'll be unloaded first when he arrives at his destination.

- **Get your rabbit a place in the cabin.** Most airlines allow only one or two pets to fly in the cabin of the plane, as long as the pet's carrier fits under the passenger's seat. Again, not all airlines allow rabbits in the cabin. Call ahead to ask. In order to secure a place in the cabin for your rabbit, make your reservations way ahead of time.
- **Do not sedate your rabbit for the flight.** In the event of heat or another problem with your pet's flight environment, tranquilizers can send your rabbit over the edge. While sedatives may sound like a great idea, you should use these drugs only under constant veterinary supervision, as reactions to these drugs in stressful situations can be unpredictable.
- **Prepare your rabbit for the flight by making sure that he's completely comfortable in his carrier.** Follow the steps in the "Carrier comfy" section, earlier in this chapter, to get your rabbit used to being confined in an airline carrier weeks before you take your flight.
- **Prepare your rabbit's crate so that your bunny has everything he needs during the flight.** If your rabbit is flying in the cargo hold, equip his crate with his favorite towel or blanket, a gravity water bottle attached on the inside of the crate door filled with fresh water, a good amount of fresh hay, and favorite fresh veggies to help him stay hydrated.
- **Clearly mark the outside of the crate with contact information.** Put more than one person's information in case of an emergency and friendly information, such as, "Hi, my name is Thumper, and I'm a lop-eared rabbit. I'm traveling for the first time, so please treat me gently." This type of note catches the attention of the handlers. Also, put a tag on your pet's crate with your name, address, and cell-phone number, along with care instructions in the event your pet becomes separated from you.
- **Make sure that you have appropriate health certificates.** All airlines and state health officials require a USDA (United States Department of Agriculture) health certificate issued by a licensed veterinarian prior to travel. Airlines vary on how far in advance they want health certificates. Certificates for interstate travel are generally good for 30 days. (Again, that's decided by the destination state in question.). It's best to check with your airline on their exact requirements.
- **If you absolutely have to put your rabbit on a plane without you, book your pet's flight in the cooler weather for his safety.** In other words, a December trip from New York to Chicago would be a better bet than a summer trip from California to Texas.

- **Use a professional pet shipper, if necessary**. You may have to book your rabbit's flight through a professional pet shipper if the airline doesn't allow pet owners to make pet reservations (see the Appendix for more information).

### Being a law-abiding bunny

If you're taking your rabbit out of state or the country or flying on a plane, call the agricultural authorities where you're going at least 6 weeks in advance to find out the regulations regarding rabbits in that area. You may need a USDA health certificate issued by a licensed veterinarian before you can bring a rabbit into the area, or you may find that you can't bring rabbits into the area at all.

You can go online to the animal welfare section of the U.S. Department of Agriculture's Web site at `www.aphis.usda.gov/animal_welfare/pet_travel/pet_travel.shtml` for more information on government regulations on interstate and international travel with pets.

Some places, such as Hawaii and the United Kingdom, have strict *quarantine* restrictions, requiring that rabbits spend considerable amounts of time in a quarantine facility when they're first brought into the area. This separation ensures that they're free of illness before mingling with the rest of the rabbit population. Find out whether the place you're going has these kinds of rules and what following them entails.

## Staying at a Five-Carrot Hotel

These days, hotels have spas, room service, and Internet access. What else do you need? Your rabbit! Who cares if a mint is on your pillow if you can't stay there with your pet? If you have to stay somewhere overnight, you need to find a bunny-friendly hotel along your route. Not to worry — plenty of them are out there.

Be prepared to pay a pet deposit, which is refunded if your room is void of pet-related damage after you leave. You may also have to pay a small fee (usually $5 to $15 per night) for the privilege of keeping your pet with you for the night.

### Booking a reservation

The best way to find the right hotel or motel is to use a pet-friendly hotel/motel guide. A number of these books have been published for hotels and motels around the United States. Although not labeled specifically for rabbit owners (some even refer only to dog-friendly places), the pets-okay policies at these lodges are often applicable to rabbits as well. (Refer to the guides listed in the Appendix.)

If you don't want to go to your bookstore and purchase a guide, you can do research on the Internet. By simply typing "pet-friendly hotel" in any search engine, you get a list of Web sites to the kinds of places you're looking for.

After you find the listing, call the hotel to make sure that rabbits are indeed allowed. Don't count on that hotel or motel having available rooms on the night you plan to stay. Book while you're on the phone to make sure that you have a place to stay — don't just show up with bunny in tow!

## Being a good guest

When you stay at a pet-friendly hotel or motel with your rabbit, be a good guest. The impression you leave on the manager and staff is vital because it determines whether future rabbit owners will be allowed to bring their pets to this facility in the future.

Follow these guidelines when staying in a hotel or motel with your rabbit:

- **Control your pet.** Don't let your rabbit run amuck in a hotel room. Rabbits are inclined to dig carpet, poop and pee under the bed, and chew on the wooden furniture if left to their own devices. By all means, give your rabbit some exercise but keep a close eye on him to make sure that he doesn't damage the room.
- **Clean up after your pet.** If your rabbit has an accident on the rug, clean it thoroughly. Scoop up any hay or litter that spills out of your pet's carrier. Avoid using room towels to clean up pet messes. If you didn't bring paper towels along with you (tsk, tsk!), run to the store and buy some if you need them or get a bunch of paper napkins from the hotel restaurant. (Chapter 5 tells you how to get rid of urine on the floor.)
- **Confine your rabbit.** This one is for the safety of the room and your pet's safety, too. Whenever you aren't in the room, keep your rabbit in his carrier. You don't want the maid to accidentally let your pet out of the room, and you certainly don't want your rabbit destroying carpet or furniture or disappearing into the box spring or some other nook or cranny.

# Part V
# The Part of Tens

"Let me guess – the vet's analysis of the rabbit's fleas showed them to be of the 100 percent fresh ground Colombian decaf variety."

## In this part . . .

This part is a hodgepodge of information. These chapters tackle knowing when you should take your rabbit to the vet, pronto. On the fun side, ten of the best rabbit Web sites are listed as well as ten ways to brighten your bunny's day.

# Chapter 17

# Ten Signs That Require Emergency Action

### *In This Chapter*

- Coping with a pet emergency
- Knowing when to rush to the vet
- Discovering the signs of a sick rabbit

Just like other pets (and people, too) rabbits can require emergency treatment. An illness or injury may mean that your rabbit needs immediate help, even before you take him to a veterinarian. Of course, everyone knows an ounce of prevention is worth a pound of cure. So if you want to do right by your rabbit, check out Chapters 9 and 10 for more health information and some preventive medicine.

Suddenly seeing that your bunny is sick or injured can be pretty scary. Thinking straight in these kinds of situations is often difficult. Before taking any action:

- **Stay calm.**
- **Consult your emergency cheat sheet.** Using the sheet provided in the front of this book (you should have already filled this out and posted it by your telephone), check for the address and phone number for your vet clinic, as well as the phone numbers for a 24-hour emergency pet hospital and ASPCA Animal Poison Control Center.

One way to keep calm is to prepare in advance for an emergency. This chapter helps you figure out how to handle the most common rabbit emergencies. If you ever find that your rabbit needs emergency care, you may be surprised at how well your memory serves you.

## Blood in Urine

Red blood in the urine is a serious sign of disease. Causes include uterine disease (in females), bladder stones, bladder cancer, and trauma to the bladder. Blood that appears at the end of urination and as a separate puddle is most likely caused by a uterine problem. Excess blood loss can be a life-threatening condition. Bloody urine should be reported to your veterinarian immediately, particularly if it is associated with

- Straining to urinate
- Frequent urination
- Weakness
- Depression

Normal rabbit urine can range in color from yellow to rusty orange due to pigments produced in the bladder and from the plants the rabbit eats. However, blood in the urine is distinctly red. If you're in doubt about your rabbit's urine color, take a sample to your veterinarian for evaluation.

## Diarrhea

True diarrhea in the rabbit is characterized by stool that is

- Profuse
- Watery
- Sometimes bloody in the absence of normal stool

Diarrhea is most often caused by a serious disruption of the flora normally in your rabbit's gastrointestinal tract. In addition, the pet will become dehydrated and go into shock. If your rabbit has diarrhea, don't attempt to treat it yourself. Take your bunny to a veterinarian as soon as possible. A serious disease of the GI tract — not a change in diet — causes diarrhea.

Rabbits can also develop soft, pudding-like stools often mixed with normal hard, round droppings. These stools aren't true diarrhea, and although they do represent a disease of the gastrointestinal tract that should be addressed, it's not a dire emergency. This condition is most often related to diet.

# Excessive Salivation

Dental disease is the most common cause of excessive salivation. If the rabbit is drooling because of dental disease, it means he's in pain, and the condition should be attended to as soon as possible. Other possible signs of dental disease can include

- Not eating well
- Quickly losing weight
- Constantly wet fur around the mouth and neck

Excessive salivation can also be caused by certain types of poisons. If this condition is accompanied by generalized weakness, you need to seek veterinary attention immediately.

# Poisoning

Rabbit owners do their very best to keep dangerous plants and chemicals away from their furry companions, but accidents happen. A long list of plants (see Chapter 8), as well as lead, pesticides, and household chemicals can be toxic to rabbits. A rabbit that has eaten something poisonous can be affected in ways that range from stomach upset to death. Symptoms may include

- Diarrhea
- Seizures
- Drooling or foaming at the mouth
- Ulcers in the mouth
- Weakness
- Burned lips, mouth or skin
- Abnormal mental state

Keep in mind that some toxins (daffodils, for example) can cause delayed symptoms, so take action even if your rabbit seems fine. Whenever possible, bring the suspected poison with you if your vet recommends you go to the emergency room. Be sure that your emergency Cheat Sheet (a handy tear-out included in the front of this book) includes the phone number for a reliable Animal Poison Control Center (for example, the ASPCA Animal Poison Control Center, at 1-888-426-4435).

# Heatstroke

Rabbits are susceptible to heatstroke and can tolerate cold weather better than hot. A hot and humid day can be all it takes to send a rabbit into heat exhaustion, even a rabbit who lives indoors without air conditioning. See Chapter 5 for information about housing tips for preventing heatstroke. Signs of heatstroke include labored breathing, extreme lethargy, and an elevated body temperature.

If your rabbit has been exposed to high temperatures and you suspect she's suffering from heatstroke, do the following to help her cool down:

1. **Get her out of the heat and into an air-conditioned or shady area.**
2. **Wrap her ears in a cool, wet towel.**
3. **Rush her to a veterinarian immediately.**

# Labored Breathing

A variety of serious problems can cause *labored breathing* (visible difficulty moving air in and out of the lungs) in rabbits. Anything from pneumonia to shock to heatstroke can cause labored breathing.

Labored breathing in a rabbit is a serious emergency. Rush your pet to a veterinarian as soon as possible. If it's hot outside, run the car air conditioner first because hot air is difficult for the rabbit to breath and will cause further difficulties.

# No Stool

If a rabbit doesn't produce any stool for 24 hours, particularly if any of the following signs accompany it, he's in need of immediate medical attention. The most common cause is a complete or partial obstruction to the gastrointestinal (GI) tract or a complete shutdown of the GI tract caused by a chronic GI motility problem.

- Bloated abdomen (may feel tight or like it's filled with fluid, like a water balloon)
- Constant tooth grinding
- Dull appearance to the eyes
- Hunched posture
- Loss of appetite
- Reluctance to move
- Weakness

This is a dire emergency, so seek medical attention immediately. These conditions are fatal within 48 hours if left untreated. If an obstruction is present, your rabbit needs emergency surgery.

## Pain

If your rabbit is in pain, he should be rushed to a vet immediately to determine the cause of pain.

The following are signs of pain in a rabbit:

- Depression
- Excessive salivation
- Frequent grinding of the teeth (Occasional tooth grinding can be normal.)
- Inability to sleep
- Loss of appetite
- Rapid or labored breathing
- Reluctance to move
- Sitting in a hunched posture all the time (particularly with dull, half-closed eyes)
- Unexplained aggression
- Unusual body posture

# Injury

Rabbits can get hurt in a variety of ways, such as when other animals attack them. When being handled improperly, rabbits are often hurt, and when really frightened, they'll do anything to escape — including injure themselves. (Chapter 7 helps you understand how to properly handle your rabbit.) If you didn't see the injury occur, you may not be certain as to what's wrong. Look for the signs of injury described in the following sections.

## Bleeding

Bleeding can result from a predatory attack or from catching the skin on a sharp surface.

If your rabbit is bleeding profusely, put pressure on the wound using your hand or finger with a clean gauze pad or small towel. Try to stop or slow the bleeding.

If the blood is coming out in a steady flow, the injury is less serious. If the blood spurts out in rhythm, your rabbit has a damaged artery. In the latter case, stopping the blood flow is difficult, and more pressure and time is required. Meanwhile, try to get your rabbit to an emergency veterinary facility.

## Broken bone

Broken bones occur from some type of trauma. The fracture causes pain, and if it occurs in the legs, the rabbit might limp or drag or hold his leg up. If the fracture is in the spine, you'll see dragging (usually the hind legs) or difficulty standing. Most fractures occur under the skin, but sometimes the bone can protrude through the skin, causing bleeding and increasing the possibility of infection.

All fractures should be seen by a veterinarian as soon as possible, because your pet is in great pain with this condition. Prepare a small deep box or carrier with thick blankets or towels padding the bottom and gently place your pet inside. Try not to jostle the rabbit's body unless absolutely necessary. Doing so may cause further injury. Do not splint or immobilize the fractured leg because the rabbit may struggle with pain, causing more damage. The rabbit will get himself in the position that is most comfortable for the ride.

### Burns

Rabbits who manage to nibble on electrical cords can be seriously burned or electrocuted. If you find a cord that's been chewed on or through, check your rabbit carefully — in particular for burns of the mouth — and call your vet immediately. Any rabbit found unresponsive near a chewed cord should be taken to a vet right away.

### Paralysis

An inability to move two or more legs can be paralysis — the result of a spinal injury. If your rabbit is conscious but unable to move part or all of her body, gently place your rabbit on a folded towel and blanket. Then carefully place your bunny, still lying on the towel and blanket, in a large carrier or open box.

## Head Tilt and Seizures

*Head tilt* is a neurological emergency that you might encounter with your rabbit. (See Chapter 9 for more on this condition.) As the name suggests, the primary symptom is a rabbit holding her head to the side. The quicker head tilt is diagnosed and treated, the greater chance for full recovery. Even if your rabbit is only showing mild signs of head tilt, you need to have her checked by your veterinarian as soon as possible.

Head tilt can be caused by an inner ear infection, trauma to the head, or a problem in the brain due to stroke, cancer, infection, parasitic disease, or other disease. Onset of head tilt symptoms can be gradual or fast. A rabbit with head tilt may also not interact as usual, hide in a dark corner, stop eating normally, or stop eating at all.

*Seizures* can be frightening to see. A rabbit who is having a seizure lays on his side, jerking and twitching uncontrollably. Even though it appears that she's struggling, remember that the rabbit is unconscious during these moments and isn't feeling any pain. Try covering the head and body of the bunny loosely with a lightweight towel to cut out visual stimulus and light, which may help shorten the seizure. Gently lift the rabbit and place her in a large carrier or open box that's been fitted with a blanket, towel, or other soft material.

Do not restrain the rabbit while she's convulsing because you may cause further injury. Do not put your hands near her mouth.

## Sudden Weakness

Any number of problems, all serious, can cause sudden weakness. Heatstroke, blood loss, shock, overwhelming infection, neurological disorder, intestinal obstruction, poisoning, trauma to the spine or legs, and metabolic diseases are just a few of the conditions that result in weakness.

If your rabbit can't stand up, don't try to force him. Instead, to make him comfortable, place him on a towel or blanket and take him to the veterinarian immediately.

# Chapter 18

# Ten Great Rabbit Web Sites

## *In This Chapter*

- Finding out about rabbit breeds and behavior
- Getting more information on rabbit care
- Networking with other rabbit owners

Rabbits have a huge presence on the Internet. And why not? Everything else does. What's great about computer-literate rabbit aficionados is that they enjoy welcoming newcomers to the world of rabbits. Most are dedicated to providing novice rabbit owners with all the information that they need so that their new pets get the best possible care.

The following Web sites contain a plethora of information that may help you to understand and care for your rabbit. If you visit any of these sites on a regular basis, your bunny's life may be enriched. Check out the links on these sites to be transported deeper into the rabbit web.

The Web sites listed in this chapter, which are just a sampling of what's on the Internet, aren't intended as an endorsement. The Internet isn't regulated, so people can put up any information they like and call it fact. Use discretion and check more than one source for information.

## www.arba.net

In the world of American rabbit shows, **The American Rabbit Breeders Association, Inc.** (ARBA) is the grand overseer. The organization registers nearly 50 different purebred rabbit breeds, manages the standards of each breed, and sanctions rabbit shows around the country.

If you're into purebred rabbits and even rabbit shows, pay a visit to the ARBA Web site. This site provides a window into the organization and provides loads of information on purebred rabbits. Take, for example, the "Breed Photos" area: A photograph of each recognized breed is pictured, along with a hot link that takes you to that breed's national club Web site — if one is available, that is. Not all national clubs have sites up yet.

Be aware that ARBA promotes *all* uses of rabbits, including commercial fur production and food production. Read its statement on its home page.

## www.binkybunny.com

If you're looking for tips and tricks for living with house rabbits, **Binky Bunny** is the place for you!

The creator of Binky Bunny came up with the idea of the site as a way to share the tried and true methods of coping with the common issues that lead many frustrated owners to give up their rabbits. The site has built up a community of rabbit folks who share what they've learned about their own experiences with house rabbits — and the joys and challenges involved with their behaviors.

The site features bunny info on bonding, rabbit-proofing, litter box training, and more; forums and chatting; and a wide variety of products.

## www.bio.miami.edu/hare/etherbun.html

**Etherbun** is an electronic mailing list devoted to care, health, and behavior of domestic companion rabbits. The list, which is free, is a wonderful resource for those interested in learning more about rabbit medical care and general health.

Most of those who participate in Etherbun are rabbit folk or seasoned rabbit rescuers. (Keep in mind, however, that the list isn't a replacement for veterinary care.) You can go to the Web site of the Houserabbit Adoption Rescue and Education organization to sign up for Etherbun.

## www.leithpetwerks.com

**Leith Petwerks,** a family-owned company of rabbit lovers, carries a full line of toys, supplies and care products for rabbits and small animals. Leith, which supports rabbit rescue groups, is known for its Bunny Abode Condos — the specially designed bunny homes that come in single-, double-, and triple-level models designed to "fit almost every rabbit and every home."

# www.myhouserabbit.com

**My House Rabbit** is dedicated to celebrating house rabbits and providing useful news and articles that cover rabbit care, adoption, behavior, and general rabbit information. Browse through this site for articles about proper diet, litter box training, housing, nail clipping, spaying and neutering, and even the environmental benefits of living with a bunny!

You can also check out the site's cute bunny photos and videos (and share your own). And don't miss the bunny blog and bunny lover gift shop.

# www.oxbowanimalhealth.com

**Oxbow Animal Health,** one of the largest suppliers of healthy diets for rabbits, small animals, and other exotics, is a valued and respected resource for many rabbit owners. In response to evolving beliefs regarding rabbit care (from livestock to companion, for example), the company has changed and improved their products. The Web site features a variety of fresh grass hays, quality pellets, and accessories, as well as litters and beddings. Although the site doesn't offer online ordering, it connects users to local stores that carry Oxbow products; the site can also connect users to veterinarians that recommend Oxbow products.

# www.rabbit.org

The **House Rabbit Society** (HRS) is an all-volunteer, nonprofit organization devoted to the rescue of rabbits and the education of the public on rabbit care. The HRS not only has chapters all over the country and even the world, but it also has an impressive presence on the Internet.

The House Rabbit Society home page is a veritable feast of information for rabbit lovers. You could literally spend hours browsing through all the information — housing, healthcare, behavior, and so on — provided on this wonderful site.

You can also get a list of all the HRS chapters in the United States and how to contact the one nearest you. And then there are the sections on kids and rabbits, links to other rabbit sites, and a page of adorable bunny shots. Truth is, if you have a thing for rabbits, you just might get lost in the HRS site and never come out. They have veterinary referral lists as well.

## www.rabbitnetwork.org

The **House Rabbit Network** offers information on rabbit adoption, as well as a listing of veterinarians in the northeastern United States. Hailing from Massachusetts, New Hampshire, and Connecticut, this excellent and complete Web site offers many solid educational articles regarding rabbit health, from weight watching to eye care. You can also make your own bunny e-card on this site, too.

## www.rainbowsbridge.com

Although not exclusively a rabbit Web site, the **Rainbows Bridge** is in this list because it's an important place on the Internet for rabbit owners — and pet owners of any kind.

The Rainbows Bridge is a site where grieving bunny owners can go to find solace and support as they try to cope with the loss of their pet. Plain and simple: If you lose your pet bunny, spend some time here. You'll find it a healing place. When visiting the Rainbows Bridge, you can look at the names of deceased bunnies and read their owners' sentiments or add your own. You can also participate in an online grief loss support group, chat, and even post your pet's story or a poem in honor of your bunny on the site. For many rabbit owners, the Rainbows Bridge site is the only place they can go to be understood in their moment of grief. For that reason, this site is worth its weight in gold.

## www.veterinarypartner.com

**Veterinary Partners** hosts hundreds of articles and links to information on all species of animals. This large library of rabbit information includes lots of information on diseases, behavior, and more.

# Chapter 19

# Ten Ways to Make Your Bunny's Day

### *In This Chapter*

- Adding a healthy dose of fresh foods
- Having a good time, bunny style
- Trying bunny massage
- Spending quality time together

Sure, the demands of life can be overwhelming, but not so much that you can't take a few moments to do something special for your rabbit. Not only will you strengthen the bond you have, but you'll show her just how much you appreciate her as a source of joy, comfort, and companionship.

In this chapter, we list some ways to put a hop, skip, and a jump in your bunny's step. None of the things on this list require a great deal of money or time, but they pack a big punch in terms of bunny rewards. Give them a try and see for yourself.

## Get Fresh

Feeding your rabbit the best, freshest diet of grass hay and greens is one of the most important things you can do to prevent a whole host of health problems. On top of that, fresh foods simply make bunnies happy!

Hay is probably the most important part of your rabbit's diet, and not just any hay will do. Be sure to give your rabbit an unlimited supply of fresh, grass hay (Timothy, for example). Chapter 6 describes how you can tell if hay is fresh or past its prime.

Fresh, moist greens, such as kale, parsley, endive, cilantro, and dark leaf lettuces, do a great deal to maintain a healthy rabbit intestine. Experiment to see which greens are a hit. Try a new vegetable, whether it's one you've grown in your garden or one from the market. Better yet, plant an organic garden devoted entirely to your bunny and let him graze as he chooses (safely, of course).

Speaking of fresh, don't forget to give your rabbit fresh water every day.

## Take a Peek

It may not be pretty, but your rabbit's urine and waste droppings can tell you a lot about what's going on with her health. (See Chapter 9 for more information.) For example, changes in urine color or urination habits may be sign of dietary changes or disease.

Changes in size and consistency of droppings can indicate a gastrointestinal problem. Soft stools (not the normal cecotropes) are often caused by a diet too low in fiber and/or too high in carbohydrates. Diarrhea, with no formed droppings and watery feces, is a different story, most likely a serious or even fatal condition. Call your vet right away.

## Get Fit

Your rabbit needs plenty of exercise and free time out of her cage. She needs at least three to four hours of time to hop, run, and play. Not only is exercise a fun diversion for your rabbit, it also helps prevent obesity, sore hocks, poor muscle tone, problems with gastrointestinal and urinary function, and even behavioral problems.

If your rabbit is like many humans and doesn't seem naturally inclined to exercise, take a look at Chapter 14, which describes a bunch of games and homemade toys that may help bring out the athlete in your bunny.

## Breathe Some Fresh Air

This book makes it clear that outdoor living is not ideal for domesticated rabbits (cold, heat, predators, disease, and so on), but a bit of fresh air does wonders for us all, including house rabbits. (Before you embark on any sort of outdoor excursion, check out the safety precautions outlined in Chapter 8.)

Once you've provided a safe (and supervised) outdoor environment, you've opened up a whole new world of sensory experiences for your rabbit. Think about the fun your rabbit might have in a patch of garden, an outdoor run, or a portable exercise pen. New smells? Yes! New snacks? Yes!

## Check on Health

Make it a part of your daily routine to handle your rabbit and check for any unusual discharge, lumps, sores, or skin problems. (Chapter 9 includes a checklist for home exams.)

Make a point of taking your bunny to a great veterinarian at least once a year for a check up. Don't balk at the cost; there's a good chance that an annual check up may prevent you from an emergency (and costly) situation.

## Make Time for Playtime

Rabbits of all ages need playtime, both for mental and physical reasons. Not only will playtime keep bunny muscles strong and bodies limber, but it will keep their minds stimulated and engaged.

A bored bunny is an unhappy bunny! Rabbits love to play games and play with toys. They'll play with you, other rabbits, and other pets (safely, of course). Experiment with different games (see Chapter 14) to see which ones tickle your bunny's fancy.

As for toys, it won't take long to figure out what your rabbit likes. (The toys he destroys or throws around the house are his favorites!) It can't hurt, however, to rotate toys into the mix or try something new.

## Listen to Your Rabbit

In nature, rabbits communicate with each other using sounds and body movements. Listen to what your rabbit may be saying to you: clucks, purrs, and snorts all have meaning ("that was delicious," "I'm feeling good," and "I'm so annoyed").

Watch her body language for subtle (and not-so-subtle) messages. Chapter 11 describes many of the common moves and what they might mean: chinning, leaping, presenting, kicking, and head butting. Enjoy!

# Schedule Spa Time

Squeeze in an extra grooming session. Brush out loose hair, check and trim nails, and check ears for mites or other problems. Short (or long) grooming sessions are great for bonding as well as another way to stay in touch with what's going on with your bunny's body.

If your rabbit appreciates petting, consider a gentle massage in the morning or evening. It may take some time to find the best location; I'd suggest a fluffy towel on a table or the floor. In the same way, you may need to experiment to find the technique that best suits your bunny, but here's a start. (Begin with a few minutes and work up to longer as he becomes more accustomed to the routine.)

1. **Wash your hands and gather up a towel and small spray bottle of water.**
2. **Point your rabbit's face away from you and move your hands down his body, from face to hind end; repeat this step up to four times.**

   Keep one hand on the bunny at all times to help him feel secure and safe.
3. **Stroke gently between your rabbit's nose, around the eyes and down the back of the head and then softly stroke the ears from the base to the tips.**

   (Remember to always be mindful of any sensitive areas.) By now your rabbit should have relaxed.
4. **Start making small circles with your thumb along the right side of your rabbit's spine (never on the spinal bones!), working your way down from the shoulder area to the hip; repeat on the left side.**
5. **Finish with another three or four sweeps of your hand from the head to hind end.**
6. **Spray your hands with a mist of water from the bottle, then sweep down the body once again, removing the loose fur.**

   Offer a fresh veggie treat as a reward!

# Clean Up

Get serious once a week about cleaning. In addition to your daily chores, thoroughly clean and disinfect your rabbit's digs and accessories once a week to keep her in good health.

## Spend Quality Time

Your rabbit craves a social life, so do what makes her happy. For some rabbits, happiness means petting on the couch; for others, a mutual grooming session on the floor, or just sitting near each other while you read or talk on phone. Whatever her fancy, make time for these special moments during each day.

## Appendix

# Rabbit Resources

The resources in this Appendix are worth scoping out. Many of these clubs and associations can provide invaluable information to help you become a better rabbit owner.

## Educational Organizations

The idea that information is power certainly applies to living with and caring for rabbits. Don't go it alone — rely on those with experience to guide you along the way.

**House Rabbit Society,** 148 Broadway, Richmond, CA 94804. Phone: (510) 970-7575. Web site: www.rabbit.org

**Ontario Rabbit Education Organization,** P.O. Box 314, 31 Adelaide St. E., Toronto, Ontario, Canada M5C 2J4. Web site: www.ontariorabbits.org

## Veterinary Organizations

Finding a vet who has experience with rabbits is one of the most important things a new owner must do. The following organizations can guide you through the process of finding a qualified exotic animal veterinarian:

**American Board of Veterinary Practitioners**, 618 Church St., Suite 220, Nashville, TN 37219. Phone: (800) 697-3583. Web site: www.abvp.com

**Association of Exotic Mammal Veterinarians,** P.O. Box 396, Weare, NH 03281-0396. Web site: www.aemv.org

## Activity Clubs

If you're looking to get together with other folks who love their bunnies, you may be a good candidate for membership in a rabbit-related organization or club.

**Rabbit Hopping Organization of America,** Linda J. Hoover, P.O. Box 184, Veneta, OR 97487

**National 4-H Headquarters,** 1400 Independence Ave. SW, Washington DC 20250-2225. Web site: www.national4-hheadquarters.gov

## Rabbit Rescue Groups

Because so many abandoned rabbits need homes, think about looking for a rabbit through one of the many rabbit rescue groups out there. These groups are always looking for volunteers to help with the good work they do for bunnies in need.

**House Rabbit Network,** P.O. Box 2602, Woburn, MA 01888-1102. Phone: (781) 431-1211. Web site: www.rabbitnetwork.org

**House Rabbit Resource Network,** P.O. Box 152432, Austin, TX 78715. Phone: (512) 444-3277. Web site: www.rabbitresource.org

**Brambley Hedge Rabbit Rescue,** P.O. Box 54506, Phoenix, AZ 85078-4506. Phone: (480) 443-3990. Web site: www.bhrabbitrescue.org

**Rabbit Rescue of Utah,** P.O Box 613, Draper, Utah 84020-0613. Web site: www.utahrabbitrescue.com

**Zooh Corner Rabbit Rescue,** P.O. Box 2192, San Gabriel, CA 91778. Web site: www.mybunny.org

## Rabbit Publications

Looking for some reading material? Check out the following publications for photos, articles, personal stories, and interesting information about rabbits.

**Rabbits U.S.A. (Annual publication),** P.O. Box 6050, Mission Viejo, CA 92690. Phone: (800) 738-2665. Web site: www.animalnetwork.com

**Rabbit Tracks (Free quarterly publication of the House Rabbit Network),** P.O. Box 2602, Woburn, MA 01888-1102. Web site: www.rabbitnetwork.org/tracks.shtml

# Rabbit Specialty Supply Outlets

Not just any hay will do, nor will just any old toy. Look to tried-and-true rabbit-supply outlets to equip, feed, and entertain your bunny companion.

**Bass Equipment,** P.O. Box 352, Monett, MO 65708. Phone: (417) 235-7557. Web site: www.bassequipment.com

**Best Little Rabbit, Rodent & Ferret House,** 14317 Lake City Way NE, Seattle, WA 98125. Phone: (206) 365-9105. Web site: www.rabbitrodentferret.org

**Leith Petworks,** P.O. Box 13520, Salem, OR 97309. Phone: (800) 956-3576. Web site: www.leithpetwerks.com

**Oxbow Animal Health, Inc.,** 29012 Mill Rd., Murdock, NE 68407. Phone: (800) 249-0366. Web site: www.oxbowanimalhealth.com

**PetMarket.com,** P.O. Box 523, Laurel, DE 19956. Phone: (888) PET-MRKT. Web site: www.petmarket.com

**West Coast Pet Supply,** 3660 Soquel Dr., Soquel, CA 95073-2035. Phone: (800) 604-2263, www.westcoastpetsupply.com

# Pet Loss Hotlines

The loss of a pet can be incredibly traumatic. Compassionate listeners are available to answer questions and offer emotional support over the telephone. Some services even send supportive materials through the mail.

**University of California, Davis:** (530) 752-4200

**Cummings School of Veterinary Medicine (Massachusetts):** (508) 839-7966

**Virginia-Maryland Regional College of Veterinary Medicine:** (540) 231-8038

**Cornell University College of Veterinary Medicine (New York):** (607) 253-3932

**Michigan State University College of Veterinary Medicine:** (517) 432-2696

**Washington State University College of Veterinary Medicine:** (509) 335-5704

**Chicago Veterinary Medical Association:** (630) 325-1600

# Travel Guides

On the Internet, you can go to www.petswelcome.com, a Web site featuring hotel listings for pet owners. However, the rest of the guides in this section are actual printed materials. Bon voyage with your bunny!

**North America:**

*Traveling with Your Pet: The AAA Petbook.* Edited and published by American Automobile Association, May 2008.

*Vacationing with Your Pet.* Written by Eileen Barish. Pet Friendly Publications, Inc., September 2006.

*No Pet Left Behind: The Sherpa Guide for Traveling with Your Best Friend.* Written by Gayle Martz. Thomas Nelson Publications, February 2008.

*Mobil Travel Guide: On the Road With Your Pet.* AMC Publications, March 2008.

**United Kingdom:**

AA Pet Friendly Places to Stay 2008. AA Publishing, November 2007.

# Pet-Sitting Associations

If you must travel and you've made the decision to spare your bunny the trouble of going along, in-home professionals can take care of all your pet-sitting needs.

**National Association of Professional Pet Sitters,** 15000 Commerce Parkway, Suite C, Mt. Laurel, NJ 08054. Phone: (856) 439-0324. Web site: www.petsitters.org

**Pet Sitters International,** 201 East King Street, King, NC 27021-9161. Phone: (336) 983-9222. Web site: www.petsit.com

# Pet-Shipping Options

Rabbit owners sometimes have no choice but to ship their bunny companions on commercial airlines (especially for relocations). Much like a travel agent, a professional pet-shipping company can help simplify the process. You need to find a reputable company, however, and the following organization can guide you through the process.

**The Independent Pet and Animal Transportation Association International, Inc.,** 745 Winding Trail, Holly Lake Ranch, TX 75755. Phone: (903) 769-2267. Web site: www.ipata.com

# Rabbit Registries

For information on showing and breeding in both the United States and abroad, consult with the following membership organizations. Please note that these groups support many uses of rabbits (exhibition, pet, and commercial).

**American Rabbit Breeders Association, Inc. (ARBA),** 8 Westport Ct., Bloomington, IL 61704. Phone: (309) 664-7500. Web site: www.arba.net

**British Rabbit Council,** Purefoy House, 7 Kirkgate, Newark, Notts NG24 1AD England. Web site: www.thebrc.org

# National Specialty Breed Clubs

If a particular breed strikes your fancy, you can contact the individual specialty breed club for more information (breeders, care tips, showing, breed history, and more).

**American Belgian Hare Club,** Frank Zaloudek, 90206 N. Harrington Rd., West Richland, WA 99353. Phone: (509) 967-3688. Web site: www.belgianhareclub.com

**American Beveren Rabbit Club.** Web site: www.freewebs.com/beverens/clubinfo.htm

**American Blue & White Rabbit Club,** Alan Schrader, 7433 North SR 59, Brazil, IN 47834. Phone: (812) 448-2304 Web site: www.rabbitgeek.com/abwrc.html

**American Britannia Petite Rabbit Society,** Ron Rohrig, 601 Sheridan Street, Richmond, IN 47374. Phone: (765) 966-4226 Web site: www.britanniapetites.com

**American Checkered Giant Rabbit Club, Inc.,** David Freeman, 1119 Klondyke Rd., Milford, OH 45150 Web site: www.acgrc.com

**American Chinchilla Rabbit Breeders Association,** Crystal Krienke-Bonkoski, R16827 Cherry Rd., Ringle, WI 54771. E-mail: clkrienke@yahoo.com

**American Dutch Rabbit Club, Inc.,** Barb Kline, 4664 S. Co. Rd. 591, New Riegel, OH 44853. Phone: (419) 595-2050 Web site: www.dutchrabbit.com

**American Dwarf Hotot Rabbit Club,** Sharon Toon, 4061 Tremont Ave, Egg Harbor Township, NJ 08234-9421. Phone: (609) 641-8839. Web site: www.adhrc.com

**American English Spot Rabbit Club,** Michael Wiley, Sr., 5772 Owenton Rd., Stamping Ground, KY 40379-9614. Phone: (502) 535-7051. Web site: www.aesrc.com

**American Federation of New Zealand Rabbit Breeders,** John Neff, 1351 Holder Lane, Geneva, FL 32732. Phone: (407) 349-0450. Web site: www.newzealandrabbitclub.com

**American Fuzzy Lop Rabbit Club,** Muriel Keyes, 14255 SE Stephens, Portland, OR 97233. Phone: (503) 254-2902 Web site: http://users.connections.net/fuzzylop/

**American Harlequin Rabbit Club,** Pam Granderson, 14991 Opera Rd., Leopold, IN 47551. Phone: (812) 843-5460. Web site: www.americanharlequinrabbitclub.com

**American Himalayan Rabbit Association,** Errean Kratochvil, 7715 Callan Ct., New Port Richey, FL 34654. Phone: 727-847-1001. E-mail: himi1@yahoo.com

**American Netherland Dwarf Rabbit Club,** Sue Travis-Shutter, 326 Travis Lane, Rockwall, TX 75032, 972-771-4394. **E-mail:** TravisDwar@aol.com

**American Polish Rabbit Club,** Patti Walthrop, 2405 Greenridge Ct., Euless, TX 76039. Phone: (817) 312-0305. Web site: www.polishrabbitclub.com

**American Sable Rabbit Society,** Richard King, 3360 Graham Rd, Rising Sun, OH 43457. Phone: 419-288-3296. Web site: www.geocities.com/american_sable

**American Satin Rabbit Breeders Association,** Clarence Linsey, 316 South Mahaffie, Olathe, KS 66061. Phone: (913) 764-1531. Web site: www.asrba.com

**American Standard Chinchilla Rabbit Association,** Robert Bowman, 7905 Thompson Twp Rd 81, Bellevue, OH 44811. Phone: (419) 483-1009. E-mail: bowman@cros.net

**American Tan Rabbit Club,** Virginia Akin, 718 CR 216, Sweetwater, TX 79556. Phone: (325) 236-4032. Web site: www.atrsc.org

**American Thrianta Rabbit Breeders' Association,** Carrol Hooks, 8761 Aycock Rd., Moody, TX 76557. Phone: (254) 986-2331. Web site: www.atrba.net

**Californian Rabbit Specialty Club,** Donald Mersiovsky, 1156 Elm Grove Spur, Belton, Texas 76513. Phone: (254) 939-0345. Web site: www.nationalcalclub.com

**Champagne d'Argent Rabbit Federation,** Wayne Cleer, 1704 Heisel Ave., Pekin, IL 61554. Phone: (309) 347-1347. E-mail: cleerchamp@grics.net

**Cinnamon Rabbit Breeders Association.** Web site: www.crbaonline.com

**Créme d'Argent Rabbit Federation,** Travis West, 2293 Factory Rd, Albany, OH 45710. Phone: (740) 698-7285. Web site: www.cremedargentfederation.com

**Florida White Rabbit Breeders Association,** Jane Meyer, 1795 N 1800 E Rd., Thawville, IL 60968. Web site: www.geocities.com/fwrba

**Giant Chinchilla Rabbit Association,** Larry Miley, 4195 County Rd. 115, Mt. Gilead, OH 43338. Phone: (419) 864-7936. Web site: www.giantchinchilla.com

**Havana Rabbit Breeders Association,** Suzanne Hemsath, 7677 W. Jefferson Rd., Magna, UT 84044. Web site: www.havanarb.com

**Holland Lop Rabbit Specialty Club,** Pandora Allen, 2633 Seven Eleven Rd., Chesapeake, VA 23322. Phone: (757) 421-9607. Web site: www.hlrsc.com

**Hotot Rabbit Breeders International.** Web site: www.geocities.com/blancdehototclub

**Lop Rabbit Club of America,** Jeanne Welch, P.O. Box 236, Hornbrook, CA 96044. Phone: (530) 475-3371. Web site: www.nordickrabbits.net/lops

**Mini Lop Rabbit Club of America,** Pennie Grotheer, P.O. Box 17, Pittsburg, KS 66762. Phone: (417) 842-3317. Web site: www.minilop.org

**National Angora Rabbit Breeders Club.** Web site: www.nationalangorarabbitbreeders.com

**National Federation of Flemish Giant Rabbit Breeders.** Web site: www.nffgrb.com

**National Jersey Wooly Rabbit Club,** Amanda Pitsch, P.O. Box 264, Marne, MI 49435. Phone: (616) 498-2330. E-mail: amanda@pitschfork.com. Web site: www.njwrc.net

**National Lilac Rabbit Club of America,** Judy Bustle, 132 Farmers Lane, State Road, NC 28676. Phone: (336) 874-7438. Web site: www.geocities.com/nlrca2002

**National Mini Rex Rabbit Club,** Jennifer Whaley, P.O. Box 712499, Santee, CA 92072. Phone: (619) 933-6505. Web site: www.nmrrc.net

**National Rex Rabbit Club,** Arlyse DeLoyola, 117 Allegheny Ct., San Marcos, TX 78666. Phone: (512) 392-6033. Web site: www.nationalrexrc.org/index.html

**National Silver Rabbit Club,** Laura Atkins, 1030 SW KK Hwy, Holden, MO, 64040-8221. Phone: (816) 732-6208. Web site: http://natlsilverrabbitclub.tripod.com

**National Silver Fox Rabbit Club,** Judith Oldenburg-Graf, P.O. Box 31, Lockridge, IA 52635. Phone: (319) 696-2604. Web site: www.nationalsilverfoxrabbitclub.org

**Palomino Rabbit Co-Breeders Association,** Deb Morrison, 396202 W. 4000 Rd., Skiatook, OK 74070. Phone: (918) 396-3587. Web site: www.geocities.com/Petsburgh/Park/4198

**Rhinelander Rabbit Club of America,** Linda Carter, 1560 Vine St., El Centro, CA 92243. Phone: (760) 352-652. Web site: http://hop.to/rhinelanders

**Silver Marten Rabbit Club,** Curtis VanLeur, P.O. Box 238, So. St. Paul, MN 55075, (651) 438-3826. Web site: www.silvermarten.com

# Index

## • A •

## • B •

# • C •

• E •

• H •

## • I •

## • J •



## • K •



## • L •



## • M •

## • P •

## • S •

## • T •

• Y •



• Z •

WILEY

## INTERNET & DIGITAL MEDIA

**AdWords For Dummies**
978-0-470-15252-2

**Blogging For Dummies, 2nd Edition**
978-0-470-23017-6

**Digital Photography All-in-One Desk Reference For Dummies, 3rd Edition**
978-0-470-03743-0

**Digital Photography For Dummies, 5th Edition**
978-0-7645-9802-9

**Digital SLR Cameras & Photography For Dummies, 2nd Edition**
978-0-470-14927-0

**eBay Business All-in-One Desk Reference For Dummies**
978-0-7645-8438-1

**eBay For Dummies, 5th Edition***
978-0-470-04529-9

**eBay Listings That Sell For Dummies**
978-0-471-78912-3

**Facebook For Dummies**
978-0-470-26273-3

**The Internet For Dummies, 11th Edition**
978-0-470-12174-0

**Investing Online For Dummies, 5th Edition**
978-0-7645-8456-5

**iPod & iTunes For Dummies, 5th Edition**
978-0-470-17474-6

**MySpace For Dummies**
978-0-470-09529-4

**Podcasting For Dummies**
978-0-471-74898-4

**Search Engine Optimization For Dummies, 2nd Edition**
978-0-471-97998-2

**Second Life For Dummies**
978-0-470-18025-9

**Starting an eBay Business For Dummies, 3rd Edition†**
978-0-470-14924-9

## GRAPHICS, DESIGN & WEB DEVELOPMENT

**Adobe Creative Suite 3 Design Premium All-in-One Desk Reference For Dummies**
978-0-470-11724-8

**Adobe Web Suite CS3 All-in-One Desk Reference For Dummies**
978-0-470-12099-6

**AutoCAD 2008 For Dummies**
978-0-470-11650-0

**Building a Web Site For Dummies, 3rd Edition**
978-0-470-14928-7

**Creating Web Pages All-in-One Desk Reference For Dummies, 3rd Edition**
978-0-470-09629-1

**Creating Web Pages For Dummies, 8th Edition**
978-0-470-08030-6

**Dreamweaver CS3 For Dummies**
978-0-470-11490-2

**Flash CS3 For Dummies**
978-0-470-12100-9

**Google SketchUp For Dummies**
978-0-470-13744-4

**InDesign CS3 For Dummies**
978-0-470-11865-8

**Photoshop CS3 All-in-One Desk Reference For Dummies**
978-0-470-11195-6

**Photoshop CS3 For Dummies**
978-0-470-11193-2

**Photoshop Elements 5 For Dummies**
978-0-470-09810-3

**SolidWorks For Dummies**
978-0-7645-9555-4

**Visio 2007 For Dummies**
978-0-470-08983-5

**Web Design For Dummies, 2nd Edition**
978-0-471-78117-2

**Web Sites Do-It-Yourself For Dummies**
978-0-470-16903-2

**Web Stores Do-It-Yourself For Dummies**
978-0-470-17443-2

## LANGUAGES, RELIGION & SPIRITUALITY

**Arabic For Dummies**
978-0-471-77270-5

**Chinese For Dummies, Audio Set**
978-0-470-12766-7

**French For Dummies**
978-0-7645-5193-2

**German For Dummies**
978-0-7645-5195-6

**Hebrew For Dummies**
978-0-7645-5489-6

**Ingles Para Dummies**
978-0-7645-5427-8

**Italian For Dummies, Audio Set**
978-0-470-09586-7

**Italian Verbs For Dummies**
978-0-471-77389-4

**Japanese For Dummies**
978-0-7645-5429-2

**Latin For Dummies**
978-0-7645-5431-5

**Portuguese For Dummies**
978-0-471-78738-9

**Russian For Dummies**
978-0-471-78001-4

**Spanish Phrases For Dummies**
978-0-7645-7204-3

**Spanish For Dummies**
978-0-7645-5194-9

**Spanish For Dummies, Audio Set**
978-0-470-09585-0

**The Bible For Dummies**
978-0-7645-5296-0

**Catholicism For Dummies**
978-0-7645-5391-2

**The Historical Jesus For Dummies**
978-0-470-16785-4

**Islam For Dummies**
978-0-7645-5503-9

**Spirituality For Dummies, 2nd Edition**
978-0-470-19142-2

## NETWORKING AND PROGRAMMING

**ASP.NET 3.5 For Dummies**
978-0-470-19592-5

**C# 2008 For Dummies**
978-0-470-19109-5

**Hacking For Dummies, 2nd Edition**
978-0-470-05235-8

**Home Networking For Dummies, 4th Edition**
978-0-470-11806-1

**Java For Dummies, 4th Edition**
978-0-470-08716-9

**Microsoft® SQL Server™ 2008 All-in-One Desk Reference For Dummies**
978-0-470-17954-3

**Networking All-in-One Desk Reference For Dummies, 2nd Edition**
978-0-7645-9939-2

**Networking For Dummies, 8th Edition**
978-0-470-05620-2

**SharePoint 2007 For Dummies**
978-0-470-09941-4

**Wireless Home Networking For Dummies, 2nd Edition**
978-0-471-74940-0

## OPERATING SYSTEMS & COMPUTER BASICS

**iMac For Dummies, 5th Edition**
978-0-7645-8458-9

**Laptops For Dummies, 2nd Edition**
978-0-470-05432-1

**Linux For Dummies, 8th Edition**
978-0-470-11649-4

**MacBook For Dummies**
978-0-470-04859-7

**Mac OS X Leopard All-in-One Desk Reference For Dummies**
978-0-470-05434-5

**Mac OS X Leopard For Dummies**
978 0 470 05433 8

**Macs For Dummies, 9th Edition**
978-0-470-04849-8

**PCs For Dummies, 11th Edition**
978-0-470-13728-4

**Windows® Home Server For Dummies**
978-0-470-18592-6

**Windows Server 2008 For Dummies**
978-0-470-18043-3

**Windows Vista All-in-One Desk Reference For Dummies**
978-0-471-74941-7

**Windows Vista For Dummies**
978-0-471-75421-3

**Windows Vista Security For Dummies**
978-0-470-11805-4

## SPORTS, FITNESS & MUSIC

**Coaching Hockey For Dummies**
978-0-470-83685-9

**Coaching Soccer For Dummies**
978-0-471-77381-8

**Fitness For Dummies, 3rd Edition**
978-0-7645-7851-9

**Football For Dummies, 3rd Edition**
978-0-470-12536-6

**GarageBand For Dummies**
978-0-7645-7323-1

**Golf For Dummies, 3rd Edition**
978-0-471-76871-5

**Guitar For Dummies, 2nd Edition**
978-0-7645-9904-0

**Home Recording For Musicians For Dummies, 2nd Edition**
978-0-7645-8884-6

**iPod & iTunes For Dummies, 5th Edition**
978-0-470-17474-6

**Music Theory For Dummies**
978-0-7645-7838-0

**Stretching For Dummies**
978-0-470-06741-3

# Get smart @ dummies.com®

- **Find a full list of Dummies titles**
- **Look into loads of FREE on-site articles**
- **Sign up for FREE eTips e-mailed to you weekly**
- **See what other products carry the Dummies name**
- **Shop directly from the Dummies bookstore**
- **Enter to win new prizes every month!**

*** Separate Canadian edition also available**
**† Separate U.K. edition also available**

Available wherever books are sold. For more information or to order direct: U.S. customers visit www.dummies.com or call 1-877-762-2974.
U.K. customers visit www.wileyeurope.com or call (0) 1243 843291. Canadian customers visit www.wiley.ca or call 1-800-567-4797.

# Do More with Dummies Products for the Rest of Us!

**DVDs • Music • Games • DIY**
**Consumer Electronics • Software • Crafts**
**Hobbies • Cookware • and more!**

**Check out the Dummies Product Shop at www.dummies.com for more information!**